AF361387

Supreme Court Policymaking and Race

Supreme Court Policymaking and Race

Origins and Development

BARBARA L. GRAHAM

Published by State University of New York Press, Albany

EU GPSR Authorised Representative:
Logos Europe, 9 rue Nicolas Poussin, 17000, La Rochelle, France
contact@logoseurope.eu

For information, contact State University of New York Press, Albany, NY
www.sunypress.edu

Library of Congress Cataloging-in-Publication Data

Name: Graham, Barbara L., 1956– author.
Title: Supreme Court policymaking and race : origins and development /
    Barbara L. Graham.
Description: Albany : State University of New York Press, [2026]. | Series:
    SUNY series in American constitutionalism | Includes bibliographical
    references and index.
Identifiers: LCCN 2025034739 | ISBN 9798855805864 (hardcover : alk. paper) |
    ISBN 9798855807158 (epub) | ISBN 9798855805888 (PDF)
Subjects: LCSH: Race discrimination—Law and legislation—United
    States—History. | Race discrimination—Government policy—United
    States—History. | United States. Supreme Court—Decision making. |
    Constitutional history—United States. | LCGFT: Law materials.
Classification: LCC KF4755 .G725 2026 | DDC 342.7308/73—dc23/eng/20250811
LC record available at https://lccn.loc.gov/2025034739

To Matthew, Christopher, and Rhonda

Contents

Tables

Acknowledgments

Near the completion of this book, I realized that it is a product of three decades of teaching, research, and reflecting on the subject of race, politics, and the law. I owe a huge intellectual debt to many scholars in the disciplines of political science, history, and law who have influenced my thinking about the institutional role of the Supreme Court in American constitutional democracy. I would like to acknowledge and express my gratitude to the anonymous reviewers who read the manuscript and gave very helpful comments and suggestions for improvement. Of course, the publication of this book would not have been possible without the support of Dr. Michael Rinella, senior acquisitions editor at SUNY Press. Finally, I would like to thank my sons Christopher and Matthew for putting up with me during the inordinate amount of time I spent on researching and writing this book.

Introduction

While serving as US solicitor general, Robert Jackson (1941, xii) observed that "nearly every significant decision of the Supreme Court has to do with power—power of government, power of officials—and hence it is always concerned with the social and economic interests involved in the allocation, denial, or recognition of power." The primary objective of this book is to present a comprehensive and systematic account of the origins and development of the Supreme Court's exercise of power in the policy context of race. Conflicts about race have been a fixture on the American political agenda since the nation's founding. Racial slavery was firmly rooted in the colonies prior to the American Revolution and the Framers protected the institution of racial enslavement in the 1787 Constitution. The important questions that have been debated throughout the course of American constitutional development concerning the proper balance of power between the national government and the states, the meaning of freedom, who is entitled to citizenship, who should vote and how to protect it and how should equal protection of the laws be defined and guaranteed have been shaped by the enduring issue of race. The inability of government to reach a broad consensus on contested racial issues increases the likelihood that they will be transformed into legal questions and presented to the Supreme Court for resolution.

Scholars have attempted to determine and assess the policymaking role of the Supreme Court with regard to race from competing disciplinary, theoretical and normative perspectives. The classic explanation of judicial power is found in Alexander Hamilton's Federalist no. 78 where he argued that the granting of life tenure to federal judges would insulate them from majoritarian political pressures and guard the rights of individuals from the effects of oppression by unjust and partial laws. Because the Supreme Court is situated at the apex of the federal judicial system, the court exercises its power of judicial review by striking down unconstitutional actions that fail to protect the rights of minorities. Chief Justice John Marshall laid the foundation for the court's image as a protector of minority rights in *Marbury v. Madison* (1803) by declaring that "the Supreme Court is constitutionally obligated to nullify actions of the majoritarian branches that impermissibly interfere with rights guaranteed to minorities by the Constitution." McCloskey (1960) and Cover (1982) pointed out that the narrative of the court as a protector of minority rights began in 1938 after popular government and mass institutions failed to correct antidemocratic injustices perpetrated against racial groups at home.

Several factors work against the Hamiltonian model to effectively appraise the court's exercise of power in race cases. It is unlikely that Hamilton had the rights of racial minorities in mind when he wrote Federalist no. 78. Hamilton offered judicial review as the solution to the problem of protecting minority rights as used in the Madisonian sense—to losing economic or sectional interests (Cover 1982, 1295). The highly politicized nature of the federal judicial recruitment and selection process operates against the view that federal judges are immune from political pressures. Scholars have interrogated the Hamiltonian model from a variety of nuanced perspectives. Spann (1993, 5) presented a highly skeptical view of the countermajoritarian model of judicial review and argued that "the Supreme Court functions to perpetuate the subordination of racial minorities in the United States." Goldstein (2017) compared the record of the Supreme Court to the record of the elected branches from the Marshall Court era to the mid-1990s to determine which branch was more capable of protecting the rights of racial minorities. Goldstein (2017, 399) found that during the first two hundred years the court exercised its power "to protect rights of one or another racial minority group to a greater degree than elected branches have been willing to do so." Rosenberg (2008) interrogated the Hamiltonian model by asking whether the Supreme Court is capable of producing significant social change. He depicted the Hamiltonian view of the court as a constrained court—one that is weak, ineffective, and powerless in producing social reform with nationwide impact.

Historical-legal accounts that chronicle the struggle for racial equality in the United States inform this study because they identify the dominant racial issues, policy debates, racial divisions, and shifts or reformulations of racial ideologies that are needed to assess the court's response to racial conflicts over time (Howard 1999; Klarman 2004; Browne-Marshall 2013).

Two recent civil rights histories written by Nieman (2020) and Burton and Derfner (2021) show how the path to racial equality has been marked by a series of defeats and few victories. Nieman's primary argument was that the court's embrace of colorblind constitutionalism has limited effective remedies to address institutional racism. By highlighting the racial equality gains African Americans won during the civil rights movement, Nieman argued that social movements like Black Lives Matter have the capability to build new coalitions that could effectively resist the court's restrictive racial agenda. Nieman's account minimizes the consequential role of life tenured justices who are driven by their preferences in making decisions whether to uphold or dismantle racial hierarchy as a member of the governing coalition. Burton and Derfner (2021) examined the Supreme Court's role in the nation's racial history by showing how the justices made deliberate choices to slow racial progress and to wash away civil rights protections. Although Burton and Derfner's account is rich in political context and substantive analysis, they rejected the use of ideological labels as a meaningful way to explain why the court decided race cases along a dividing line based on broad and narrow interpretations of the Reconstruction Amendments and civil rights laws. Despite their penetrating critique of the court's race decisions, Burton and Derfner failed to address any changes that would inhibit the court from consistently falling short in the area of race.

Political, historical, and legal accounts have established that the Supreme Court can be a friend or foe in the pursuit of racial equality in the United States. In this book, I take a closer look at this claim by utilizing three analytic frameworks: racial institutional orders, partisan regimes, and jurisprudential regimes. Political scientists Desmond King and Rogers Smith (2005; Smith and King 2024) formulated a racial institutional orders framework for understanding racial politics in the United States. In their seminal article "Racial Orders in American Political Development," King and Smith (2005, 75) argued that American political development has been historically constituted by two sets of evolving but linked racial institutional orders: a set of white supremacist orders and a competing set of transformative egalitarian orders. Racial institutional orders are comprised of political actors and governing institutions that take opposing positions on the major racial issues of their eras (Smith and King 2024, 7–8). They maintain that the clashes between the two racial orders over predominant era-defining racial issues have been an enduring driver of American political development. Smith and King (2024, 8) argued that it makes sense to speak of aggregate patterns of national and state racial policies in different eras as constituting the American racial order of their times. For the purposes of this study, I identified five era-defining racial policy dichotomies to assess whether the Supreme Court's decisions advanced the policy goals of the rival racial orders: slavery versus emancipation, formal equality versus civil rights, caste and exclusion versus equal rights of citizenship, racial discrimination versus equal rights under law, and colorblindness versus race consciousness.

Racial institutional orders have distinct phases, they are complex, but they are also breakable. King and Smith (2005, 79) explained that meaningful development occurs "when one predominant order gives way to another, or when the prevailing order's leading concepts of racial goals, rules, roles, and boundaries are substantially revised." Because this study assumes that the court's collective policy preferences will serve the interests of the rival racial orders, I resorted to the political science literature that views the Supreme Court as a member of the partisan regimes that dominate policymaking (Clayton and May 1999; Gillman 2002, 2006). Gillman (2006, 107) defined regime politics as "the various ways in which governing coalitions organize their power and advance their political agenda within a system of interrelated institutions." A basic tenet of the regime politics literature is that partisan coalitions direct their power to strategically construct and populate federal courts, especially the Supreme Court, to advance favored policy and electoral goals and craft litigating strategies designed to achieve favored legal outcomes in cases (Devins and Baum 2016; Peretti 2020; Greenhouse 2022). Justices serve the partisan coalitions that appointed them by invalidating laws enacted by ideologically distant political coalitions. Regime politics scholars do not claim that the policy goals of the elected branches dictate the outcomes of court decisions or that the court does not behave independently, but rather the court functions in ways that legitimate and protect the policy agenda of the governing partisan coalition that appointed the justices.

The origin of regime politics theory can be traced to Robert Dahl's (1957) seminal article "Decision-Making in a Democracy: The Supreme Court as a National Policy-Maker." To appraise the role of the Supreme Court as a national policymaking institution, Dahl asserted that justices are not appointed primarily for their judicial qualities without regard to their attitudes on fundamental questions of public policy. The source of the Supreme Court's collective policy preferences was derived from the president's power to make appointments with Senate confirmation on a regular basis. Because "the Supreme Court is inevitably a part of the dominant national alliance," Dahl (285) argued that "the policy views dominant on the Court are never for long out of line with the policy views dominant among the lawmaking majorities of the United States." He explained that the court is not "simply an *agent* of the alliance," but "it is an essential part of the leadership and possesses some bases of power of its own, the most important of which is the unique legitimacy attributed to its interpretations of the Constitution." Dahl found that the court seldom rules against the governing coalition except for short-lived transitional periods when old governing coalitions are disintegrating and new ones are taking control.

Dahl's account assumed that the justices vote according to the attitudinal model proposed by Segal and Spaeth (2002) that posits that the key to unlocking their decisional behavior is their sincere ideological preferences. Segal and Spaeth (86) argued that the justices vote the way they do because they are either more liberal or more conservative considering the facts of a given case. Epstein, Knight, and Martin (2001) argued that Dahl's claim did not consider the role of justices as sophisticated decision-makers who must pay attention to the actions and preferences of other institutions and actors if they want to generate enduring policy. The scholars found that justices vote their sincere preferences when they are similar to the preferences held by members of the ruling regime but they adjust their decisions in anticipation of the potential responses of the other branches of government at the individual and aggregate levels.

My account of court policymaking takes into consideration the way justices "translate their political ideologies and identities into a preferred legal analysis" (Gillman 2006, 114). Pacelle (2009, 180) found that Supreme Court doctrine evolves from a number of cases over time, and justices who want to see their preferences put into the law are institutionally obligated to build doctrine in a coherent fashion. Richards and Kritzer (2002) introduced the concept of jurisprudential regimes as an organizing framework to explain the influence of the law and legal change in Supreme Court decision-making. Richards and Kritzer (308) conceptualized a jurisprudential regime as "a key precedent, or a set of related precedents, that structures the way in which the Supreme Court justices evaluate key elements of cases in arriving at decisions in a particular legal area." They argued that law matters in court decision making in ways that are specifically jurisprudential, and justices must contend with both policy goals and jurisprudential regimes in deciding cases. When Bartels and O'Geen (2015, 891–92) applied jurisprudential regimes theory to investigate the nature of legal change in freedom of expression cases, they concluded that "legal change over many years is complex and nuanced. The Supreme Court can produce drastic change in one facet of an issue, induce evolutionary change on another facet, and impose legal stability on yet another facet—all within the same issue area."

Gillman (2006, 114–15) argued that jurisprudential regimes are related to regime politics in two important ways: they are designed to influence decision making in a favored direction, and party leaders in the White House and Senate evaluate judicial nominees based on their beliefs that the nominees will fortify or undermine favored precedents that represent these regimes. When justices from a new governing coalition view inherited doctrines, tests, and approaches as inconsistent with their sincere preferences and goals, they will dispose of the old ones and create new ones. I applied jurisprudential regime theory to this study to identify the landmark precedents that were the main drivers of legal change with regard to race: *Prigg v. Pennsylvania* (1842), *Dred Scott v. Sandford* (1857), *Slaughter-House Cases* (1873), *Strauder v. West Virginia* (1880), *Civil Rights Cases* (1883), *Williams v. Mississippi* (1898), *Chae Chan Ping v. United States* (1889), *Plessy v. Ferguson* (1896), *Bailey v. Alabama* (1911), *Moore v. Dempsey* (1923), *Powell v. Alabama* (1932), *Missouri ex rel. Gaines v. Canada* (1938), *Smith v. Allwright* (1944), *Korematsu v. United States* (1944), *Shelley v. Kraemer* (1948), *Hernandez v. Texas* (1954), *Brown v. Board of Education* (1954), *NAACP v. Alabama ex rel. Patterson* (1958), *Heart of Atlanta Motel v. United States* (1964), *New York Times v. Sullivan* (1964), *Swain v. Alabama* (1965), *South Carolina v. Katzenbach* (1966), *Jones v. Alfred H. Mayer Co.* (1968), *Swann v. Charlotte-Mecklenburg Board of Education* (1971), *Griggs v. Duke Power Co.* (1971), *Furman v. Georgia* (1972), *San Antonio Independent School District v. Rodriguez* (1973), *Washington v. Davis* (1976), *Regents of the University of California v. Bakke* (1978), *Thornburg v. Gingles* (1986), *Batson v. Kentucky* (1986), *McCleskey v. Kemp* (1987), *Freeman v. Pitts* (1992), *Shaw v. Reno* (1993), *Adarand Constructors v. Peña* (1995), *Shelby County v. Holder* (2013), and *Students for Fair Admissions v. Harvard College* (2023). I selected the thirty-seven landmark precedents based on their construction of racial policies from decisions, how their doctrines influenced law, and how they impacted legal change in the issue area of race.

Organization, Methodology, and Chapter Overview

To explore the origins and development of Supreme Court policymaking within the confines of the racial orders institutional framework, I break down the rival racial orders into distinct phases that correspond to the fourteen Chief Justice tenures that operated during recognizable historical periods: the first white supremacist order (Marshall and Taney Courts, slavery era), the first transformative egalitarian order (Chase and Waite Courts, Reconstruction era), the second white supremacist order (Fuller, White, and Taft Courts, progressive era), the first phase of the second transformative egalitarian order (Hughes, Stone, and Vinson Courts, New Deal era), the second phase of the second transformative egalitarian order (Warren and Burger Courts, civil rights movement era), and the anti-transformative racial order (Rehnquist and Roberts Courts, New Right conservatism era).

The Supreme Court Database (Spaeth et al. 2024) was used to select cases based on the issues and legal provisions that were decided between the 1801 and 2024 terms. The database did not include any slave trade or slavery cases decided by the Jay, Rutledge, and Ellsworth Courts (1789 to 1801). American Indian cases are not included in this study because of their distinct legal status due to their ties to the Indigenous people of North America and their federal recognition as separate sovereign nations. Cases disposed of on jurisdictional or procedural grounds were not included in the study. This selection process yielded 441 constitutional and statutory race cases decided over a 224-year period. The ideological direction of the decision variable was used to determine whether a case outcome was decided in favor of people of color or pro–civil rights claimants (liberal) and the reverse for an outcome decided against people of color or pro–civil rights claimants (conservative). To present the case outcomes in a structured way, tables were created that list the case names, the votes, a brief statement of the holdings, and a designation of the ideological direction of the outcome. Cases that do not appear in the tables are presented in the chapter discussions.

I cover the origins and development of court policymaking in eight chapters: Marshall and Taney Courts (chapter 1), Chase and Waite Courts (chapter 2), Fuller, White, and Taft Courts (chapter 3), Hughes, Stone, and Vinson Courts (chapter 4), Warren Court (chapter 5), Burger Court (chapter 6), Rehnquist Court (chapter 7), and the Roberts Court (chapter 8). In each chapter, I explore the nature and extent to which the court supported the policy goals of the rival racial orders and whether the case outcomes favored people of color or pro–civil rights claimants. In the conclusion, I review my findings and reveal what has been learned about the Supreme Court's response to people of color when they brought legal challenges to have their constitutional and statutory rights vindicated. Because negative landmark precedents can affect legal change for decades, I explain why reforms are needed to make the Supreme Court more accountable to the democratic values expressed in the Constitution.

Chapter 1

The Marshall and Taney Courts, 1801–1864

This chapter begins at the formation of the American slaveholding republic and ends with its demise by means of a civil war. The enslavement of Africans and people of African descent existed in North America as early as the 1560s in Spanish Florida (Davis 2006). By the mid-1600s, American colonies had enacted legal codes to justify the racial basis for slavery, to protect slave owners' economic interests in slavery and to place limitations on the rights of the enslaved. The colonial legal codes covered a variety of slave regulations: a system of heritable slavery based on the status of the mother, rules that discouraged slave owners from freeing their slaves, prohibitions on interracial marriage, the denial of voting rights, the requirement of passes to travel, prohibitions on the carrying of arms, slaves could not testify against whites, and codes that permitted extreme forms of corporal punishment (whipping, branding, and other forms of bodily mutilation). Colonial court decisions established legal doctrines that were consistent with the objectives of the slave codes. Slavery was legal in all thirteen colonies prior to the American Revolution (Higginbotham 1978, 313).

By the time the fifty-five delegates met in the summer of 1787 to draft a new constitution to replace the Articles of Confederation, the institutions of racial slavery and the slave trade were firmly entrenched in America. The fact that the economies of Southern states were built and maintained by free labor meant that Southern delegates would not accept a constitution that threatened their economic self-interests. The Framers' deliberations resulted in the creation of a document that contained mechanisms and provisions that benefitted slave owners politically and prevented the national government from interfering with the institution of slavery where it existed (Wiecek

1977). Although the Framers' Constitution never used the words "slave" or "slavery," Wiecek (1977, 62–63) and Finkelman (2001, 6–10) found that the document directly sanctioned slavery in five provisions: the three-fifths clause (Article I, § 2, Clause 3), the slave trade clause (Article I, § 9, Clause 1), the fugitive slave clause (Article IV, § 2, Clause 3), the clause that declared that direct and capitation taxes had to take into account the three-fifths clause (Article I, § 9, Clause 4), and Article V that prohibited the ratification of any constitutional amendment involving the slave trade before 1808. The legal historians also identified several provisions that indirectly protected slavery: the electoral college system, which gave slave states disproportionate influence in presidential elections (Article II, § 1, Clause 2), the domestic insurrections clause, which granted Congress the power to call forth the militia to suppress insurrections, including slave rebellions (Article I, § 8, Clause 15), and the requirement that three-fourths of the states ratify amendments, which guaranteed that the slaveholding states would have veto power over constitutional changes (Article V). Article I, § 9, Clause 5, and Article I, § 10, Clause 2, prohibited the federal government and the states from taxing the exported products of slave labor.

According to King and Smith's (2005, 77) theory of racialized policy development, the political coalition that existed at the nation's founding gained sufficient power to direct governing institutions and actors in ways that established a white supremacist institutional order based on beliefs in racial inferiority, racial hierarchy, and chattel slavery. The proslavery regime was formed and maintained by Faustian bargains and compromises struck in the Framers' Constitution, policies of the federal government, and the political power of the slaveholding states. In Article III, the Framers created a national court, the Supreme Court, and granted Congress the authority to establish a system of lower federal courts. Article II, § 2, Clause 2, granted the president the power to appoint federal judges with the advice and consent of the Senate. The newly created Supreme Court was asked to decide policy conflicts that arose from the slavery compromises in the Framers' Constitution. The era-defining racial policy dichotomy used to determine whether the court advanced the policy goals of the predominant ruling regime was slavery versus emancipation. The fact that the proslavery ruling regime appointed justices to the court from 1801 until 1862 guaranteed that the court would exercise its power against emancipation. In this chapter, the court's policymaking role is appraised based on outcomes in cases involving the liberty of the enslaved, the slave trade, slave rendition, the spread of slavery into the territories, and the citizenship status of blacks in America.

The Marshall Court, 1801–1835

THE COMPOSITION OF THE MARSHALL COURT

The Federalists held national political power until the 1800 election when the Jeffersonian-Republicans swept into power and became the dominant national coalition. Six weeks before President John Adams left office in 1801, he appointed his secretary of state, John Marshall, to become the fourth chief justice, to carry out his Federalist policies. Marshall was born into a middle-class, slaveholding Virginia family. He served as a soldier in the American Revolution, he practiced law in Virginia, and held various positions in state and national government. As chief justice, Marshall established institutional boundaries, he regularized court procedures and enhanced the court's prestige. Marshall's legacy as "the Great Chief Justice" is largely based on his contributions to American constitutional development in the areas of judicial power, federalism, the commerce power, and property rights. Finkelman (2018) argued that most biographies of Marshall overlooked or gave limited attention to his economic investment in slavery and his proslavery opinions. Finkelman found that Marshall owned over one hundred slaves in Henrico and Fauquier Counties in Virginia, he believed in white supremacy, and he used his power as chief justice to fashion slavery jurisprudence according to his proslavery views. Finkelman (29) argued that Marshall's slavery jurisprudence cannot be simply explained away by "the need to preserve the Union or fend off proslavery southerners' claims of states' rights." He found that slaves "were a constant factor in his personal life, his economic success, and his children's future. He was personally fully invested in slavery" (48).

Six presidents appointed thirteen justices to the Marshall Court: John Marshall, Bushrod Washington, Alfred Moore, William Johnson, Henry Livingston, Thomas Todd, Gabriel Duvall, Joseph Story, Smith Thompson, Robert Trimble, Henry Baldwin, John McLean, and James Wayne. A majority of Marshall Court justices owned slaves at some point. Of the six presidents who made appointments to the Marshall Court—John Adams, Thomas Jefferson, James Madison, James Monroe, John Quincy Adams, and Andrew Jackson—Jefferson, Madison, Monroe, and Jackson were slave owners.

FREEDOM SUITS

Under the institution of racial slavery, enslavement was the rule and liberty for the enslaved was the exception. The extralegal path to freedom was escape. Slave manumission—the freeing of persons while the institution of slavery persisted—was legally permitted by legislation, wills, deeds, hereditary lineage, purchased freedom, and residence on free soil. Most slavery cases were adjudicated at the state level, but the circuit court in the District of Columbia heard slave manumission cases, which provided a route of appeal to the Supreme Court. It was extremely difficult for the enslaved to bring freedom lawsuits for a variety of reasons: slaves were illiterate, they were isolated on country plantations, they were not aware that they could sue their owners in court, they had limited access to the local courts, they had to obtain and pay for legal counsel, and their suits were subject to discretionary dismissal. Despite these enormous barriers, the enslaved used the legal process to gain and preserve their freedom (VanderVelde 2014; Twitty 2016; Thomas 2020).

Freedom suits raised four issues: free status based on matrilineage, manumission by will or deed, illegal importation of slaves under state law, and residence on free soil based on a federal statute. The Marshall Court placed obstacles in the path of enslaved people of color who attempted to legally contest their bondage based on matrilineal laws of slavery. During the late eighteenth and early nineteenth centuries, some Southern courts permitted the use of hearsay testimony to establish evidence of family history, reputation, or pedigree (Fede 2017, 7–27). Mima Queen sought her freedom on the ground that she was the descendant of a free woman of color. In *Mima Queen and Child v. Hepburn* (1813), Chief Justice Marshall rejected the use of hearsay evidence in Queen's freedom petition because she could not establish specific facts to support her claim and hearsay evidence was susceptible to fraud. Justice Gabriel Duvall dissented on the ground that Maryland permitted the use of hearsay evidence in freedom suits and to "exclude hearsay in such cases, would leave the party interested without a remedy. . . . And people of color, from their helpless condition under the uncontrolled authority of a master, are entitled to all reasonable protection."

The court was more likely to defer to the wishes of the slave owner as expressed in wills or deeds in freedom suits. In 1810, Bennett Darnall, a slave owner, devised to his son Nicholas 596 acres of land. Nicholas's mother was an enslaved woman owned by Darnall (Condon 2001). After Darnall died in 1814, Nicholas took possession of the property in 1826 and entered into a contract with Claudius Le Grand for the sale of a portion of the land for $13,112. Le Grand began to have doubts about the sale and filed a lawsuit that claimed that Nicholas was unable to convey to him a good title under the land because he was not legally manumitted under Maryland law. In *Le Grand v. Darnall* (1829), the court unanimously upheld Maryland's high court's ruling that Nicholas was entitled to his freedom under state law. Justice Duvall found that Nicholas and his brother had guardians appointed, they were well educated and living in affluence and he was capable in law to sell and dispose of any part of his estate and to convey a sufficient title to the purchase.

In Article VI of Northwest Ordinance of 1787, the Confederation Congress prohibited slavery in the land north and west of the Ohio River, but it provided for the return of escaped slaves. In 1789, the first Congress affirmed the ordinance with few modifications and left the free soil provision in place. By the 1830s, sectional conflicts became more intense over the issue of slavery in the territories. Two cases reached the Marshall Court that raised the question whether the Northwest Ordinance's free soil provision was a legal route for the enslaved to obtain their freedom. Both cases were precursors to the sort of claim Dred and Harriet Scott would raise in their freedom suit sixteen years later. In *LaGrange v. Chouteau* (1830) and *Menard v. Aspasia* (1831), the court dismissed both cases as lacking jurisdiction under § 25 of the Judiciary Act of 1789. An enslaved woman was granted her freedom in the *Menard* case because the lower ruled in her favor. Freedom suits pitted human rights against the property rights of the slave owner. The case outcomes presented in table 1.1 show that in most cases, the Marshall Court protected the property rights of slave owners.

Slave Trade Cases

A national political consensus existed in America to ban the international slave trade but not a corresponding consensus to abolish domestic slavery. The slave trade clause prohibited Congress from banning the slave trade before 1808; and in March 1807, Congress passed a law that prohibited the importation of slaves into any port or place within the jurisdiction of the United States. The law took effect on January 1, 1808. Despite subsequent congressional legislation to enforce the ban, the international slave trade persisted due to weak enforcement efforts. The Marshall Court's most important slavery case, the *Antelope* (1825), was a complex international slave trade case that was litigated over several years and produced three court opinions. In 1820, a Spanish slave ship from Cuba, the *Antelope*,

Table 1.1. Marshall Court Freedom Suit Cases, 1801–1835

Case	Vote	Outcome
Scott v. Negro London (1806)*	5–0	Found no illegal importation of a slave under Virginia law; freedom petition denied (C)
Scott v. Negro Ben (1810)*	5–0	Found no illegal importation of a slave under Maryland law; freedom petition denied (C)
Wood v. Davis (1812)*	7–0	Enslaved children failed to prove their free status based on matrilineage; freedom petition denied (C)
Mima Queen and Child v. Hepburn (1813)*	5–1	Rejected the use of hearsay evidence in a freedom petition (C)
Negress Sally Henry v. Ball (1816)*	7–0	Found no illegal importation of a slave under Maryland law; freedom petition denied (C)
Negro John Davis v. Wood (1816)*	7–0	Failed to prove free status based on matrilineage; freedom petition denied (C)
Mason v. Matilda (1827)	7–0	Found no illegal importation of a slave under Virginia law; freedom petition denied (C)
Le Grand v. Darnall (1829)	6–0	Held that a young boy of color was legally manumitted by will and held good title to inherited land (L)
LaGrange v. Chouteau (1830)*	7–0	Residence on free soil lawsuit dismissed for lack of jurisdiction (C)
Menard v. Aspasia (1831)	7–0	Residence on free soil lawsuit dismissed for lack of jurisdiction; enslaved woman granted freedom (L)
McCutchen v. Marshall (1834)	6–0	Failed to prove free status based on matrilineage; freedom petition denied (C)
Lee v. Lee (1834)	6–0	Found no illegal importation of a slave under Maryland law; freedom petition denied (C)
Fenwick v. Chapman (1835)	6–0	Slaves were legally manumitted by will (L)
Wallingsford v. Allen (1836)	5–0	Slaves were legally manumitted by deed (L)

Source: Created by the author.

Note: C for conservative outcomes, L for liberal outcomes.

*Chief Justice Marshall wrote the opinion of the court or the majority opinion.

was captured while it was adrift off the coast of Spanish Florida. The ship was brought to the port of Savannah, Georgia, where American authorities found 281 young African captives on board to be sold on the Southern market. The *Antelope*'s crew was charged with piracy under American law. The claimants, Spain, Portugal, and the captain of the ship, sought restitution for the captured Africans.

The federal government argued that the Africans were free because they had been captured by slave traders who intended to sell them in America in violation of the Slave Trade Act of 1819. The federal government's legal argument was based on a circuit court opinion written by Justice Joseph Story in *United States v. La Jeune Eugenie* (1822). The *La Jeune Eugenie* was captured off the West African coast by an American naval cruiser on the suspicion that it was an American ship even though it flew a French flag. The question before the circuit court was whether the *La Jeune Eugenie* was an American ship engaged in the slave trade in violation of federal law or whether it was a French slave ship captured because of its involvement in the slave trade in violation of the law of nations. Although Justice Story strongly condemned the international slave trade based on natural law principles, he ruled that the *La Jeune Eugenie* was a French ship and the court lacked jurisdiction to hear foreign cases.

Chief Justice Marshall wrote the unanimous decision in the first *Antelope* case. At the outset, Marshall acknowledged the conflict between the sacred rights of liberty and property raised in the case. He asserted that the slave trade was "contrary to the law of nature" because that "every man has a natural right to the fruits of his own labour, is generally admitted; and that no other person can rightfully deprive him of those fruits and appropriate them against his will, seems to be the necessary result of this admission." Marshall explained that war has existed throughout history and even among the "most enlightened nations of antiquity" the "victor might enslave the vanquished." Because this "was the usage of all," slavery could not be repugnant by the law of nations because "that which has received the assent of all, must be the law of all." Marshall went on to say that in the continent of Africa, "it is still the law of nations that prisoners are slaves." Marshall found that the slave trade was legal, that both Europe and America embarked in it for nearly two centuries, and that "it was carried on without opposition and without censure." He concluded that the slave trade was considered commerce under the law of nations and every nation had an equal right to engage in it.

Chief Justice Marshall applied natural rights principles to property rights cases, but he refused to do so in the *Antelope* case. Marshall understood that natural law doctrine would lead to the release of the captured Africans, which would upset the proslavery regime if the doctrine was applied to domestic slavery. In the *Antelope*, Marshall sanctioned one of the worst crimes against humanity—the economic enterprise of the international slave trade. Despite laws and international treaties to suppress the slave trade, table 1.2 shows that the Marshall Court amassed a mixed record with regard to upholding the prosecutions of slave traders.

Table 1.2. Marshall Court Slave Trade Cases, 1801–1835

Case	Vote	Outcome
Adams v. Woods (1805)*	4–0	Statute of limitations barred fines against a slave trader (C)
United States v. Schooner Sally (1805)	4–0	Affirmed the acquittal of a defendant accused of violating the Slave Trade Act of 1794 (C)
Amiable Lucy v. United States (1810)	5–0	Reversed the conviction of a defendant accused of violating the Slave Trade Act of 1803 (C)
Brig Caroline v. United States (1813)	7–0	Reversed the sentence of forfeiture of a slave trader's ship because the libel charge was too vague (C)
Brig Alerta v. Moran (1815)	6–0	Held that a federal court had jurisdiction to return slaves to a Spanish slave trader captured by a French ship (C)
Josefa Segunda (1820)	7–0	Upheld the seizure and forfeiture of property of a slave ship (L)
Mary Ann (1823)*	5–0	Reversed a decree ordering the forfeiture of a slave trader's ship (C)
Emily and the Caroline (1824)	6–0	Held that the ships were properly forfeited under Slave Trade Acts of 1794 and 1807 (L)
Merino (1824)	6–0	Held that the evidence did not support slave trading charges against all ships, but amended slave trading charges were allowed (L)
St. Jago de Cuba (1824)	6–0	Upheld charges against a slave trader under the 1794 and 1818 Slave Trading Acts (L)
Plattsburgh (1825)	6–0	Held that a seized slave trading ship must be forfeited under the 1794 and 1800 Slave Trading Acts (L)

Case	Vote	Outcome
Antelope (1825)*	6–0	Held that the international slave trade did not violate the law of nations (C)
United States v. Gooding (1827)	7–0	Found indictments against some slave traders defective but not others under the 1818 Slave Trade Act (L)
Sundry African Slaves v. Madrazo (1828)*	6–1	Held that the Eleventh Amendment barred claims for confiscated slaves against the governor of Georgia (C)

Source: Created by the author.

Note: C for conservative outcomes, L for liberal outcomes. A slave trade case is listed only once even if it returned to the court to clarify earlier holdings or presented new issues.

*Chief Justice Marshall wrote the opinion of the court or the majority opinion.

The Taney Court, 1836–1864

THE COMPOSITION OF THE TANEY COURT

After Justice Gabriel Duvall retired from the court in 1835, President Andrew Jackson nominated Roger Brooke Taney as his successor. The Whigs in the Senate refused to confirm Taney because they feared that a Jackson appointment would eventually dismantle Marshall's nationalist jurisprudence. In March 1836, the Senate confirmed Jackson's second choice, Phillip Barbour, to succeed Duvall. The Marshall Court ended on July 6, 1835, when John Marshall died at the age of 79 from declining health. In December 1835, Jackson nominated Taney to succeed Marshall and the Jacksonian-controlled Senate confirmed him in March 1836 by a 29–15 vote. Born in Calvert County, Maryland, Taney came from a wealthy slaveholding family that made its fortune in tobacco. During his early career, Taney practiced law and served in the Maryland legislature. Taney was a politically polarizing figure during his service in the Jackson administration as secretary of war, attorney general, and secretary of the treasury.

Eight presidents made sixteen appointments to the Taney Court: Andrew Jackson, Martin Van Buren, John Tyler, James Polk, Millard Fillmore, Franklin Pierce, James Buchanan, and Abraham Lincoln. Four of the presidents were slave owners: Jackson, Van Buren, Polk, and Tyler. Five Marshall Court holdovers served on the Taney Court: Story, Thompson, Baldwin, McLean, and Wayne. Thirteen justices were subsequently appointed after Taney was confirmed as chief justice: John Catron, John McKinley, Samuel Nelson, Peter Daniel, Levi Woodbury, Robert Grier, Benjamin Curtis, John Campbell, Nathan Clifford, Samuel Miller, David Davis, Noah Swayne, and Stephen Field. Most of the justices who served on the Taney Court were Southerners and doughface Northerners. Finkelman (2018, 172) labeled Roger Taney as "Slavery's Great Chief Justice." Taney's proslavery jurisprudence was rooted in principles of dual federalism and state sovereignty unless they would lead to undesirable policy outcomes. In those instances, Taney espoused nationalist views to protect the institution of slavery. Taney took an intensely partisan approach to slavery cases, and he was consistently hostile to the rights of free blacks. The Taney Court addressed three slavery issues: the slave trade, slave rendition, and claims to freedom based on residence on free soil. The court's decisions under Taney's leadership intensified sectional conflict and tipped the balance of the scales in favor of the South.

Slave Trade Cases

During the tenure of the Taney Court, enforcement of international slave trade bans remained a problem because the illegal trade in captured Africans was a lucrative business enterprise. A sensational case about the fate of African captives who physically resisted their enslaved status aboard a Spanish slave ship galvanized the antislavery movement in America. In *United States v. Amistad* (1841), Justice Story found that the African captives were never the lawful slaves of the slave traders because they were kidnaped in violation of the laws and treaties banning the international slave trade. Despite the fact that the African captives won their freedom, the *Amistad* decision had no impact on domestic slavery in America.

Transatlantic travel to France provided an opportunity for the enslaved who traveled with their owners to obtain their freedom (Schafer 1994). In *United States v. Ship Garonne* (1837), Chief Justice Taney found that an enslaved domestic servant's right to freedom under French law was not material to the case. Taney explained that the Slave Trade Act of 1818 did not prohibit slave owners from traveling to foreign countries and returning to the United States with their slaves who were inhabitants or held to service by the laws of the states or territories of the United States after a temporary absence. Taney's proslavery views in *Garonne* signaled how he might decide freedom suits based on residence on free soil in the United States.

In *Groves v. Slaughter* (1841), the Taney Court avoided a constitutional conflict over the power of states to regulate the domestic slave trade.

Groves was a commercial case that involved a conflict between the buyer and seller of slaves over the payment of promissory notes in Mississippi. The court's decision failed to address a question connected to the case: whether Mississippi's ban on the importation of slaves violated the commerce clause. In his concurring opinion, Justice John McLean expressed the view that Northern states had the right to prevent slave owners from bringing their slaves to the North. Chief Justice Taney agreed with McLean that the power over slavery belongs to the state, but he added that Congress could not regulate slavery under the commerce clause or any other provision in the Constitution. Taney's concurrence shed insight on how he would vote when the question of federal power versus state power to regulate slavery in the territories was directly presented to the court.

SLAVE RENDITION

The fugitive slave clause protected slave owners' economic interests by prohibiting free states from using their antislavery laws to grant freedom to escaped slaves. To implement the clause, Congress passed the Fugitive Slave Act of 1793, which authorized slaveowners or their agents to capture escaped slaves across state lines and bring them before a state or federal magistrate to obtain a certificate of removal that would allow their return. The law also penalized any person who provided assistance to escaped slaves. Northern states enacted personal liberty laws that established legal procedures to facilitate the return of escaped slaves and to prohibit the kidnaping of free blacks. Edward Prigg and three other slave catchers were convicted of violating Pennsylvania's personal liberty law after he captured Margaret Morgan and her children and returned them to slavery in Maryland without obtaining a certificate of removal from a state judicial officer. Prigg appealed his conviction on the ground that the personal liberty law violated his rights established by the Fugitive Slave Act of 1793.

In *Prigg v. Pennsylvania* (1842), Justice Joseph Story wrote the sweeping majority opinion that upheld the Fugitive Slave Act of 1793 on two grounds: the fugitive slave clause guaranteed the slave owner's right to recapture fugitive slaves from anywhere in the United States, and Congress had exclusive power to enforce the clause. Story explained that the "true design" of the fugitive slave clause "was to guard against the doctrines and principles prevalent in the non-slaveholding states, by preventing them from intermeddling with, or obstructing, or abolishing the rights of the owners of slaves." The remaining question addressed in *Prigg* was whether the Fugitive Slave Act was exclusive to the national government or whether it was concurrent in the states. Story asserted that the slaveholding states would not have been satisfied with leaving this power of regulation in the nonslaveholding states, which "would or might practically amount to a power to destroy the rights of the owner." He explained that the police power belonged to the states in virtue of their sovereignty but "such regulations can never be permitted to interfere with or to obstruct the just rights of the owner to reclaim his slave, derived from the Constitution of the United States; or with the remedies prescribed by Congress to aid and enforce the same." Story concluded that "under and in virtue of the Constitution, the owner of a slave is clothed with entire authority, in every state in the Union, to seize and recapture his slave, whenever he can do it without any breach of the peace, or any illegal violence."

Chief Justice Taney concurred in the result in *Prigg*. He objected to Story's pro-nationalist conclusion that state authorities did not have the power to enforce the Fugitive Slave Act. He asserted that it was the duty of the states to protect and support the slave owner when he attempted to obtain possession of his property after the slave has escaped and taken refuge in another state. In his dissent, Justice McLean rejected the right of recapture, because blacks who resided in Northern states were presumed to be free and states had the right to enact personal liberty laws to protect them. *Prigg v. Pennsylvania* was the court's first landmark slavery precedent that established that the nation was governed by a proslavery Constitution. The Taney Court used national power to protect the South's interest in slavery, and the decision jeopardized the liberty of free blacks who were at risk of being captured by slave catchers. Northerners denounced the decision as an assault on the rights of states to exercise their police powers and provide for civil liberties (Finkelman 1994).

During the Fillmore administration, Congress passed a more oppressive fugitive slave law, the Fugitive Slave Act of 1850, which made rendition a federal matter by prohibiting state officials from interfering with the process, blacks who were accused of being escaped slaves were denied the right to petition the court for a writ of habeas corpus and heavy civil penalties were imposed on private citizens who interfered with the rendition process. In 1854, a group of Milwaukee abolitionists were arrested by federal marshals after they stormed a jail and freed an escaped slave. Sherman Booth challenged his detention on the ground that the Fugitive Slave Act of 1850 was unconstitutional. In *Ableman v. Booth* (1859), Chief Justice Taney found that "the act of Congress commonly called the fugitive slave law is, in all of its provisions, fully authorized by the Constitution of the United States; that the commissioner had lawful authority to issue the warrant and commit the party, and its proceedings were regular and conformable to law." In contrast to his strongly held states' rights position, Taney relied on the primacy of national authority to preserve slave ownership in *Ableman*. As the outcomes in table 1.3 indicate, the Taney Court's slave rendition decisions secured the Southern states' grip on the institution of slavery.

FREEDOM SUITS

The Taney Court did not prohibit manumission by will or deed as a path to freedom for the enslaved. In *Williams v. Ash* (1842), Chief Justice Taney ruled in favor of a slave who sued the executor of his former owner's estate when the executor broke the terms of the will by selling him to a slave trader. The will stipulated that none of the enslaved persons could be sold or removed from Maryland; otherwise, they would be free for life. Taney rejected the executor's argument that the terms of the will infringed on the property rights of the heirs and, because slaves were property, Ash could not receive a bequest of freedom. Taney held that "the bequest of freedom to a slave is a specific legacy, and undoubtedly this is its true legal character."

The failure of the Compromise of 1850 to settle the debate over the expansion of slavery into the western territories resulted in another legislative

Table 1.3. Taney Court Rendition Cases, 1836–1864

Case	Vote	Outcome
Prigg v. Pennsylvania (1842)	8–1	Struck down Pennsylvania's personal liberty law and upheld the Fugitive Slave Act of 1793 (C)
Jones v. Van Zandt (1847)	9–0	Upheld the constitutionality of the Fugitive Slave Act of 1793 on the authority of *Prigg* (C)
Moore v. Illinois (1852)	7–1	Held that states have concurrent powers to enact fugitive slave laws (C)
Ableman v. Booth (1859)	9–0	Held that the Fugitive Slave Act of 1850 was constitutional based on the primacy of national authority (C)

Source: Created by the author.

Note: C for conservative outcomes, L for liberal outcomes.

attempt, the Kansas-Nebraska Act of 1854. Senator Stephen Douglas authored the legislation, which transferred authority from Congress to the voters to decide whether the Kansas and Nebraska territories would be free states or slave states. Douglas insisted that popular sovereignty was the democratic solution to the conflict over slavery in the territories. In reality, the law caused immediate political upheaval between free soilers, who were firmly opposed to territorial expansion of slavery, and slaveowners, who sought to increase their national power by promoting the expansion of slavery into the new territories. Opposition to the Kansas-Nebraska Act led to the formation of a new political party, the Republican Party.

The Taney Court initially dodged the question whether residence on free soil was a legal path to freedom for enslaved blacks. In *Strader v. Graham* (1851), a Kentucky slaveowner permitted three slaves to work for wages as musicians in Ohio and Indiana. When the slaves returned to Louisville, they were taken aboard a steamboat and transported to Cincinnati where they escaped to Canada. The slaveowner sued the operator of the steamboat under a Kentucky law that allowed for the recovery of damages when a steamboat owner took slaves out of state without the owner's permission. The Kentucky Court of Appeals ruled that the Northwest Ordinance did not grant the slaves their freedom due to their short stays in Ohio and Indiana because their status was determined by Kentucky law. Chief Justice Taney dismissed the case for lack of jurisdiction under § 25 of the Judiciary Act of 1789 because the state's high court ruling was not against the validity of a federal law. The resolution of the case on jurisdictional grounds did not prevent Taney from asserting his view that the Northwest Ordinance of 1787 was unconstitutional. Taney expressed support for total state power over the status of slaves, and he declared that slavery could not be limited by Congress in the new states.

In 1846, an enslaved couple, Dred and Harriet Scott, filed separate freedom suits in a St. Louis, Missouri, circuit court based on their extended stays on free soil in Illinois and Wisconsin (Fehrenbacher 1981; Finkelman 1997). Under Missouri law, slaves could sue their owners if they had reasonable grounds to believe that they were free. VanderVelde (2014, 20–21) found that of three hundred original court filings in St. Louis, over one hundred enslaved litigants were granted their freedom in the years leading up to the *Dred Scott* case. In 1847, the St. Louis circuit court consolidated the Scotts' freedom petitions and granted their freedom from Irene Sanford Emerson, the widow of the Scotts' owner John Emerson, who died in 1843. By the time Irene Emerson's appeal reached the Missouri Supreme Court, it had been transformed into a proslavery court due to changes in its personnel. The Scotts lost their case before the Missouri Supreme Court on the ground that residence on free soil did not entitle their freedom upon return to Missouri. After obtaining new lawyers in 1853, the Scotts sued New York resident John Sanford, Irene Emerson's brother, in a federal circuit court in Missouri under Article III's diversity jurisdiction to obtain their freedom. Sanford sought to have Scott's freedom suit dismissed on jurisdictional grounds because Scott was a slave and not a citizen of the United States. The circuit court allowed the case to proceed because Scott was a resident of Missouri for the purposes of Article III jurisdiction, but the court made it clear that its ruling did not extend citizenship status to the Scotts. On the merits of the case, the federal circuit court ruled against the Scotts' freedom, citing the Missouri Supreme Court ruling and the *Strader* decision.

The Scotts' freedom rested in the hands of the Taney Court justices: Roger Taney, James Wayne, John Catron, Peter Daniel, Samuel Nelson, Robert Grier, John Campbell, John McLean, and Benjamin Curtis. With regard to sectional representation, five justices were appointed from slave states (Taney, Wayne, Catron, Daniel, and Campbell) and four justices were appointed from free states (Nelson, Grier, McLean, and Curtis). Eight of the nine justices were appointed by Democratic presidents, except Curtis who was appointed by Whig President Millard Fillmore. The Southern justices came from slaveholding families and they owned slaves themselves at some point. John McLean, the only justice on the Taney Court who openly opposed slavery, had become a Republican by the time the case was decided. Two of the Northern justices on the court, Nelson and Grier, were doughfaces, and Curtis was a Northern conservative who strongly supported the enforcement of fugitive slave laws. Based on the ideological and partisan composition of the Taney Court, the Scotts had no chance of winning their freedom suit.

In *Dred Scott v. Sandford* (1857), Chief Justice Taney wrote the sweeping majority opinion that ruled against the Scotts' freedom in a 241-page, 7–2 decision that produced nine separate opinions. Fehrenbacher (1981, 186) argued that Taney used the case "to vindicate his extreme views at length and graft them authoritatively onto American constitutional law." According to Fehrenbacher's account, free blacks in the South were a problem for slave owners, and Taney was determined to protect the South by separating the black race absolutely from the rights bestowed in the federal Constitution whether free or slave. To put his policy preferences into law, Taney framed the question as: "Can a negro, whose ancestors were imported into this country, and sold as slaves, become a member of the political community formed and brought into existence by the Constitution of the United States, and as such become entitled to all the rights, and privileges, and immunities, guarantied by that instrument to the citizen?"

Before answering the question, Taney distinguished the situation of the black population from the members of the Indian nations, who were a free and independent people governed by their own laws and were treated as foreign governments. Taney stated that "if an individual should leave his nation or tribe, and take up his abode among the white population, he would be entitled to all the rights and privileges which would belong to an emigrant from any other foreign people." Taney treated the words "people of the United States" and "citizens" synonymously and asserted that they described "the political body who, according to our republican institutions, form the sovereignty, and who hold the power and conduct the Government through their representatives." Taney's response to the question presented in the case was that at the time the Constitution was adopted, blacks were "considered as a subordinate and inferior class of beings" and "who had been subjugated by the dominant race." Whether emancipated or not, blacks "were not intended to be included, under the word 'citizens' in the Constitution, and can therefore claim none of the rights and privileges which that instrument provides for and secures to citizens of the United States."

Taney proposed a novel, race-based dual citizenship theory that claimed that prior to the adoption of the Constitution, every state had the right to confer citizenship on anyone it pleased, but it was limited within the confines of the state. After the adoption of the Constitution, that person or a class of persons "would not be a citizen in the sense in which that word is used in the Constitution of the United States, nor entitled to sue as such in one of its courts, nor to the privileges and immunities of a citizen in the other States." Based on this reasoning, Taney found that the Constitution did not make blacks citizens of the Union, and even if states conferred citizenship rights upon blacks, they "would be restricted to the State which gave them." Taney made it clear that Northern states could not force its notions of citizenship on the slave states.

Taney resorted to white supremacist ideology, legislation, the history of the founding, language in the Declaration of Independence, and clauses in the Constitution to support his finding that blacks, slaves or free, were not state citizens or citizens of the United States. Taney asserted that at the time of the founding, blacks "had for more than a century before been regarded as beings of an inferior order, and altogether unfit to associate with the white race, either in social or political relations; and so far inferior, that they had no rights which the white man was bound to respect; and that the negro might justly and lawfully be reduced to slavery for his benefit." Taney explained that blacks were property—they were bought and sold and treated as merchandise whenever a profit could be made by it. According to Taney, "this opinion was at that time fixed and universal in the civilized portion of the white race." Taney cited colonial laws that banned interracial marriages as evidence that a "perpetual and impassible barrier" was created between whites and the enslaved because they were "looked upon as so far below them in the scale of created beings." After examining the language of the Declaration of Independence, Taney concluded that "it is too clear for dispute, that the enslaved African race were not to be included, and formed no part of the people who framed and adopted this declaration." Turning to the Constitution, Taney found that the slave trade clause and the fugitive slave clause "point directly and specifically to the negro race as a separate class of persons, and show clearly that they were not regarded as a portion of the people or citizens of the Government then formed." He contended that free blacks "were identified in the public mind with the race to which they belonged, and regarded as a part of the slave population rather than the free."

Taney explained that the laws of the slaveholding states established that blacks were not considered as citizens; otherwise, they would not have consented to the Constitution. He cited several federal laws to support his argument that blacks were not considered as citizens: the first naturalization law passed by Congress in 1790 that confined the right of citizenship to "aliens being free white persons," the first militia law that directed that every "free able-bodied white male citizen shall be enrolled in the militia," and the 1813 law that prohibited the employment of persons of color on board any public or private vessels of the United States. Based on his selective and biased reading of the history of the founding era, which ignored the fact that free blacks had political, legal, and property rights, Taney concluded that Scott was not a citizen of Missouri within the meaning of the Constitution, and therefore he was not entitled to sue in the federal circuit court.

Next, Taney addressed the question whether the Scotts' residence on free soil in Illinois and the Wisconsin territory changed their enslaved status to rule on the constitutionality of the Missouri Compromise. To show that Congress lacked the power to regulate or prohibit slavery, Taney made the absurd claim that the language used in the territories clause, Article IV, § 3, Clause 2, was limited to the territories that existed in 1787 and not to those territories owned by the federal government in 1857. For additional support, Taney argued that slavery was a special kind of property that deserved greater protection under the Bill of Rights and especially the Fifth Amendment's provision that no person shall be deprived of life, liberty, or property without due process of law. He asserted that the Missouri Compromise deprived slave owners of their property when they brought slaves "into a particular Territory of the United States." As the final blow to the Scotts' claim of freedom, Taney cited *Strader v. Graham* to support his finding that the Scotts were not made free when they were taken to Rock Island, Illinois, and their status "as free or slave, depended on the laws of Missouri, and not of Illinois."

The two dissenting justices, John McLean and Benjamin Curtis, addressed the weaknesses of Taney's majority opinion. McLean disagreed with Taney's white supremacist ideology as being "more of a matter of taste than of law." He accurately pointed out that free blacks could vote and were considered citizens of states. On the question whether Congress had the authority to enact laws for the territories, McLean stated that the Confederation Congress passed the Northwest Ordinance of 1787, and it intended to ban slavery in the territories. For McLean, this historical fact was consistent with the intent of the Founders and Framers of the Constitution, it meant that the Missouri Compromise was constitutional and the Scotts were made free as a result of their extended stays on free soil. Justice Curtis was highly critical of Taney's treatment of the question of black citizenship. He pointed out that free blacks were citizens of New England states at the time the Constitution was adopted, and they could vote on equal terms with other citizens in several states. Curtis believed that blacks were members of the political community, which meant that they had access to the courts. He asserted that the Missouri Compromise was valid, Congress had plenary power to regulate slavery in the territories based on the structure of the Constitution and the territories clause in Article IV, and the Scotts remained free under Missouri law. He viewed state court decisions on slavery as being politically motivated, and their decisions were not binding on the Supreme Court.

The landmark *Dred Scott* decision was the Taney Court's final policy pronouncement on slavery. The South applauded the decision because it strongly favored a proslavery interpretation of the Constitution and it indicated a policy direction that slavery would become national. Opponents of slavery expressed considerable hostility toward the decision, because they thought it would facilitate the spread of slavery into the territories and the free states by obligating them to protect slave property. Two months after the decision, abolitionist Frederick Douglass delivered a speech before the American Abolition Society in New York where he told the audience that Taney's settlement "to blot out forever the hopes of an enslaved people may be one necessary link in the chain of events preparatory to the downfall and complete overthrow of the whole slave system" (Foner 1999, 348). Douglass believed that the *Dred Scott* decision would not be the final settlement of the slavery question, because "slaveholders are in earnest, and mean to cling to their slaves as long as they can, and to the bitter end. . . . The case is one of life or death with them, and they will give up only when they must do that or do worse" (Foner 1999, 345).

John Sanford won his case but he died a few weeks after the decision. The Scotts' freedom was subsequently arranged by Irene Emerson Chaffee's new husband, Republican congressman Clifford Chaffee of Massachusetts, who learned that he was the actual owner of the Scotts under the law of coverture. Because Missouri law allowed only state residents to free a slave,

Table 1.4. Taney Court Freedom Suit Cases, 1836–1864

Case	Vote	Outcome
Williams v. Ash (1842)	9–0	Granted a slave his freedom after the executor of the owner's estate violated the terms of the will (L)
Rhodes v. Bell (1844)	9–0	Granted a slave his freedom when he was brought to Maryland from Virginia and sold in violation of Maryland law (L)
Adams v. Roberts (1844)	7–0	Granted a slave her freedom by allowing a jury to consider that she was born after her mother was manumitted by deed (L)
Miller v. Herbert (1847)	9–0	Denied two slaves their freedom because the witnesses did not sign the deed of manumission (C)
Strader v. Graham (1851)	8–1	Held that the court lacked jurisdiction to hear a claim that residence on free soil conferred freedom on blacks (C)
Dred Scott v. Sandford (1857)	7–2	Held that slaves and free blacks were not citizens and they could not sue in federal or state courts; declared the Missouri Compromise unconstitutional (C)
Vigel v. Naylor (1861)	8–0	Permitted a slave to offer conclusive evidence to the jury that she was free based on the rule of matrilineage (L)

Source: Created by the author.

Note: C for conservative outcomes, L for liberal outcomes.

ownership of the Scotts was transferred to Taylor Blow, the son of Dred Scott's original owner Peter Blow. Irene Emerson Chaffee agreed to the arrangement on the condition that she received the wages the Scotts' earned while they were rented out during the litigation. The Scotts' freedom was granted on May 26, 1857, and about fourteen months later, Dred Scott died from illness on September 17, 1858 (VanderVelde 2015, 276).

Aftermath of the *Dred Scott* Decision

Chief Justice Taney's approach to the *Dred Scott* case was more political and policy driven than legal. Taney believed that he could resolve the intense political debate over slavery in the territories by declaring that persons of African descent were not citizens, slaves were property, and Congress lacked the authority to ban slavery in the territories. Taney's miscalculation contributed to the rise of the Republican Party and unrelenting attacks on the *Dred Scott* decision. Southern Democrats believed that Northern Republicans would not accept the legitimacy of the *Dred Scott* decision; and after John Brown's failed raid at Harper's Ferry in 1859, they feared that abolitionists would stop at nothing to eradicate slavery. Southerners were outraged at a New York Court of Appeals decision, *Lemmon v. The People* (1860), which held that eight slaves who travelled to New York with their owners by steamboat only to briefly disembark and board another vessel bound to New Orleans were free. The state high court rejected Taney's premise in *Dred Scott* and applied the reasoning in *Somerset v. Stewart* (1772)—that a slave becomes free by coming into a free jurisdiction (Wiecek 1977, 57).

In 1858, the Republican US Senate candidate from Illinois, Abraham Lincoln, harshly criticized the *Dred Scott* decision in his famous House Divided Speech on the ground that it would lead to the nationalization of slavery. Lincoln lost his Senate election, but he won the 1860 presidential election in a four-way contest, which marked the beginning of the demise of the first white supremacist racial order and the rise of the transformative egalitarian racial order. Presidential elections matter and the South realized that Lincoln would carry out his pledge to restrict slave owners' access to the federal territories and he would appoint antislavery justices to the Supreme Court. Southern Democrats reached the conclusion that the only way to protect the institution of slavery was to secede from the Union and form a new slaveholding republic. By the time Lincoln was inaugurated on March 4, 1861, seven Southern states had seceded and formed a new government, the Confederate States of America. On April 12, 1861, the Confederate attack on Fort Sumter in Charleston, South Carolina, plunged the Union into a constitutional crisis and a civil war.

The sectional politics of slavery shaped the composition of the Supreme Court. About six months after *Dred Scott* was decided, Justice Curtis submitted his resignation to go into private practice. In 1858, President Buchanan appointed Roger Taney's friend Nathan Clifford to succeed Curtis. Within a two-year period, President Lincoln made four appointments to the Taney Court. In January 1862, Lincoln appointed Noah Swayne, the antislavery Quaker who succeeded John McLean after his death in 1861. In July 1862, Lincoln appointed Samuel Miller to fill Peter Daniel's vacancy after his death in 1860. When Lincoln declared that war existed three days after the attack on Fort Sumter, Justice John Campbell quickly resigned from the court to serve as assistant secretary of war for the Confederacy. In December 1862, Lincoln appointed his friend and former campaign manager, David Davis, to succeed Campbell. Congress passed the Tenth Circuit Act of 1863, which expanded the size of the Supreme Court to ten. The legislation gave Lincoln the opportunity to appoint Stephen Field, a Unionist Democrat, to fill the newly created tenth seat. Lincoln made his last appointment to the court when eighty-seven-year-old Roger Taney died on October 12, 1864, after serving twenty-eight-years as chief justice. Salmon Chase, who opposed slavery and represented escaped slaves in court, became the sixth chief justice on December 15, 1864.

The Destruction of Slavery

The destruction of the institution of racial slavery was a process that began during the Civil War. In his first inaugural address on March 4, 1861, Lincoln announced that secession was incompatible with a perpetual Union, and he restated his commitment to prevent the spread of slavery to the western territories. Lincoln believed that Chief Justice Taney's interpretation of the Constitution was not final, and under the doctrine of coordinate construction, each branch had the independent authority to interpret the Constitution. Lincoln stated that "if the policy of the Government upon vital questions affecting the whole people is to be irrevocably fixed by decisions of the Supreme Court," then "the people will have ceased to be their own rulers, having to that extent practically resigned their Government into the hands of that eminent tribunal." The Republican Congress ignored the *Dred Scott* decision when it enacted several laws that were designed to abolish slavery.

Congress passed the Confiscation Acts of 1861 and 1862, which authorized the Union military to seize and capture Confederate property, free slaves in conquered territories, and prohibit the return of fugitive slaves. In 1862, Lincoln signed the District of Columbia Compensation Emancipation Act, which abolished slavery in Washington, DC, by compensated emancipation and the Territorial Slavery Act which abolished slavery in the federal territories.

On January 1, 1863, Lincoln issued an executive order to emancipate the enslaved based on his constitutional authority as commander-in-chief. The Emancipation Proclamation declared that "all persons held as slaves within said designated States, and parts of States, are, and henceforward shall be free; and that the Executive Government of the United States, including the military and naval authorities thereof, will recognize and maintain the freedom of said persons." The order also provided that slaves abstain from all violence unless in self-defense and that they labor for reasonable wages, and it permitted the enlistment of black troops into the Union army. Emancipation did not occur immediately, because the executive order could not be enforced in states under Confederate control; nor did it apply to the four border states. Despite its limitations, the Emancipation Proclamation was a great document of human rights. The enslaved reacted jubilantly to the Proclamation, because it gave them hope that freedom was near. Du Bois ([1935] 2007, 112) wrote that "it changed all their pessimism and despair into boundless faith. It was the Coming of the Lord."

Only a constitutional amendment could formally eradicate the institution of racial slavery and destroy its legal foundations. In 1864, Lincoln expressed his support for a constitutional amendment to abolish slavery because he was concerned that the Emancipation Proclamation would be challenged before the Taney Court (Foner 2019, 45). The Thirteenth Amendment was approved by Congress on January 21, 1865: "Neither slavery nor involuntary servitude, except as a punishment for crime whereof the party shall have been duly convicted, shall exist within the United States, or any place subject to their jurisdiction." On April 9, 1865, the Civil War came to an end when Confederate general Robert E. Lee surrendered to Union general Ulysses S. Grant at the Appomattox Court House in Virginia. On the evening of April 14, Confederate sympathizer John Wilkes Booth shot President Lincoln as he watched a play at Ford's Theatre, and he died the next day. Lincoln did not live to see the ratification of the Thirteenth Amendment on December 6, 1865. The white supremacist racial order had formally come to an end. As Du Bois ([1935] 2007, 140) observed, "the paradox of a democracy founded on slavery had at last been done away with."

Conclusion

The Framers' compromises that gave formal recognition to the institution of slavery and the slave trade in the text of the 1787 Constitution cannot be defended as a sin or a moral failing. The slave trade and racial enslavement were crimes against humanity that were perpetrated against millions of captured Africans who were brought to the Americas against their will and relegated to the status of chattel property. The Framers' Constitution created America's slaveholding republic, and Southern slaveowners who profited from free labor were its primary beneficiaries until 1860. The outcomes of the slavery cases examined in this chapter show that the Marshall and Taney Courts exercised their powers to advance the policy goals of the proslavery regime. Of the forty-two slavery cases decided by the court over a sixty-three-year period, 64 percent were decided in a conservative direction (proslavery) and 36 percent were decided in a liberal direction (antislavery). The court was willing to uphold the wishes of slaveowners when the enslaved sought their freedom in lawsuits with regard to contested wills or deeds, and the court was partially supportive of the enforcement of slave trade laws. The Supreme Court did not decide a single case that threatened or weakened the institution of racial slavery.

Chief Justice Roger Taney's notorious *Dred Scott* majority opinion exacerbated sectional tensions that contributed to the rise of the Republican Party and Lincoln's ascendancy into the White House. For Southern Democrats, the only way to maintain the slaveholders' republic was to secede from the Union and fight a civil war. The consequences of the South's fateful decision were significant: the South surrendered in 1865, the enslaved received their freedom, Lincoln was assassinated, the proslavery provisions in the Framers' Constitution were rejected, and a civil war death toll over 700,000. Taney was denounced, vilified, and despised by opponents of slavery. When the US Senate debated whether Taney's bust should be placed in the Old Supreme Court Chamber in the US Capitol, Senator Charles Sumner (1865, 1012) objected, stating that "the name of Taney is to be hooted down in the page of history." Three years after Sumner's death, a bust of Taney was placed in the Old Supreme Court Chamber. As part of an effort to remove Confederate statutes and busts from public display in the US Capitol, the House of Representatives voted in 2021 to remove Taney's bust. On December 27, 2022, President Joe Biden signed legislation to replace Taney's bust with the bust of the first African American Supreme Court Justice, Thurgood Marshall—from a jurist who stripped away the citizenship rights of blacks to a jurist who fought for their right to first-class citizenship.

Chapter 2

The Chase and Waite Courts, 1864–1888

During Reconstruction, the transformative egalitarian racial order gained predominance. The Radical Republican alliance, which consisted of antislavery forces, abolitionists, and free blacks, added three amendments to the US Constitution to undo the slavery provisions of the Framers' Constitution. The egalitarian ruling regime built "new constitutional, administrative, political, economic, educational, and social institutions to promote greater racial equality" (King and Smith 2005, 77). For the first time in the nation's history, democratic values of freedom, birthright citizenship, privileges and immunities of citizenship, equal protection of the laws, and the right to vote unencumbered by race were written into the Constitution. Foner (2005, 126) pointed out that "the effort to create an interracial democracy in the aftermath of slavery was an unprecedented experiment" among the nations that abolished slavery in the nineteenth century. Du Bois ([1935] 2007) found that emancipated blacks mobilized politically, black males were elected to national, state, and local offices, blacks were educated and became educators, social institutions controlled by blacks were built, which played important religious and public roles in black communities, and blacks sought with limited success economic stability and independence from the coercive conditions of the Southern labor market.

The end of the Civil War did not eradicate the old white supremacist racial order. The ex-Confederate states attempted to institute a postwar slavery regime by enacting laws that severely curtailed the civil rights of blacks. The second founding fostered divisions among the rival racial orders over the meaning of the Thirteenth, Fourteenth, and Fifteenth Amendments and their enforcement statutes. The Radical Republican alliance favored a broad interpretation of the amendments to protect substantive civil rights, including privileges and immunities of citizenship, political equality, and public equality. Southern Democrats believed that the amendments applied only to formal equality. Their views were based on the traditional power of the states to define and regulate the rights of citizenship. The Chase and Waite Courts were asked to resolve policy conflicts about race in an environment of intense Southern social upheaval and hostility, political violence, racial terrorism, and economic depression. The questions were difficult to resolve, because the amendments were written using ambiguous language. In this chapter, I present an analysis of the first race cases decided under the amended Constitution to determine and appraise the court's exercise of power during Reconstruction.

Constitutional and Statutory Developments

On March 3, 1865, Congress passed the first Freedmen's Bureau Act to provide assistance to the emancipated people to help them transition to freedom (Belz 1976, 66–112; Schnapper 1985). A bill to extend and expand the operation of the Freedmen's Bureau in 1866 was bitterly opposed by President Andrew Johnson but Congress overrode his veto, which renewed the agency's work for two additional years. Johnson granted thousands of pardons to members of the ex-Confederate planter class and leaders who reemerged in positions of power and dominance in the South (Gordon-Reed 2011, 114–15). The Thirteenth Amendment abolished racial slavery but not the ideology that supported it. The South's response to the Thirteenth Amendment was twofold: the imposition of widespread racial terrorism and the enactment of laws known as the Black Codes (Du Bois 1910, 784). Wiecek (1989, 111–12) found that the substantive provisions of the Black Codes defined racial status and controlled the behavior of blacks in a variety of ways: blacks could not pursue certain occupations, the laws provided for a system of harsh forced labor, blacks could not own firearms, and their movement was controlled by a system of passes. The Black Codes specified an etiquette of deference to whites, they prohibited interracial marriage, and blacks would receive the death penalty for raping white women. The codes violated the civil and political rights of blacks by placing restrictions on their right to vote and hold office, and they required segregated public transportation and schools. Harsh punishments were meted out to blacks for breaking the codes.

Congress responded to the enactment of the Black Codes by passing national legislation to protect black civil rights on the basis of its § 2 authority to enact legislation to enforce the Thirteenth Amendment. Section 1 of the Civil Rights Act of 1866 declared that all persons born in the United States are citizens without regard to any previous condition of slavery or involuntary servitude. The law provided that citizens of every state and territory shall have the same right to make and enforce contracts, to sue, be parties, give evidence, to inherit, purchase, lease, sell, hold, and convey real and personal property as is enjoyed by white citizens. The Civil Rights Act abrogated the *Dred Scott* decision by establishing birthright citizenship, and, for the first time, a federal law gave civil rights a precise legal meaning. Johnson vetoed the law on white supremacy and states' rights grounds, but Congress overrode the veto and the bill became law on April 9, 1866.

Congress had to address the political consequences of slavery's destruction and establish a process to bring back the ex-Confederate states into the Union. These divisive issues were resolved in the form of a constitutional amendment to avoid a presidential veto or subsequent congressional repeal. Section 1, the heart of the Fourteenth Amendment, provides that "All persons born or naturalized in the United States, and subject to the jurisdiction thereof, are citizens of the United States and of the state wherein they reside. No state shall make or enforce any law which shall abridge the privileges or immunities of citizens of the United States; nor shall any state deprive any person of life, liberty, or property, without due process of law; nor deny to any person within its jurisdiction the equal protection of the laws." Section 1 repudiated Chief Justice Roger Taney's white supremacist vision of American identity and replaced it with the principle of birthright citizenship. Implicit in the citizenship provision is the concept of equal citizenship—blacks were equal citizens under the Constitution, and no longer would citizenship be equated with whiteness. Section 5 granted Congress the power to enforce the Fourteenth Amendment by appropriate legislation. The Fourteenth Amendment was approved by Congress on June 13, 1866, two months after the Civil Rights Act of 1866 became law.

The Military Reconstruction Act of 1867 placed the ex-Confederate states under temporary military control and established the process for readmitting them to the United States. The states were required to adopt new constitutions, select new officials, and ratify the Fourteenth Amendment. The elections that were needed to put the new Southern governments in place were based on universal male suffrage, and, for the first time, black males were allowed to vote and hold office in the South. The Fourteenth

Amendment was ratified on July 9, 1868, but thousands of black men who resided in border states and some Northern states remained disenfranchised. To address the problem, Congress approved the Fifteenth Amendment in 1869, and it was ratified a year later on February 3, 1870. Section 1 provides that "The right of citizens of the United States to vote shall not be denied or abridged by the United States or by any state on account of race, color, or previous condition of servitude." Section 2 granted Congress the power to enforce the amendment by appropriate legislation. The Fifteenth Amendment was the final constitutional command to destroy the system of racial enslavement in the United States. The amendment empowered blacks politically, especially in the South, but it was left up to the states to determine voter qualifications using nonracial requirements.

The Chase Court, 1864–1873

THE COMPOSITION OF THE CHASE COURT

On December 15, 1864, President Abraham Lincoln appointed Salmon Chase to become the sixth chief justice after the death of Roger Taney. Chase was born in New Hampshire to a prominent family and attended Dartmouth College. He became involved in the antislavery movement and represented escaped slaves in court. Chase served two nonconsecutive terms in the US Senate, he was elected governor of Ohio, and Lincoln gave him a wartime appointment as secretary of the treasury. In addition to the four Lincoln appointees—Samuel Miller, David Davis, Noah Swayne, and Stephen Field—five Taney Court holdovers served on the Chase Court—James Wayne, John Catron, Samuel Nelson, Robert Grier, and Nathan Clifford. The Judicial Circuits Act of 1866 reduced the number of seats on the court from ten to seven, which effectively prevented President Johnson from making appointments to the court (Fairman 1939, 338–39). The Judiciary Act of 1869 restored the number of seats on the court to nine, and President Ulysses Grant appointed Joseph Bradley in March 1872 to fill the new seat. Grant made two additional appointments to the court in 1872: William Strong and Ward Hunt, who succeeded Robert Grier and Samuel Nelson. A partisan and ideologically divided Chase Court had to decide cases involving wartime measures, Reconstruction policies, and the meaning of the Reconstruction Amendments.

Initial Interpretations of the Thirteenth Amendment

The first cases to interpret the Thirteenth Amendment and the Civil Rights Act of 1866 were decided by federal circuit courts. Section 3 of the Civil Rights Act of 1866 gave federal district and circuit courts jurisdiction to hear all civil and criminal cases affecting persons who were denied or could not enforce their rights secured to them by the law in state courts. In *United States v. Rhodes* (1866), the federal government prosecuted three white men for burglarizing the home of a black woman in Kentucky because blacks could not testify against whites under state law. The defendants challenged their indictments on the ground that the court lacked jurisdiction to hear the case and the 1866 law usurped the authority of the states. In his capacity as circuit justice, Justice Noah Swayne acknowledged that "crimes of the deepest dye were committed by white men with impunity" against blacks and "courts and juries were frequently hostile to the colored man." Swayne found that Congress met these evils by giving blacks everywhere the same right to testify as is enjoyed by white citizens and by giving federal courts the jurisdiction to hear all civil and criminal cases wherever they were denied the right to testify in state court. He concluded that the Thirteenth Amendment "trenches directly upon the power of the states and of the people of the states" and its enforcement provision was added to guard against the enactment of state laws which had the intent of restoring slavery. After Maryland abolished slavery in 1864, the legislature passed an apprenticeship law that bound newly freed black children to their former owners. Under its terms, black apprentices were described as property, they were denied an education, and they could be assigned and transferred at will by their former owners. In his capacity as circuit justice, Chief Justice Chase wrote the brief opinion in *In re Turner* (1867) that held that the apprenticeship system violated the Thirteenth Amendment and the Civil Rights Act of 1866.

Chief Justice Chase's influence on the court began to wane due to declining health after he suffered a stroke in 1870. He did not participate in *Blyew v. United States* (1872), the first Supreme Court case to interpret the Civil Rights Act of 1866. *Blyew* involved the horrific ax murder and mutilation of the bodies of four members of the Foster family in rural Lewis County, Kentucky. The seventeen-year-old son was mortally wounded, but his two sisters survived the attack. Local authorities arrested two Klansmen for the murders, but US marshals placed them under federal arrest and moved the case to federal circuit court for prosecution. During the trial, one of the young sisters who survived the attack gave eyewitness testimony to the murders, and the brother lived long enough to make a dying declaration that fixed the crime on the Klansmen. During the trial, the government produced evidence that the Klansmen had planned to participate in an upcoming race war against blacks. The defendants argued that the federal circuit court lacked jurisdiction to hear the case because murder was a state offense and the law usurped the state's authority to administer its own criminal laws.

The Chase Court dismissed the case on jurisdictional grounds, reversed the judgments of the Klansmen, and avoided all constitutional questions. Justice William Strong applied a formalist interpretation to § 3 of the Civil Rights Act of 1866 and found that the murdered victims were not "affected" persons whose rights would be denied in state courts because the law referred to "persons in existence"—the prosecutor and the defendants. Strong explained that Congress did not intend "to give to the District and Circuit Courts jurisdiction over all causes both civil and criminal." Justice Bradley, joined by Swayne in dissent, asserted that the case was clearly within the scope of § 3 and the majority's view of the law was "too narrow, too technical, and too forgetful of the liberal objects it had in view." Bradley went on to say that to "deprive a whole class of the community of this right, to refuse their evidence and their sworn complaints, is to brand them with a badge of slavery; is to expose them to wanton insults and fiendish assaults; is to leave their lives, their families, and their property unprotected by law." The *Blyew* decision undermined the objectives of the Civil Rights Act of 1866 by placing jurisdictional obstacles in the path of federal civil rights enforcement.

Initial Interpretations of the Fourteenth Amendment

The first federal circuit case to interpret the Fourteenth Amendment involved the Klan's political violence and racial terrorism campaign in Alabama to disrupt the November 1870 elections. In October 1870, about 150 Klansmen attended a Republican campaign meeting for the upcoming November elections at the courthouse in Eutaw, Alabama, where almost two thousand blacks were in attendance. The Klansmen verbally harassed the speakers, they fired shots into the crowd, panic ensued, which caused the deaths of four black men, and fifty-four attendees were wounded as they attempted to flee the courthouse (Trelease 1971, 271–72). Federal prosecutors charged two Klansmen with conspiracy to injure, threaten, and intimidate Republicans with the intent to prevent the exercise of their rights to freedom of speech and to peaceably assemble under § 6 of the Enforcement Act of May 31, 1870. The defendants challenged the indictment on the ground that the First Amendment did not apply to the states, nor did it apply to acts of private individuals. In *United States v. Hall* (1871), federal circuit judge William Woods found that the rights enumerated in the Bill of Rights were fundamental rights secured by the Constitution, they were protected by the privileges or immunities clause of the Fourteenth Amendment, and Congress had the power to protect them by appropriate legislation. Woods asserted that under the original Constitution, citizenship depended upon the state, but the Fourteenth Amendment reversed citizenship—citizenship in the United States is made independent of citizenship in a state, and national citizenship is paramount.

The Chase Court rejected Judge Wood's expansive interpretation of the privileges or immunities clause in the first court case to interpret the Reconstruction Amendments, the *Slaughter-House Cases* (1873). In 1869, Louisiana enacted a law that created a slaughterhouse monopoly to operate in New Orleans for twenty-five years to control health risks posed by the slaughtering of animals. The law was tainted by bribery and corruption, and approximately 1,000 butchers were affected by the law because they were deprived of their own slaughterhouses and they were forced to pay fees to work at the new slaughterhouse company. Former Taney Court justice John Campbell argued on behalf of the white butchers that the monopoly was a form of involuntary servitude under the Thirteenth Amendment, and it violated one of the privileges or immunities of citizenship under the Fourteenth Amendment—the right to labor freely in an honest avocation.

Writing for the 5–4 majority, Justice Samuel Miller presented a succinct history of the Reconstruction Amendments to determine their purpose and "the evil which they were designed to remedy." Miller found that the "overshadowing and efficient cause" of the Civil War was African slavery and the Thirteenth Amendment was added to the Constitution "to establish the freedom of four millions slaves." The phrase "involuntary servitude" was meant to "forbid all shades and conditions of African slavery" such as apprenticeship and serfdom. Because the Southern states "imposed upon the colored race onerous disabilities and burdens, and curtailed their rights in the pursuit of life, liberty, and property to such an extent that these freedoms were of little value," additional protections were placed in the Fourteenth Amendment. The former confederate states had to ratify the amendment to restore "their full participation in the government of the Union." Miller explained that the Fifteenth Amendment was ratified because the freedmen "could never be fully secured in their person and their property without the right to vote." The Fourteenth Amendment declared that blacks were citizens of the United States and the Fifteenth Amendment made them a voter in every state in the Union.

Justice Miller then turned to the butchers' claim that the privileges or immunities of citizenship clause protected their right to labor freely without state interference. Miller asserted that the citizenship clause in § 1 of the Fourteenth Amendment overturned the *Dred Scott* decision "by making all persons born within the United States and subject to its jurisdiction citizens of the United States." The phrase, "subject to its jurisdiction," was "intended to exclude from its operation children of ministers, consuls, and citizens or subjects of foreign States born within the United States." Miller's interpretation of the privileges or immunities clause was based on a dual citizenship theory that made a distinction between national citizenship and state citizenship. Miller claimed that the Fourteenth Amendment prohibited the states from abridging the privileges or immunities of national citizenship, which at the time were restricted to a limited category of rights: the right of free access to seaports, the right to life, liberty, and property on the high seas, the right to peacefully assemble, and the privilege of the writ of habeas corpus. The butchers' claim to privileges or immunities were those that belonged to citizens of the states and state governments were responsible for their security and protection. Miller declared that the butchers' interpretation of the Fourteenth Amendment would "fetter and degrade the State governments by subjecting them to the control of Congress," and it "radically changes the whole theory of the relations of the State and Federal governments to each other." He concluded that "no such results were intended by the Congress which proposed these amendments, nor by the legislatures of the States which ratified them," and to hold otherwise "would constitute this court a perpetual censor upon all legislation of the States, on the civil rights of their own citizens, with authority to nullify such as it did not approve."

Writing for the dissenters, Justice Stephen Field argued that the first clause of the Fourteenth Amendment created citizenship of the United States and made it dependent on birthright citizenship—"a citizen of a State is now only a citizen of the United States residing in that state." Field pointed out that the fundamental rights, privileges, and immunities that belong to citizens "now belong to him as a citizen of the United States, and are not dependent upon his citizenship of any state." According to the dissenters, the Fourteenth Amendment placed all privileges and immunities under the guardianship of national authority, the corporate monopoly violated the rights of citizens to pursue an ordinary trade, and the nationalization of civil rights placed limits on abusive state powers.

In the *Slaughter-House Cases*, the Chase Court had the option to decide the case on the ground that the state had the right to regulate the business of slaughtering animals for the protection of public health under its police powers. To put their own policy preferences into law, the justices applied prewar federalism doctrines to restrict the reach of the privileges or immunities clause to protect civil rights. The landmark decision effectively eviscerated the use of the privileges or immunities clause as an instrument of national civil liberties and civil rights protections and the Chase Court's interpretation of the clause remains authoritative. The practical effect of the dual citizenship theory was that protections of black civil rights would be left up to hostile Southern state governments. Opponents of Reconstruction policies based their opposition to national protection of black civil rights on the *Slaughter-House* precedent. As shown in table 2.1, the Chase Court's

Table 2.1. Chase Court Civil Rights Cases, 1864–1874

Case	Vote	Outcome
Osborn v. Nicholson (1872)	7–1	Upheld the validity of a prewar contract for the sale of a slave after the ratification of the Thirteenth Amendment (C)
White v. Hart (1872)	7–1	Held that the Georgia state constitution could not prohibit the enforcement of an 1860 promissory note for the slave of slaves (C)
Blyew v. United States (1872)	5–2	Restricted the meaning of "affected persons" in § 3 of the Civil Rights Act of 1866 to living persons in federal criminal prosecutions (C)
Slaughter-House Cases (1873)	5–4	Nullified the use of the Fourteenth Amendment's privileges or immunities clause to protect civil rights (C)
Bradwell v. Illinois (1873)	8–1	Held that the privileges or immunities clause did not protect the right of women to practice law in a state (C)
Boyce v. Tabb (1873)	8–0	Held that an 1861 promissory note for the sale of slaves was enforceable under the contract clause (C)
Railroad Company v. Brown (1873)	8–0	Upheld a judgment against a railroad company for its failure to comply with a congressional requirement that authorized the extension of a railroad line conditioned on nonsegregated railroad cars (L)

Source: Created by the author.

Note: C for conservative outcomes, L for liberal outcomes.

civil rights decisions failed to advance the policy goals of the transformative egalitarian alliance.

The Waite Court, 1874–1888

THE COMPOSITION OF THE WAITE COURT

Chief Justice Chase died approximately three weeks after *Slaughter-House* was decided on May 7, 1873, at the age of sixty-five. President Grant struggled to fill the chief justice position for eight months (Magrath 1963). Morrison Waite was confirmed on January 21, 1874, as the seventh chief justice, after several potential candidates for the position declined their nominations or withdrew their names from consideration prior to Senate confirmation. Waite was a commercial lawyer from Ohio who had never argued a case before the Supreme Court. He was viewed as a competent, noncontroversial choice for chief justice but one who lacked a national reputation. The Waite Court experienced considerable personnel turnover during its fourteen-year tenure. The Buchanan and Lincoln appointees, Nathan Clifford, Samuel Miller, David Davis, Noah Swayne, and Stephen Field, served with three Grant appointees, William Strong, Joseph Bradley, and Ward Hunt. President Rutherford Hayes appointed John Marshall Harlan in 1877 and William Woods in 1881. President James Garfield appointed Stanley Matthews in 1881, and President Chester Arthur appointed two justices in 1882—Horace Gray and Samuel Blatchford. During the Waite Court's final term, the first Southern Democratic president elected to office after the Civil War, Grover Cleveland, appointed Lucius Q. C. Lamar in 1888. Although most Waite Court justices were Northern Republicans, they voted in lockstep against federal protection of black civil rights, except for John Marshall Harlan, the Southerner and former slaveowner from Kentucky.

FEDERAL ENFORCEMENT OF CIVIL RIGHTS

Foner (1988, 425) found that "the wave of counterrevolutionary terror that swept over large parts of the South between 1868 and 1871 lacks a counterpart either in the American experience or in that of the other Western Hemisphere societies that abolished slavery in the nineteenth century." By the mid-1870s, political violence was the weapon of choice for organized racial terror groups such as the Ku Klux Klan, the Knights of the White

Camelia, and the White Leagues. Their organized efforts were intended to serve the interests of the Democratic Party, destroy Reconstruction governments, murder, terrorize, and intimidate blacks, and create a postwar regime of white supremacy in the South. The Republican Congress responded to widespread political violence by enacting legislation to enforce the Reconstruction Amendments (Wang 1995).

The Enforcement Act of May 31, 1870, was the first federal law to enforce the Fifteenth Amendment. The law made it a federal crime for state officials to deny qualified persons the right to vote on account of race. Another provision made it a crime for persons to conspire together to deprive any person of rights secured by the Constitution or laws of the United States. One month after the 1870 law was passed, Congress created the Department of Justice to administer the nation's legal business and to protect and enforce civil rights. The Enforcement Act of February 28, 1871, was designed to protect black voting rights in the North and guard against Northern election fraud. The Enforcement Act of April 20, 1871, also known as the Ku Klux Klan Act, was the federal government's most effective weapon to suppress Klan activities and to enforce black civil rights. The law defined specific practices that constituted a conspiracy to deprive persons of their civil rights, including interference with the right to vote, to serve on juries, or to enjoy equal protection of the laws, and it punished persons who aided criminal conspirators. Federal courts were given exclusive jurisdiction to try Enforcement Acts offenses.

An ongoing struggle for political control between two competing factions, Republicans and a Fusionist coalition of white supremacist Democrats and conservative Republicans, erupted during the 1872 Louisiana elections. Both sides disputed the results, they claimed election fraud, and they proceeded to set up a dual government in the state (Lane 2008, 44–62). In early March 1873, mounting tensions grew in Grant Parish over the control of the Colfax courthouse. When black Republicans found out about the Fusionists' plan to retake control of the courthouse, a group of 150 armed black militiamen had gathered to defend it. Foner (1988, 437) described the Colfax Massacre as the "bloodiest single instance of racial carnage in the Reconstruction era." On Easter Sunday, April 13, 1873, a well-armed mob of 165 ex-Confederate veterans and Klansmen attacked the black militiamen. After they refused to surrender, the mob set fire to the courthouse and killed them as they fled the burning building. William Cruikshank and other Klansmen decided to take revenge by executing and mutilating the bodies of a few dozen black prisoners who had survived the attack. Lane's

(2008, 265–66) account of the massacre indicated that three white men were killed and the death toll for blacks varied from a minimum of 62 to a maximum of 81 (Lane 2008, 266).

In June 1873, a New Orleans federal grand jury initially indicted ninety-seven white men for thirty-two violations of §§ 6 and 7 of the 1870 Enforcement Act (Kaczorowski 2005, 143–44). The lengthy and complex proceedings, which included 140 black prosecution witnesses and stretched over four months, ended in mistrials and acquittals. A year later, Cruikshank and two Klansmen were convicted of sixteen counts of conspiracy to interfere with the constitutional rights of two black Republicans under the 1870 Enforcement Act. A motion was made by the defendants' counsel to set aside the convictions on the ground that the Enforcement Act was unconstitutional because it was "municipal in its character, operating directly on the conduct of individuals, and taking the place of ordinary state legislation." Two judges were assigned to rule on the motion: Justice Bradley in his capacity as circuit justice and Judge Woods. Bradley ruled in favor of the motion, but Woods voted to reject it. In *United States v. Cruikshank* (1874), Bradley wrote the circuit court opinion that overturned the Colfax conspirators' convictions on three grounds: the dual citizenship theory advanced in the *Slaughter-House Cases*, the counts not expressly alleging a racial motivation, and when a racial motivation was specified, the counts being vague and too general.

To make his opinion widely available, Bradley sent copies "to his colleagues on the Supreme Court, members of the cabinet, congressional leaders, major newspapers and law journals. He mailed one each to five federal judges across the Fifth Circuit, to guide them in Enforcement Act cases until the Supreme Court ruled" (Lane 2008, 213). For Southern blacks, Bradley's decision meant that the federal government's efforts to enforce their civil rights would be sufficiently curtailed. For white supremacists, Bradley's decision established the rule that no white man would be punished for killing blacks. The *Cruikshank* decision ushered in a new wave of racial terrorism and political violence in the South (Keith 2008, 140). After celebrating the release of the Colfax prisoners, a group of whites on their way to Colfax sought revenge as they terrorized black homes and shot and cut the throats of two black men (Keith 2008, 148). Despite the attempt to prosecute the terrorists, no one would testify against them. During the summer of 1874, the White League paramilitary group launched a wave of political violence and racial terror across Louisiana to force Republicans out of power (Hogue

2006). Acts of racial terror, political violence, and voting intimidation and suppression quickly spread to Mississippi, South Carolina, and subsequently throughout the South (Kaczorowski 2005, 150–60; Lane 2008, 215–62).

The Waite Court upheld Bradley's circuit court ruling in *United States v. Cruikshank* (1876). Chief Justice Waite's majority opinion was almost identical to Bradley's opinion. Neither opinion recounted the horrific factual background of the Colfax massacre. Both opinions applied *Slaughter-House*'s dual citizenship theory to limit national authority to protect the civil rights and safety of blacks, and both opinions asserted that the Reconstruction Amendments had not fundamentally altered the structure of federalism. Waite found all sixteen counts of the indictment defective on several grounds: the rights hindered or prevented in the case were not granted or secured by the Constitution or federal laws, it was the duty of the states to punish for a conspiracy to murder, the counts did not expressly allege a racial motivation, and when a racial motivation was specified, the counts were vague and too general, because they did not specify any right within the meaning of the Enforcement Act that was violated by the conspirators.

Lower court judges responded to the *Cruikshank* decision by imposing an onerous burden of proof requirement in federal civil rights prosecutions (Pope 2014, 428–32). None of the participants in the Colfax massacre went to prison, and federal prosecutors dropped all charges against them in 1880 (Lane 2008, 256). On June 14, 1951, Louisiana erected a historical marker on the grounds of the Grant Parish courthouse in Colfax to present a whitewashed version of the massacre. The marker read, "On this site occurred the Colfax Riot in which three white men and 150 negroes were slain. This event on April 13, 1873 marked the end of the carpetbag misrule in the South." With the approval of Democratic governor John Bel Edwards, the historical marker was removed in May 2021.

On the same day *Cruikshank* was decided, the Waite Court dealt a serious blow to federal voting rights enforcement in *United States v. Reese* (1876)—the first case to address black voting rights under the Fifteenth Amendment and the Enforcement Act of 1870. The Kentucky legislature enacted a law that required the payment of a $1.50 poll tax in municipal elections. The law disenfranchised Lexington's black voters because they were either unable to pay the tax or they could be denied the right to vote subject to the discretion of election inspectors. In 1873, federal indictments were brought against two Democratic election inspectors when they refused to allow William Garner to vote in a municipal election despite his attempts to pay the poll tax. In

Reese, the Waite Court dismissed the indictments and declared §§ 3 and 4 of the Enforcement Act of May 31, 1870, unconstitutional. Writing for the 8–1 majority, Chief Justice Waite explained that "the Fifteenth Amendment does not confer the right of suffrage upon anyone" and §§ 3 and 4 impermissibly covered voting discrimination that had nothing to do with race. In his dissent, Justice Ward Hunt characterized Waite's Fifteenth Amendment analysis as "unsound." Hunt asserted that the Enforcement Act perfectly fit the circumstances of the case and the decision would leave blacks with "practically no remedy" against "hostile legislation and personal prejudice."

The *Cruikshank* and *Reese* decisions indicated that the court was willing to abandon Reconstruction policies. Wang (1997, 130) found that the decisions did not foreclose all prosecutions under the Enforcement Act, but they clearly jeopardized and discouraged federal civil rights enforcement. Both decisions emboldened white supremacist groups to escalate their campaign of political violence and racial terrorism to prevent blacks from voting in the 1876 presidential election. The election was marred by widespread voter fraud by both parties, which prevented the Republican candidate, Rutherford Hayes, from winning the election outright against the Democratic candidate, Samuel Tilden. Congress created an electoral commission to decide the outcome of the disputed election results, and Justice Bradley, who was a member of the commission, cast the deciding vote in favor of Hayes along party lines. Backroom negotiations took place between Republican and Democratic leaders to prevent Democrats from repudiating the commission's decision. The bargain struck between the parties included an agreement that Hayes would become president and Republicans would turn over control of Southern governments to Democrats. Woodward (1951, 246) found that the Compromise of 1877 "did not restore the old order in the South but "it did assure the dominant whites political autonomy and nonintervention in matters of race policy." These developments signaled the demise of the first phase of the transformative egalitarian racial order.

Initial Interpretations of the Equal Protection Clause

In the *Slaughter-House Cases*, Justice Miller's historical account of the Fourteenth Amendment established that the intent of the equal protection clause was to remedy the evil of laws "which discriminated with gross injustice and hardship" against blacks "as a class." The Waite Court activated the Fourteenth Amendment's equal protection clause in cases involving the exclusion of blacks from juries. Although black men were qualified to serve as jurors on state courts, state laws mandated all-white juries and their exclusion

Table 2.2. Waite Court Civil Rights Enforcement Cases, 1874–1888

Case	Vote	Outcome
Minor v. Happersett (1875)	9–0	Held that the privileges and immunities clause did not protect the right of women to vote (C)
United States v. Reese (1876)	8–1	Held that §§ 3 and 4 of the 1870 Enforcement Act were unconstitutional because the provisions exceeded the scope of the Fifteenth Amendment (C)
United States v. Cruikshank (1876)	8–1	Overturned the Colfax conspirators' federal convictions on two main grounds: it was the duty of the states to punish for a conspiracy to murder, and the counts in the indictment were too vague and general because they did not expressly allege a racial motivation under the Enforcement Act (C)
Ex parte Siebold (1880)	7–2	Upheld the convictions of election officials for stuffing and destroying ballots in a congressional election under the elections clause (L)
United States v. Harris (1883)	8–1	Held that the conspiracy statute, § 5519 (formerly § 2 of the KKK Act of 1871), was unconstitutional on state action grounds in a case involving mob violence between two feuding white families (C)
Ex parte Yarbrough (1884)	9–0	Held that Congress had the power to protect and enforce the right to vote in national elections against Klan violence under the Elections Clause and the Fifteenth Amendment (L)
Baldwin v. Franks (1887)	6–2	Held that § 5519 could not be used to punish a white mob that attacked Chinese laborers to expel them from Nicholas, California (C)
Hall v. United States (1876)	9–0	Held that the end of slavery had no effect on a rule that a slave could not enter into a contract (C)

Source: Created by the author.

Note: C for conservative outcomes, L for liberal outcomes.

was nearly total in the South (Schmidt 1983, 1406–14). The theory that the Fourteenth Amendment protected only civil rights but not political rights such as voting and jury service meant that states had unfettered discretion to keep blacks off juries (Alschuler and Deiss 1994, 887–89). In Southern criminal courts, all-white juries would punish black defendants more harshly or all-white juries would refuse to convict white defendants who committed crimes against blacks. To limit the power of racially hostile juries, blacks had to participate in the criminal justice system as jurors and witnesses on an equal basis with whites. Section 4 of the Civil Rights Act of 1875 established a right and remedy to serve on state and federal juries without discrimination based on race. Section 641 of the Revised Statutes of 1875, a recodification of § 3 of the Civil Rights Act of 1866, permitted the removal of cases from state court to federal court when any person was denied "any right secured to him by any law providing for the equal civil rights of citizens of the United States."

Strauder v. West Virginia (1880) addressed a challenge to a West Virginia statute that permitted only white male citizens who were twenty-one years old or older to serve on grand and petit juries. When Taylor Strauder was indicted for the brutal murder of his wife in state court, he petitioned to have his case moved to federal court under § 641 on the ground that the exclusion of blacks from juries prevented him from having the full and equal benefit of all laws and proceedings in the state as is enjoyed by white citizens under the Constitution and federal laws. The trial court denied his motion and Strauder was convicted and sentenced to prison. The Waite Court was asked to decide whether every citizen has a right to a trial by jury selected and impaneled without discrimination on the basis of race or color.

Writing for the 7–2 majority, Justice William Strong found that the West Virginia law violated the equal protection clause. Strong began his analysis by reviewing the history of the Fourteenth Amendment to ascertain the "true spirit and meaning" of the equal protection clause. He found that discrimination against blacks "had been habitual" and they needed "protection against unfriendly action in the States where they were resident." Strong asserted that the "colored race, as a race, was abject and ignorant, and in that condition was unfitted to command the respect of those who had superior intelligence. Their training had left them as mere children, and as such they needed the protection which a wise government extends to those who are unable to protect themselves." Strong explained that the Fourteenth Amendment was framed and adopted "to assure to the colored race the enjoyment of all the civil rights that under the law are enjoyed by white persons, and to give to that race the protection of the general government, in that enjoyment, whenever it should be denied by the States." Strong asserted that the equal protection clause declared that "the law in the States shall be the same for the black as for the white; that all persons, whether colored or white, shall stand equal before the laws of the States, and, in regard to the colored race, for whose protection the amendment was primarily designed, that no discrimination shall be made against them by law because of their color." Strong found that blacks were singled out and expressly denied the right to participate in the administration of the law as jurors because of their color even though they were qualified to serve. Strong upheld the removal provision because prejudice against particular classes in the community could sway the judgment of jurors, and change of venue was "an ordinary mode of protecting rights and immunities conferred by the Federal Constitution and laws."

In *Ex parte Virginia* (1880), the court rejected an attack on the constitutionality of § 4 of the Civil Rights Act of 1875 that prohibited racial discrimination in the selection of state and federal juries. Grand juries indicted fourteen county judges for refusing to allow qualified blacks to serve as jurors in Virginia. Pittsylvania County judge James Coles claimed that his conduct was a judicial act that was beyond the reach of federal power to punish him for his failure to obey the law. He petitioned the Supreme Court to direct a federal judge to release him on the ground that the federal court lacked jurisdiction to hear the case and § 4 was unconstitutional on state sovereignty grounds. Justice Strong rejected the states' rights attack on the law, and he reaffirmed the principle that "an equal right to an impartial jury trial, and such an immunity from unfriendly discrimination" may be enforced by Congress by means of appropriate legislation. Strong made it clear that the prohibitions of the Fourteenth Amendment were directed to the states and Judge Coles was a state actor who was prohibited from denying any person the equal protection of the laws. Justices Field and Clifford dissented in *Strauder* and *Ex parte Virginia*. They advanced two main arguments: that § 4 violated the Tenth Amendment on the theory of state sovereignty, and the equal protection clause protected only civil rights, not political rights such as jury service.

In *Neal v. Delaware* (1881), the court considered the evidence needed to prove systematic exclusion of blacks from state juries. William Neal was tried, convicted, and sentenced to death by all-white grand and petit juries in New Castle County, Delaware, for raping a white woman. Neal was not permitted to move his case to federal court, nor was he allowed to present evidence and witnesses to establish pervasive racial discrimination in Delaware's jury selection system. Justice John Marshall Harlan found that Neal was entitled to appeal for a violation of his "constitutional equality of civil rights." Harlan found that the motion to quash the indictment should have been sustained based on the evidence presented in Neal's affidavit that no black citizen had ever served as a juror in Delaware despite its large black population, and disparaging statements made by the state's chief justice that black men were utterly unqualified to serve on juries. Harlan added that the clerk and bailiff could have testified as witnesses to either clearly sustain or disprove the allegations that blacks were excluded from serving on juries on account of race. Harlan found that Neal presented prima facie evidence of systematic exclusion of blacks from grand and petit jurors.

Schmidt (1983, 1428–29) explained that "*Strauder's* achievement is that at the earliest opportunity the Court freed the fourteenth amendment from the narrowest readings of its legislative history and looked for meaning in the language of the amendment and the broad purposes that the language connoted rather than to the statements of Congressman Wilson and Senator Trumbull. This enabled the Court to measure the sweep of equal protection in a functional and broadly historical perspective rather than through a probing of the specific anxieties of 1866." Levinson (2018, 603) asserted that *Strauder* was "the most illuminating single case ever decided by the Supreme Court regarding the doctrinal implications of the Equal Protection Clause for the ever-controversial topics of race and, in our time, ethnicity." *Strauder's* anti-discrimination principle was rarely applied in subsequent jury discrimination cases until the court changed its policy direction in the 1930s (Alschuler and Deiss 1994, 894–95). Table 2.3 shows that most jury discrimination cases advanced the policy goals of the transformative egalitarian alliance.

Table 2.3. Waite Court Jury Discrimination Cases, 1874–1888

Case	Vote	Outcome
Strauder v. West Virginia (1880)	7–2	Held that the exclusion of blacks from jury service on account of race violated the equal protection clause (L)
Ex parte Virginia (1880)	7–2	Held that state judges were prohibited from excluding blacks from jury service (L)
Virginia v. Rives (1880)	9–0	Held that § 641's removal provision did not extend to all cases in which equal protection of the laws was denied to a black defendant (C)
Neal v. Delaware (1881)	4–2	Held that a prima facie case of systematic exclusion of blacks from juries was established by showing that they were excluded for long periods of time and there were numerous qualified blacks in the community to serve on juries (L)
Bush v. Kentucky (1883)	6–3	Reversed a black defendant's murder conviction on the ground that state laws permitted the exclusion of blacks from juries (L)

Source: Created by the author.

Note: C for conservative outcomes, L for liberal outcomes.

Social Equality

During Reconstruction, apartheid was justified by an invented category of rights called social equality. Social equality was a vague phrase often used to promote fear among whites that civil rights laws would be used to mandate unwanted "race mixing" with regard to forcing whites and blacks to socialize together in public and private spaces. The most feared aspect of social equality was interracial intimate relationships and marriage, and Southern states responded to those fears by enacting so-called anti-miscegenation statutes to enforce the regime of white supremacy. In *Pace v. Alabama* (1883), the court upheld an 1867 Alabama law that prohibited marriages, adultery, or fornication between blacks and whites on the ground that the "punishment of each offending person, whether white or black, is the same." Without providing any justification for upholding the Alabama law, the court allowed an equal application exception to the equal protection clause.

Caste distinctions restricted the social equality rights of blacks to enjoy equal access to businesses serving the public, including railroads, steamships, street cars, and hotels. Blacks fought back by challenging the denial of their equal public rights in court. In 1868, the biracial government of Louisiana adopted a constitution that declared that its citizens would be guaranteed the same civil, political, and public rights independent of race or color in all places of public accommodations, public transportation, and business. In 1872, the white owner of a steamboat refused to issue a ticket for a ladies' cabin reserved for white women to a prominent Créole woman of color, Josephine Decuir. Josephine Decuir and her husband Antoine came from a background of slaveholding wealth—they owned a plantation with 112 enslaved persons (Scott 2020, 543). Decuir relied on her racial identity, gender, and class to demonstrate that she was a well-respected woman who should have access to the ladies' cabin. She sued the steamboat owner under the 1869 equal public rights implementing law that gave persons of color the right to sue for damages for violating the law. Decuir won her case at trial and the Louisiana Supreme Court upheld the law on the ground that the segregation regulation was unreasonable because it was founded on prejudice. In *Hall v. Decuir* (1878), the court ruled that the equal public rights law was an undue burden on interstate commerce. Writing for a unanimous court, Chief Justice Waite found that Decuir's travel on the Mississippi River was unavoidably of an interstate character even though her journey began and ended in Louisiana. Waite asserted that in the absence of congressional legislation, the steamboat owner was at liberty to adopt reasonable rules and regulations for the disposition of passengers on his boat.

Waite avoided the issue of equal public rights, but Justice Nathan Clifford wrote a twenty-six-page concurring opinion that articulated a reasonableness defense for segregated public accommodations.

In 1870, Senator Charles Sumner introduced a far-reaching civil rights bill that went beyond political equality and protection against racial violence. Sumner believed that meaningful equality before the law encompassed a claim to the right to dignity in the pursuit of everyday business and to be free from the stigma of caste. Sumner introduced testimony into the record by blacks, including Frederick Douglass and black legislators, that addressed the evils of exclusion and how blacks were denied access to ordinary accommodations in railroad cars, streetcars, hotels, and restaurants. From the perspective of blacks, apartheid was synonymous with inequality and separate facilities were not equal. After Sumner's death in 1874, the Republican Congress enacted a narrower version of his civil rights bill, the Civil Rights Act of 1875, before the newly elected Democratic Congress took control. Section 1 of the law prohibited racial discrimination by private businesses in the enjoyment of public accommodations on land and water. Section 2 subjected violators of the law to fines and imprisonment, and it gave persons of color the right to sue for damages. The constitutionality of §§ 1 and 2 was challenged in the controversial social equality case, the *Civil Rights Cases* (1883). Five separate test cases were consolidated for review that challenged caste discrimination with regard to the exclusion of blacks from a dining room of an inn in Topeka, Kansas; hotel accommodations in Jefferson City, Missouri; a theater in San Francisco; an opera house in New York City; and access to a ladies' car on a train. The black plaintiffs claimed that the owners of the private businesses violated their rights to the full and equal enjoyment of public accommodations on account of race or color. Solicitor General Samuel Philips argued on behalf of the federal government that the law was constitutional under the Thirteenth and Fourteenth Amendments.

Opponents of the 1875 act derided it for promoting social equality. Fairman (1987, 565–66) uncovered an undated writing by Justice Joseph Bradley that recorded his private thoughts about the law. Bradley wrote that the law "was passed to prevent discrimination on account of race and color," but it would also "deprive white people of the right of choosing their own company" and "introduce another kind of slavery." The Civil Rights Act of 1866 had already guaranteed blacks "the right of buying, selling and holding property, and of equal protection of the laws." He posed the question—"Are not these the essentials of freedom? Surely a white lady cannot be enforced by Congressional enactment to admit colored persons to her ball or assembly or dinner party." Bradley believed that the "essentials to the enjoyment of citizenship" did not extend to the rights of blacks to attend "a white man's theater," or a "white man's carriage or railroad car" or a "white man's hotel" if he is free to have his own theater, carriage, railroad car, or hotel. Bradley argued against compelling whites to "lodge and eat and sit with the negro" because "the antipathy of race cannot be crushed and annihilated by legal enactment" and the Thirteenth and Fourteenth Amendments "were never intended to aim at such an impossibility." He believed that freedom, privileges, and immunities and the equal protection of the laws for blacks did not "require the slavery of the whites" and "enforced fellowship would be that."

In the *Civil Rights Cases*, Justice Bradley wrote the 8–1 decision that declared §§ 1 and 2 of the Civil Rights Act of 1875 unconstitutional. Bradley's visceral, antiblack private views about civil rights were mostly absent from his majority opinion in the *Civil Rights Cases*. He restricted the application of § 1 of the Fourteenth Amendment to state laws and actions by its officers or agents that discriminated on the basis of race. Bradley found that the 1875 law violated the Tenth Amendment because Congress could not "with equal show of authority enact a code of laws for the enforcement and vindication of all rights of life, liberty, and property." The federal government argued that the law violated the Thirteenth Amendment because Congress had the power to enact all laws necessary for abolishing badges and incidents of slavery in the United States and restrictions on the mobility of blacks could be construed as imposing conditions that constitute badges and incidents of slavery. Bradley's response was that the refusal of private businesses to offer accommodations to blacks in public places had "nothing to do with slavery or involuntary servitude," and it "would be running the slavery argument into the ground to make it apply to every act of discrimination which a person may see fit to make as to the guests he will entertain, or as to the people he will take into his coach or cab or car, or admit to his concert or theatre, or deal with in other matters of intercourse or business." Bradley explained that the Civil Rights Act of 1866 defined badges and incidents of slavery as civil rights and not to "what may be called social rights of men and races in the community." He went on to say that "when a man has emerged from slavery, and by the aid of beneficent legislation has shaken off the inseparable concomitants of that state, there must be some stage in the progress of his elevation when he takes the rank of a mere citizen, and ceases to be the special favorite of the laws." Bradley refused to expand the definition of freedom beyond that which existed for free blacks prior to the Civil War, because at that time "mere discriminations on account of race or color were not regarded as badges of slavery."

Justice Harlan wrote a thirty-six-page dissent that criticized Bradley's interpretation of the Thirteenth and Fourteenth Amendments as being "entirely too narrow and artificial" and that the substance and spirit of the amendments had been "sacrificed by a subtle and ingenious verbal criticism." Harlan believed that Bradley's reasoning was flawed because it "departed from the familiar rule requiring, in the interpretation of constitutional provisions, that full effect be given to the intent with which they were adopted." Harlan reminded Bradley that if the court's prewar decisions established that Congress had the power to legislate directly on individuals to protect slavery, then Congress should not have less power to legislate directly or under its implied power to eradicate the badges and incidents of slavery by prohibiting racial discrimination in public places by private individuals. Harlan was especially critical of Bradley's state action limitation on protections of rights secured by the Fourteenth Amendment. He asserted that § 5 of the Fourteenth Amendment gave Congress the power to enforce all of its provisions, and it was the responsibility of Congress, not the judiciary, to say what legislation was appropriate or for what end. Harlan explained that the Civil Rights Act of 1875 secured and protected legal rights, not social rights, and "no government ever has brought or ever can bring, its people into social intercourse against their wishes." With regard to Bradley's assertion that blacks had been the special favorite of the laws, Harlan explained that the law was "for the benefit of citizens of every race and color," and what Congress sought to accomplish was "what had already been done in every State of the Union for the white race" and nothing more. Harlan concluded that "if the constitutional amendments be enforced, according to the intent with which, as I conceive, they were adopted, there cannot be, in this republic, any class of human beings in practical subjection to another class, with power in the latter to dole out to the former just such privileges as they may choose to grant."

The *Civil Rights Cases* decision attracted considerable press attention and national interest. Fairman's (1987, 568–86) examination of the editorial content of sixty-seven newspapers and journals that reported on the decision indicated that a consensus existed among whites that the *Civil Rights Cases* was correctly decided. Lado's (1995) analysis of the reactions to the decision by black political and religious leaders and black newspaper editors revealed universal condemnation of the decision. The landmark decision established that Congress lacked the power under the Thirteenth and Fourteenth Amendments to prohibit private acts of racial discrimination. Bradley's opinion relied on the concept of state action to divest Congress of any authority to remedy or punish discrimination by private individuals. One week after the decision was announced, Frederick Douglass ([1883] 1966, 298–306) delivered a fiery critique of Bradley's opinion at a civil rights meeting in

Table 2.4. Waite Court Social Equality Cases, 1874–1888

Case	Vote	Outcome
Walker v. Sauvinet (1876)	7–2	Upheld a damage award to a man of color against a business owner who violated Louisiana's equal public rights statute (L)
Hall v. Decuir (1878)	8–0	Held that Louisiana's equal public rights law encroached on Congress's commerce clause authority (C)
Civil Rights Cases (1883)	8–1	Held that §§ 1 and 2 of the Civil Rights Act of 1875 were unconstitutional under the Thirteenth and Fourteenth Amendments (C)
Pace v. Alabama (1883)	9–0	Upheld state criminalization of interracial sexual relationships under the equal protection clause (C)

Source: Created by the author.

Note: C for conservative outcomes, L for liberal outcomes.

Washington, DC. Douglass accurately predicted that Congress would enact another public accommodations statute that would not be struck down by the court. Eighty-one years later, Congress enacted legislation that prohibited private acts of racial discrimination in public places under its commerce clause authority that was upheld by the Supreme Court.

Racial Discrimination against Chinese Immigrants

In the 1850s, Chinese immigrants came to America to meet the demands for labor in mining, the construction of the transcontinental railroad, and the agricultural industry for very low wages (McClain 1984, 534–35). During Reconstruction, blacks and Chinese immigrants were treated similarly in some respects: both groups faced racial discrimination, they were viewed as inferior, and they were subjected to extreme forms of racial terrorism, threats, and intimidation (Maltz 1994; McClain 1985). Unlike blacks, Chinese immigrants were not citizens, and they were attacked by whites because of their culture, religion, perceived inability to assimilate, and perceived loyalties to China. Two federal laws protected the civil rights of Chinese immigrants. The Burlingame Treaty of 1868 provided that "Chinese subjects visiting or residing in the United States, shall enjoy the same privileges, immunities, and exemptions in respect to travel or residence as may there be enjoyed by the citizens or subjects of the most favored nation." When Congress passed the Enforcement Act of May 31, 1870, § 16 of the law was added to protect the rights of Chinese immigrants (Wang 1995, 1032; Maltz 1994, 235–36).

Politicians played into white workers' fears and anxieties about Chinese laborers, which resulted in the enactment of discriminatory state and local laws designed to curtail their settlement or to exclude them from working in certain occupations. Because their employment opportunities were limited, the commercial laundry business was one occupation that was open to Chinese ownership. Local governments responded to their dominance in the commercial laundry business by enacting facially neutral laws to force Chinese-owned laundries out of business. The regulations were justified on public health and safety grounds as reasonable exercises of the police power. In *Soon Hing v. Crowley* (1885), a Chinese laundryman was arrested for violating a San Francisco ordinance that prohibited laundries from operating after 10:00 p.m. or before 6:00 p.m. within city limits. In a unanimous decision, Justice Stephen Field rejected Soon Hing's claim that the laundry regulation deprived him of the right to labor. Field asserted that liberty can be restricted as long as the laws were just and impartial "unless in its enforcement it is made to operate only against the class mentioned."

Lee Yick and Wo Lee were among 150 Chinese laundrymen arrested and convicted of violating San Francisco ordinances that prohibited the operation of commercial laundries in any building not made of brick or stone without having first obtained a license from the board of supervisors. The ordinances were directed at Chinese-owned commercial laundries that mainly operated in wooden buildings. The laundrymen challenged their convictions on the ground that the ordinances discriminated against them on account of race under the Fourteenth Amendment and the Burlingame Treaty. In *Yick Wo v. Hopkins* (1886), the court unanimously agreed that the ordinances illegally discriminated against Chinese laundrymen as a class. Linking race to property interests, Justice Stanley Matthews asserted that "the very idea that one man may be compelled to hold his life, or the means of living, or any material right essential to the enjoyment of life, at the mere will of another, seems to be intolerable in any country where freedom prevails" and is "the essence of slavery itself." Matthews found that public authorities administered the ordinances exclusively against the class of Chinese persons in violation of the equal protection of the laws. He declared that "though the law itself be fair on its face and impartial in appearance, yet, if it is applied and administered by public authority with an evil eye and an unequal hand, so as practically to make unjust and illegal discriminations between persons in similar circumstances, material to their rights, the denial of equal justice is still within the prohibition of the Constitution." The *Yick Wo* decision had little impact on the enactment of discriminatory laws intended to drive Chinese immigrants out of the labor market or discrimination against the Chinese community (Chin 2008).

Conclusion

The addition of the Thirteenth, Fourteenth, and Fifteenth Amendments to the Constitution brought about regime change in the United States. The amended Constitution guaranteed freedom from enslavement, birthright citizenship, the privileges or immunities of citizenship, equal protection of the laws, and voting rights—civil and political rights that were nonexistent in the Framers' Constitution of 1787. The second founding provided a new jurisprudential regime for the Reconstruction era court to rid itself of the stigma of institutional illegitimacy associated with the proslavery decisions of the Marshall and Taney Courts. In response to the amended Constitution, the justices applied a jurisprudential regime framework to the first race cases that countered the transformative egalitarian policy goals of the Radical Republican alliance. The justices made deliberate policy choices that favored prewar interpretations of federalism and constitutional theories advanced by Southern Democrats while ignoring the intentions of the Republican coalition that was responsible for drafting the amendments. The Chase and Waite Court justices simply refused to push the constitutional interpretation reset button during Reconstruction.

Of the twenty-six race cases decided by the Reconstruction era court, 65 percent were decided in a conservative direction in favor of pro-Southern interests and 35 percent were decided in a liberal direction in favor of the civil rights interests of blacks and Chinese immigrants. The case outcomes reveal that the Chase and Waite Courts exercised their power independently of the transformative egalitarian ruling regime to defeat Reconstruction policies and to strengthen the power of the modified white supremacist racial order. In the *Slaughter-House Cases*, *United States v. Cruikshank*, *United States v. Reese*, and the *Civil Rights Cases*, the justices restricted the national authority of Congress to enact laws that enforced and protected civil rights. *Strauder v. West Virginia* was the sole exception to the court's pattern of restricting civil rights under the Reconstruction amendments. The conservative case outcomes guaranteed that Southern blacks would remain in a state of racial subordination and caste at a time when they held out hope for ameliorative conditions. The Reconstruction era decisions built the constitutional foundation for the second phase of the predominant white supremacist racial order, which lasted until the 1930s.

Chapter 3

The Fuller, White, and Taft Courts, 1888–1930

Historian Rayford Logan (1965, 62) found that "the last decade of the nineteenth century and the opening of the twentieth century marked the nadir of the Negro's status in American society." The defeat of congressional Republicans in the 1888 and 1892 elections foreclosed any prospect for the enactment of additional federal civil rights legislation. By the late 1880s, Southern legislatures had enacted a variety of electoral schemes to disenfranchise black voters. Horrific acts of racial terrorism were the extralegal instruments used to enforce the regime of white supremacy. The second phase of the white supremacist racial order coincided with the progressive era—a period in American history characterized by sweeping social, economic, political, and technological transformation in the United States. These changes were attributed to a variety of factors: industrialization, urbanization, war, corruption, migration, immigration, xenophobia, and race, gender, and class divisions. Scientific racism theories and eugenics dominated scientific, intellectual, and popular thought. An antiblack propaganda campaign portrayed black people as subhuman. In 1915, Hollywood's first box office hit, *The Birth of a Nation*, which premiered at the White House during the Wilson administration, presented a grotesque racist depiction of black political achievements during Reconstruction. Confederate statutes were erected to advance "Lost Cause" revisionist interpretations of the Civil War. The writings of prominent historians such as William Dunning reflected revisionist, white supremacist interpretations of Reconstruction that influenced intellectual thought and the teaching of American history for decades.

How to alter the subordinate position of blacks during the progressive era was a subject of debate. Frederick Douglass, who had pressed for full

59

equality for blacks during Reconstruction, died on February 20, 1895. Seven months later, Booker T. Washington delivered his controversial speech in Atlanta where he urged Southern blacks to accept their subordinate status while proving themselves worthy of equality. The black community understood that it had to rely on a variety of strategies to combat the oppressive ruling regime. In 1885, a group of black lawyers in Baltimore formed the Brotherhood of Liberty in response to the *Civil Rights Cases* (1883) decision. The group was among the first civil rights organizations in the nation formed to attack racial inequality, but it was short lived (Halpin 2019). In response to Washington's accommodationist strategy, W. E. B. Du Bois and William Trotter founded the Niagara Movement in 1905 to advance full political, civil, and social rights for blacks. By 1909, the Niagara Movement had collapsed, but it became an important precursor to an organization that would become known as the National Association for the Advancement of Colored People (NAACP). Kellogg (1967, x) found that the "aim of the 'new abolitionists' was to fight the 'new slavery' by means which were then considered radical—non-violent agitation, well-publicized protest, propaganda and legal action."

Three courts operated during the progressive era—the Fuller Court (1888–1910), the White Court (1910–1921), and the Taft Court (1921–1930). Congress strengthened the institutional power of the court when it enacted several federal court reorganization and reform laws. The most significant reform legislation, the Judiciary Act of 1891 (the Evarts Act), created the structure of the modern federal judiciary. The law relieved the court of its caseload burden and abolished the justices' circuit riding responsibilities. The court was also given more control over its discretionary agenda when it received the power to grant petitions for writs of certiorari.

From 1888 until 1930, the era-defining policy dichotomy of the rival racial orders was caste and exclusion versus equal rights of American citizenship. As shown in this chapter, the court exercised its expanded powers to advance the policy goals of the modified white supremacist regime. The Waite Court's restrictive interpretations of the Reconstruction amendments laid the doctrinal foundation for the progressive era court to implement its negative racial equality agenda in the issue areas of apartheid, race-based immigration and naturalization restrictions, disenfranchisement, peonage, jury discrimination, and racial terrorism. The decisions examined in this chapter will show that the progressive era court was anything but progressive—its policies were hostile toward people of color and nonwhite immigrants, and they strengthened the color line in the United States.

The Composition of the Fuller, White, and Taft Courts

The Reconstruction era court ended on March 23, 1888, when Chief Justice Morrison Waite died of pneumonia at the age of seventy-one. President Grover Cleveland nominated Melville Fuller to succeed Waite as the eighth Chief Justice. Fuller was a successful commercial lawyer who specialized in the fields of corporate and real estate law in Chicago, but he never held a judicial position or any high office at the state or federal level. The Republican controlled Senate attempted to delay Fuller's confirmation because of his lack of support for President Lincoln's wartime policies, abolitionism, and black voting rights, but he was eventually confirmed by a 41–20 vote. Five presidents appointed thirteen justices to the Fuller Court during its twenty-two-year tenure. Cleveland appointed three additional justices to the court: Lucius Q. C. Lamar (1888), Edward Douglass White (1894), and Rufus Peckham (1896). Benjamin Harrison appointed four justices: David Brewer (1890), Henry Brown (1891), George Shiras (1892), and Howell Jackson (1893). William McKinley appointed Joseph McKenna in 1898, and Theodore Roosevelt appointed Oliver Wendell Holmes, Jr. (1902), William Day (1903), and William Moody (1906).

On July 4, 1910, Chief Justice Fuller died of heart disease at the age of seventy-eight. On December 12, 1910, Taft nominated associate justice Edward White to become the ninth Chief Justice. White was confirmed by a voice vote on the same day, and he became the first associate justice to be elevated to the position of chief justice. White was born in Louisiana, and he fought for the Confederacy. He was a successful lawyer and served as US Senator from Louisiana prior to his initial appointment in 1894. The White Court experienced rapid personnel turnover during its brief eleven-year tenure. Taft appointed five additional justices to the court: Horace Lurton (1909), Charles Evans Hughes (1910), Joseph Lamar (1911), Willis Van Devanter (1911), and Mahlon Pitney (1912). Woodrow Wilson made three appointments to the White Court: James McReynolds (1914), Louis Brandeis (1916), and John Clarke (1916). After Chief Justice White died on May 19, 1921, from a heart attack at the age of seventy-five, President Harding nominated William Taft to become the tenth chief justice. Taft, who had lobbied for his dream job, was confirmed on June 30, 1921, by a 61–4 vote. Taft became the first person to serve as president of the United States and chief justice. Harding made three additional appointments to the court: George Sutherland (1922), Edward Sanford (1923), and Pierce Butler (1923). In 1925, Calvin Coolidge appointed Harlan Fiske Stone to the court. The numerous personnel changes that occurred on the progressive era court failed to alter the policy direction of the outcomes in race cases.

Apartheid

Woodward (1974, 17–22) pointed out that one of the strangest aspects of American apartheid was that it originated in the free states of the North and eventually moved to the free Midwestern and Western states. After 1865, Southern legislatures enacted racial segregation laws as part of the Black Codes, and by the late 1880s, the formal system of laws and practices that separated people based on racial categories had proliferated in Southern and border states. Segregation laws were accompanied by informal practices and customs that affected people of color in all aspects of their lives. Woodward (101–102) found that the "extremes to which caste penalties and separation were carried out in parts of the South could hardly find a counterpart short of the latitudes of India and South Africa."

TRANSPORTATION

The first legal challenges to segregated public transportation were brought by Northern blacks a decade prior to the Civil War (Litwack 1961). Between 1890–1907, most Southern and border states had enacted some form of mandatory segregated travel on railways, streetcars, and steamboats (Lofgren 1987, 21–23). Blacks resisted exclusionary practices on common carriers by bringing civil lawsuits for violations of separate coach laws. Most of the private damage suits involved three types of challenges: assault in enforcing the law, inferior accommodations, and failure to keep whites out of black coaches (Welke 2001, 359). When Congress was considering legislation to regulate the railroads in 1886, Southern Democrats attempted to prevent the black representative from North Carolina, Republican James O'Hara, from offering an amendment to ban racial discrimination by railroads in interstate travel (Welke 2001, 344). In its final form, § 3 of the Interstate Commerce Act of 1887 made it "unlawful for any common carrier . . . to subject any particular person . . . to any undue or unreasonable prejudice or disadvantage in any respect whatsoever."

Laws that mandated segregated railway transportation forced railroad companies to act as agents of the state to enforce racial segregation. In response to the loss of power over their operations, railroad companies sued

Southern states on the ground that the laws violated the commerce clause. In *Louisville, New Orleans & Texas Railway Company v. Mississippi* (1890), the Fuller Court distinguished *Hall v. Decuir* (1878) from *Louisville* to rule that a Mississippi law that required segregated railroad accommodations for intrastate travel did not violate the commerce clause. Two months after *Louisville* was decided, a bill was introduced in the Louisiana legislature that required segregated railway accommodations. In 1890, the Separate Car Act was enacted over the objections of eighteen black members of the legislature and the railroads. The law required all railway companies to separate black and white passengers by providing separate coaches or divide them with partitions. Railroad employees were granted the power to assign passengers to the coach or compartment based on their race. Passengers and railroad employees who refused to comply with the law were subjected to fines or imprisonment.

New Orleans Creoles enjoyed social and economic advantages because of their mixed-race identity, and apartheid threatened their culture and community. Two members of the Creole community, Louis Martinet and Rodolphe Desdunes, formed a committee to test the legality of the law. The leaders hired the prominent white equal rights advocate Albion Tourgée as lead counsel. Tourgée was the author of six novels about his experience during Reconstruction, he served in the Union Army, he was a leader in the Republican Party, and he served as a superior court judge (Elliott 2006). Tourgée's legal strategy to invalidate the law centered on the power of railroad employees to determine the race of passengers for coach assignments. Tourgée sought a racially ambiguous Creole to serve as the plaintiff. Homer Plessy, who self-identified as having "seven-eighths Caucasian and one-eighth African blood," agreed to participate in the case. All aspects of the test case were planned in advance. Plessy purchased a first-class, intrastate train ticket to travel on the East Louisiana Railway from New Orleans to Covington, Louisiana. Plessy informed the conductor that he was "colored" and he took a seat in the whites-only passenger coach. When Plessy refused to comply with the conductor's order to vacate the seat and take one reserved for black passengers, the conductor alerted a detective and Plessy was arrested and charged with violating the Separate Car Act. Orleans Parish Criminal Court judge John Ferguson upheld the constitutionality of the law and the Louisiana Supreme Court found that the statute was a reasonable exercise of the state's police power under the Fourteenth Amendment.

Plessy v. Ferguson (1896) was decided by the ultraconservative Fuller Court. The court was mostly comprised of Northern Gilded Age justices who exercised their power to protect the moneyed classes, corporations, and railroads until they consented to the rights of blacks to ride in the same coaches as whites for economic reasons. In his legal brief, Tourgée argued that the Separate Car Act was unconstitutional on Thirteenth and Fourteenth Amendment grounds. Justice Henry Brown, a former federal judge in Michigan who came from a privileged Massachusetts background, was assigned to write the majority opinion. Justice David Brewer, the nephew of sitting justice Stephen Field, did not participate in the case. In a 7–1 decision, the court upheld the constitutionality of the Separate Car Act. At the outset, Justice Brown dismissed Tourgée's (1895, 31–33) Thirteenth Amendment argument that racial distinctions in the law imposed a badge of servitude and a condition of inferiority on black citizens. Brown asserted that the law implied "merely a legal distinction between the white and colored races—a distinction which is founded in the color of the two races, and which must always exist so long as white men are distinguished from the other race by color—has no tendency to destroy the legal equality of the two races, or reestablish a state of involuntary servitude."

Tourgée (14) advanced several arguments to show that the Separate Car Act violated the Fourteenth Amendment. He asserted that the law impermissibly sorted citizens on the basis of race, which interfered with their personal liberty, and it legalized caste. States could enact absurd segregation laws to "humiliate or degrade one race in order to promote the rise of ascendancy in another." Justice Brown replied that the Fourteenth Amendment was not intended "to abolish distinctions based on color, or to enforce social, as distinguished from political equality, or a commingling of the two races upon terms unsatisfactory to either." Segregation laws "do not necessarily imply the inferiority of either race to the other," and they were valid as long as they were reasonable and based on "established usages, customs and traditions of the people, and with a view to the promotion of their comfort, and the preservation of the public peace and good order." Brown cited state and federal cases that upheld segregated schools and laws prohibiting racial intermarriage to support his position.

Tourgée (8–9) asserted that the lack of a statutory definition of race impeded the ability of railroad employees to comply with the law, especially "in a community where race admixture is a frequent thing." Justice Brown dismissed the question of racial determination because it was not raised in the case and it was left up to the states to legally define who is black or white. Tourgée made the novel argument that the law deprived the Creole community of its property right to whiteness because "the reputation of being white" is "the most valuable sort of property, being the master-key that unlocks the golden door of opportunity." Brown replied that Plessy had not been deprived of property "since he is not lawfully entitled to the reputation of being a white man." Brown also dismissed Tourgée's (26) argument that the intent of the law was to separate blacks from whites "for the gratification and recognition of the sentiment of white superiority and white supremacy of right and power." Brown replied that if "the enforced separation of the two races stamps the colored race with a badge of inferiority," it is "solely because the colored race chooses to put that construction upon it." He asserted that "legislation is powerless to eradicate racial instincts or to abolish distinctions based upon physical differences. If one race be inferior to the other socially, the Constitution of the United States cannot put them upon the same plane." Brown concluded that the racial classification in the law was for the public good and therefore reasonable under the equal protection clause.

Justice John Marshall Harlan wrote the sole dissent in *Plessy*. Harlan's arguments were less radical and egalitarian compared to Tourgée's arguments, but there were several similarities in their positions (Elliott 2001, 326). Harlan argued that the true intent of the Thirteenth and Fourteenth Amendments was to protect all civil rights that pertain to freedom and citizenship. He believed that the Constitution prohibited any public authority to know the race of those entitled to be protected in the enjoyment of civil rights because it was inconsistent with the personal liberty enjoyed by everyone in the United States. It was obvious to Harlan that the law was conceived in hostility and enacted for the purpose of humiliating black citizens because the law made an exception for nurses attending children of the other races. He found that prior court decisions established that the amendments "removed the race line from our governmental systems" and declared that "the law in the States shall be the same for the black as for the white." Harlan pointed out that the railroad was a public highway and the law interfered with the personal freedom of blacks and whites to choose to occupy the same public conveyance. He dismissed Brown's contention that the Fourteenth Amendment protects civil equality and not social equality as "scarcely worthy of consideration."

Justice Harlan criticized the majority's application of the reasonableness standard to the law because it could lead to absurd state laws regulating the separation of races in other contexts. His main concern was that the reasonableness standard would reinstate a system of racial caste in the United States:

> But in view of the Constitution, in the eye of the law, there is in this country no superior, dominant, ruling class of citizens. There is no caste here. Our Constitution is color-blind, and neither knows nor tolerates classes among citizens. In respect of civil rights, all citizens are equal before the law. The humblest is the peer of the most powerful. The law regards man as man, and takes no account of his surroundings or of his color when his civil rights as guaranteed by the supreme law of the land are involved. It is, therefore, to be regretted that this high tribunal, the final expositor of the fundamental law of the land, has reached the conclusion that it is competent for a State to regulate the enjoyment by citizens of their civil rights solely upon the basis of race.

Harlan borrowed the concept of a color-blind Constitution from Tourgée's (19) brief where he characterized the Separate Car Act as class legislation "intended to promote the happiness of one class by asserting the supremacy and the inferiority of another class. Justice is pictured blind and her daughter, the Law, ought to be color-blind." Elliott (2006, 4) found that Tourgée used the color-blind phrase repeatedly in his writings and speeches on race and citizenship, and "Justice Harlan never elaborated on his color-blindness doctrine outside of his *Plessy* dissent; he never used this phase either before or after it."

The *Plessy* decision produced two competing visions of American citizenship under the equal protection clause. The majority viewed the citizenship status of blacks through the lens of racial instincts and black inferiority, which permitted the states to use their police powers to enact reasonable laws to separate the races. Justice Harlan viewed the citizenship status of blacks through the lens of equal rights of American citizenship. He believed that laws separating the races placed blacks in a condition of legal inferiority and they were inconsistent with the true intent of the Thirteenth and Fourteenth Amendments. Harlan speculated that the decision would "prove to be quite as pernicious as *Dred Scott*." Despite its nationwide impact, the *Plessy* decision received little national press attention compared to the *Civil Rights Cases*, but the decision was denounced in the black press (Woodward 1987, 173). Lofgren (1987, 202) summed up the policy impact of *Plessy* in a single statement: "From hospitals before birth to cemeteries after death, separate-but-equal set the legal status of blacks." After the decision was announced, Homer Plessy pleaded guilty to violating the Separate Car Act and paid the $25 fine. One hundred twenty-six years later, Democratic Governor John Bel Edwards of Louisiana granted Homer Plessy a posthumous pardon (Grossman 2022).

Barnes (1983, 10) found that several Southern states enacted railroad segregation statutes that applied to all aspects of transit in response to the *Plessy* decision. The statutes were assumed to be valid as long as they provided equal services. In 1907, the Oklahoma legislature enacted a separate coach law that included a provision that exempted railroads from providing luxury Pullman car and dining services for black passengers as long as there was no substantial demand for them. Before the law took effect, Edward McCabe, a black politician and businessman from Oklahoma, filed a class action lawsuit against five railroad companies to prevent them from complying with the separate coach law. The lower courts agreed with the railroads that the allegations in the complaint were too vague and indefinite to warrant relief. In *McCabe v. Atchison, Topeka & Santa Fe Railway Co.* (1914), Chief Justice White assigned the opinion to Charles Evans Hughes. Hughes was the governor of New York at the time of his appointment to the White Court in 1910. He grew up in a religious family in Glenn Falls, New York, and his Welsh father was an abolitionist Baptist preacher. While serving as governor, Hughes was nicknamed "Charles the Baptist" because he became the first president of the Northern Baptist Convention in 1907. Harlan and Hughes served together on the court for a year prior to Harlan's death on October 14, 1911. Baker (1991, 473) portrayed Hughes as "slowly taking Harlan's place on race issues." Baker described Harlan as a "stump speaker," but Hughes "applied a cooler, more analytical hand to the problems at issue."

McCabe was the first railroad transportation case decided by the court after Harlan's death. Hughes dismissed the case on procedural grounds because the allegations in the complaint were "altogether too vague and indefinite" to justify the injunction sought by the black plaintiffs. When Hughes examined § 7 of the law that permitted carriers to "provide sleeping cars, dining cars and chair cars exclusively for white persons and provide no similar accommodations for negroes," he found that it was based on the reasoning "that there may not be enough persons of African descent seeking these accommodations to warrant the outlay in providing them." Hughes struck it down because he interpreted *Plessy*'s separate but equal standard to require equal accommodations. He asserted that the equal protection clause had been violated, because it "makes the constitutional right depend upon the number of persons who may be discriminated against, whereas the essence of the constitutional right is that it is a personal one." Hughes declared that "if facilities are provided, substantial equality of treatment of persons traveling under like conditions cannot be refused."

Chief Justice White and Justices Holmes, Lamar, and McReynolds concurred in the result without an opinion. Schmidt (1982a, 488–91) found a memo written by Hughes that suggested that Holmes disagreed with the substantial equality of treatment requirement. Hughes's memo stated that he could not "construe the statute as requiring the carriers to give equal, though separate, accommodations so far as sleeping cars, dining cars and chair cars are concerned." Hughes disagreed with the position that "a black man must sit-up all night just because he is black, unless there are enough blacks to make a 'black sleeping car' pay." Hughes wrote that this is not "a case calling for 'logical exactness' in enforcing equal rights, but rather as it seems to me it is a bald, wholly unjustified, discrimination against a passenger solely on account of race."

In the landmark *Plessy v. Ferguson* decision, the court devised the separate but equal doctrine that established the constitutional foundation of apartheid in the United States. In *McCabe*, Justice Hughes devised a strategy to attack the constitutional foundation of apartheid by requiring substantial equality of treatment in cases. As the outcomes in table 3.1 show, the progressive era court consistently upheld the constitutionality of segregated travel.

Table 3.1. Fuller, White, and Taft Courts Transportation Cases, 1888–1930

Case	Vote	Outcome
Louisville, New Orleans & Texas Railway Company v. Mississippi (1890) F	7–2	Held that a Mississippi law that required segregated railroad accommodations did not violate the commerce clause (C)
Plessy v. Ferguson (1896) F	7–1	Held that a Louisiana law that required separate but equal railroad coaches for black and white passengers was reasonable under the equal protection clause (C)
Chesapeake and Ohio Railway Company v. Kentucky (1900) F	8–1	Held that Kentucky's separate coach law did not violate the commerce clause on the authority of *Louisville* (C)
Chiles v. Chesapeake and Ohio Railway Company (1910) F	6–1	Held that a railroad's segregation regulation was reasonable based on the customs and usages in the state (C)

Case	Vote	Outcome
Butts v. Merchants & Miners Transportation Company (1913) W	9–0	Held that §§ 1 and 2 of the Civil Rights Act of 1875 did not apply to segregated travel on a steamship on national waters (C)
McCabe v. Atchison, Topeka & Santa Fe Railway Company (1914) W	9–0	Held that a provision in Oklahoma's separate coach law violated the substantial equality of treatment principle; case dismissed on procedural grounds (L)
South Covington & Cincinnati Street Railway Company v. Kentucky (1920) W	6–3	Held that a Kentucky law that required segregated streetcars was not an unconstitutional burden on interstate commerce (C)
Cincinnati, Covington & Erlanger Railway Company v. Kentucky (1920) W	6–3	Upheld Kentucky's separate coach law on the authority of *South Covington* (C)

Source: Created by the author.

Note: F for Fuller Court, W for White Court, and T for Taft Court. C for conservative outcomes, and L for liberal outcomes.

Education

The first education case decided by the Supreme Court, *Cumming v. Richmond County Board of Education* (1899), addressed the issue of equal funding of public schools for black and white children. When the Georgia legislature created its public school system in 1872, the law mandated segregated schools and it included a provision that was unique to the city of Augusta. The provision required the Richmond County school board to provide primary schools for black and white children, but the board was given the discretion to establish high schools. Public primary schools were free, but public high schools charged tuition. A board committee investigating the status of high schools recommended the closure of a black classical high school established by a group of racially ambiguous Augusta elites. Its leaders sought an injunction to prevent the collection of a tax and spending on white high schools that black children could not attend. Writing for the unanimous court, Justice Harlan upheld the lower court's decision, which denied the injunction. Harlan believed that the school board's decision was not based on hostility toward blacks. He asserted that the board's decision was reasonable because it was in the interest of the greater number of black children and black high school students had the option of attending existing private schools. Kousser (1980, 42–43) found that the *Cumming* decision gave Southern states the green light to discriminate in publicly funded activities, and it was not until 1945 before a full, four-year public high school for blacks was reestablished in Augusta.

Berea College v. Kentucky (1908) involved a legal attack on the choice of a private Christian college to teach black and white students in the same classroom in the South. In 1904, Kentucky passed the Day Act, which made it illegal for any person, corporation, or association of persons to teach black and white students together. Berea College was found guilty of violating the Day Act and fined $1,000. The college challenged the constitutionality of the law on the ground that it was repugnant to the state's bill of rights and the Fourteenth Amendment, which guaranteed every citizen the right to enjoy their liberty and the right to worship God according to the dictates of their own consciences. The Kentucky Court of Appeals ruled that the law was reasonable, based on white supremacist ideology. The Fuller Court upheld the constitutionality of the Day Act on the ground that Berea College was a corporation chartered by the state, and the state had the power to alter or amend charters as long as the alterations did not defeat or substantially impair the object of the grant. Writing for the 7–2 majority, Justice David Brewer found that Berea College's charter could be amended based on the language of the Day Act without destroying the power of the college to furnish education to white and black students. The law "simply separates them by time or place of instruction." In his dissent, Justice Harlan argued that the court should have decided the broad question raised in the case—whether a statute that made it a crime for a private institution to teach white and black students in the same classroom was constitutional under the Fourteenth Amendment. Harlan found that the Day Act was based on hostility toward blacks, and it violated the Fourteenth Amendment. He wrote a lengthy dissent that addressed the calamitous effects of Brewer's opinion on religious freedom and its spillover effects on race in other contexts.

The Taft Court's decision in *Gong Lum v. Rice* (1927) reinforced *Plessy's* central premise that state-mandated separation of the races was permissible under the equal protection clause. Gong Lum, a Chinese merchant who resided in the Mississippi Delta, sued the school board when his American citizen daughter was denied admission to a white public high school. The 1890 Mississippi Constitution required separate schools "for children of the white and colored races." The implementing statute defined "colored" as any race other than the Caucasian or the white race. The Mississippi Supreme Court found that the purpose of the law was to maintain the integrity and purity of the white race and Martha Lum was not entitled to attend a white public school. Chief Justice Taft wrote the brief unanimous decision, which upheld the lower court's ruling without much reasoning other than citing prior court decisions that upheld racial segregation. Taft found that the constitutionality of segregated education was a settled question.

Housing

Apartheid restricted where people of color could live and attend public schools in the United States. In cities with large black populations, public officials enacted land use regulations and exclusionary housing policies to segregate communities (Rothstein 2017). Border and Southern cities adopted racial zoning policies which prohibited blacks from moving into majority white blocks (Power 1983). In 1914, the Louisville city council enacted a segregation ordinance that prohibited black residents from occupying houses in blocks where the greater number of houses were occupied by white residents and vice versa. NAACP President Moorfield Storey argued that the ordinance, which prevented a white property owner from selling his property to a black man, violated the equal protection clause. In *Buchanan v. Warley* (1917), the White Court agreed that the law violated the Fourteenth Amendment and gave the NAACP its first legal victory in its campaign against residential segregation. Writing for the unanimous court, Justice William Day found that the ordinance "was based wholly upon color, simply that and nothing more," and its purpose was to maintain racial purity and to prevent the deterioration of property owned and occupied by whites. He determined that the zoning ordinance annulled the civil right of a white man to dispose of his property as he saw fit under the due process clause of the Fourteenth Amendment and the right of a black man to acquire property without state legislation discriminating against him under the Civil Rights Act of 1866.

Racial restrictive covenants were used to segregate neighborhoods in Northern, Midwestern, and Western urban areas. White homeowners would enter into formal private agreements to not sell or lease their properties to blacks and other racial groups. Restrictive covenant schemes were encouraged by private homeowners' associations and local real estate boards. Jones-Correa (2000) linked the spread of the use of restrictive covenants to the Great Migration when hundreds of thousands of blacks moved out of the South between 1910 and 1920. In *Corrigan v. Buckley* (1926), the Taft Court rejected the NAACP's argument that the use of restrictive covenants in Washington, DC, violated the Civil Rights Act of 1866 and the Fourteenth Amendment. Writing for the unanimous court, Justice Edward Sanford found the NAACP's argument "entirely lacking in substance or color of merit." Sanford reaffirmed the distinction between state action and private action and found that the Reconstruction Amendments did not prohibit "private individuals from entering into contracts respecting the control and disposition of their own property."

With few exceptions, the Fuller, White, and Taft Courts upheld the constitutionality of racial segregation laws in the areas of transportation, education, and housing—the most important areas of public life in the United States. The court's decisions advanced the policy goals of the ruling regime of white supremacy.

Table 3.2. Fuller, White, and Taft Courts Education and Housing Cases, 1888–1930

Case	Vote	Outcome
Cumming v. Richmond County Board of Education (1899) F	9–0	Held that a Georgia school board decision to fund public white high schools without funding black high schools did not violate the Fourteenth Amendment (C)
Berea College v. Kentucky (1908) F	7–2	Upheld a Kentucky law that prohibited a private Christian college chartered as a corporation from teaching black and white students together (C)
Buchanan v. Warley (1917) W	9–0	Held that a Louisville segregation ordinance violated the Fourteenth Amendment and the Civil Rights Act of 1866 (L)
Corrigan v. Buckley (1926) T	9–0	Dismissed a challenge to the use of restrictive covenants in Washington, DC, on jurisdictional grounds (C)
Gong Lum v. Rice (1927) T	9–0	Held that the exclusion of a Chinese American student from an all-white public high school did not violate the Fourteenth Amendment (C)
Harmon v. Tyler (1927) T	9–0	Held that a New Orleans zoning ordinance was unconstitutional on the authority of *Buchanan* (L)

Source: Created by the author.

Note: F for Fuller Court, W for White Court, and T for Taft Court. C for conservative outcomes, and L for liberal outcomes.

Race-Based Exclusion

Shortly after the ratification of the Constitution, Congress passed the Naturalization Act of 1790—"That any alien, being a free white person, who shall have resided within the limits and under the jurisdiction of the United States for the term of two years, may be admitted to become a citizen thereof." Citizenship was defined in terms of whiteness, and nonwhite immigrants had to legally fight for the opportunity to become American citizens. The citizenship clause in § 1 of the Fourteenth Amendment provided that all persons born or naturalized in the United States and subject to its jurisdiction are citizens. The Naturalization Act of 1870 extended naturalization to aliens of African nativity and to persons of African descent. Between 1870 and 1924, Congress passed several laws that barred nonwhite immigrants from entry into the United States and imposed onerous restrictions on naturalization. The laws were passed in response to the escalation of white supremacist ideology and hostility toward Chinese immigration. The Supreme Court was asked to determine the constitutionality of racist immigration and naturalization laws when nonwhite immigrants challenged them in court.

The Exclusion of Chinese Immigrants

The Burlingame Treaty of 1868 recognized the right to free Chinese immigration to the United States, but the Angell Treaty of 1880 placed limits on the numbers of Chinese laborers permitted to enter into the country. Congress passed the Chinese Exclusion Act of 1882, which barred Chinese laborers from entering the United States for a period of ten years, with few exceptions. The law placed travel restrictions on Chinese immigrants already living in America, it curbed their ability to become citizens, and they had to obtain a certificate to reenter if they left the country. The Scott Act of 1888 prevented Chinese immigrants from returning to the United States. Chae Chan Ping had lived and worked in San Francisco for a decade prior to taking a trip to China to visit his family in 1877. The Scott Act became law a few days before Ping's return to California, which annulled his certificate of reentry. Ping filed a habeas corpus petition seeking his release on the ground that the Chinese Exclusion Act and the Scott Act violated the Burlingame Treaty.

In *Chae Chan Ping v. United States* (1889), also known as the Chinese Exclusion Case, Justice Stephen Field wrote the unanimous decision, which upheld the Chinese Exclusion Act. Field was born and raised in the Northeast, but he moved to California during the Gold Rush. He was elected to the California state legislature and later served on the California Supreme Court prior to his appointment to the Supreme Court by President Lincoln. Field expressed his antipathy toward Chinese immigration and the Chinese Exclusion Act in a letter sent to Hastings Law College professor John Pomeroy dated April 14, 1882 (Graham 1938, 1104). Field stated that "it must be apparent to every one, that it would be better for both races to live apart—and that their only intercourse should be that of foreign commerce." He went on to say that "they are a different race, and, even if they could assimilate, assimilation would not be desirable." Field believed that Chinese immigration should be stopped and that he belonged to the class "who repudiate the doctrine that this country was made for the people of *all* races. On the contrary, I think it is for our race—the Caucasian race." With regard to blacks, Field stated that the country "was obliged to take care of the Africans; because we find them here, and they were brought here against their will by our fathers. Otherwise, it would be a very serious question, whether their introduction should be permitted or encouraged."

Justice Field's anti-Chinese views were prevalent throughout the decision. To put his policy preferences into law, Field had to resolve the conflict between the Chinese Exclusion Act and the Burlingame Treaty of 1868 and its 1880 revisions. Field explained that treaties were on the same plane as laws enacted by Congress, but Congress had the sovereign power to exclude aliens from the United States, which could not be surrendered by the treaty making power. He went on to say that if Congress "considers the presence of foreigners of a different race in this country, who will not assimilate with us, to be dangerous to its peace and security, their exclusion is not to be stayed because at the time there are no actual hostilities with the nation of which the foreigners are subjects." Field's deference to Congress on the power to control immigration meant that the legislative department's determination was conclusive on the judiciary. In *Ping*, Field articulated the plenary power doctrine that gave Congress sweeping power to deny entry to any immigrants it chose in this statement: "The power of exclusion of foreigners being an incident of sovereignty belonging to the government of the United States, as a part of those sovereign powers delegated by the Constitution, the right to its exercise at any time when, in the judgment of the government, the interests of the country require it, cannot be granted away or restrained on behalf of any one." Field concluded that the licenses obtained by Chinese immigrants prior to 1888 were held at the will of the federal government and revocable at any time.

Congress passed the Geary Act of 1892, which extended the Chinese Exclusion Act for another ten years. Two provisions of the law required Chinese immigrants residing in the United States to obtain and carry a certificate of residence to prove that they were in the country legally. Violators of the law could be sentenced up to a year in prison at hard labor and deported. In the Chinese deportation case *Fong Yue Ting v. United States* (1893), Justice Horace Gray expanded the plenary power of Congress to exclude immigrants to the plenary power to deport immigrants because they "rest upon one foundation, are derived from one source, are supported by the same reasons, and are in truth but parts of one and the same power." Despite his hostile views toward Chinese immigrants in *Ping*, Field wrote a passionate dissent that criticized the practice of "deportation of friendly aliens in the time of peace." He argued that once Chinese immigrants became lawful residents, Congress lacked the power to expel them without due process rights. Field characterized the deportation of the Chinese immigrants as cruel and unusual punishment that resulted in "the breaking up of all the relations of friendship, family and business." The Fuller Court's foundational immigration decisions recognized the plenary power of Congress to exclude and expel immigrants based solely on race. When the United States and China became allies during World War II, Congress passed the Magnuson Act of 1943 that repealed the Chinese Exclusion Act.

In 1894, Wong Kim Ark traveled to China to visit his family, and upon his return to the United States in 1895, a customs official barred his reentry under the Chinese Exclusion Act. Wong Kim challenged his detention on the ground that he was born in San Francisco in 1870 to Chinese immigrant parents. The federal government argued that birth in the United States did not automatically grant citizenship and Wong Kim Ark was Chinese "by reason of his race, language, color and dress." In *United States v. Wong Kim Ark* (1896), the Fuller Court ruled that the Fourteenth Amendment and the Civil Rights Act of 1866 reaffirmed the fundamental principle of citizenship by birth "in the most explicit and comprehensive terms." Justice Gray presented an extensive analysis of common law to support his finding that the Fourteenth Amendment, "in clear words and in manifest intent, includes the children born, within the territory of the United States, of all other persons, of whatever race or color, domiciled within the United States." To find otherwise "would be to deny citizenship to thousands of persons of English, Scotch, Irish, German or other European parentage, who have always been considered and treated as citizens of the United States." Gray made it clear that Congress has the power to regulate naturalization, but it has no authority to restrict birthright citizenship without amending the Constitution.

Discrimination against Japanese Immigrants

As the Chinese immigrant population decreased as a result of the Chinese Exclusion Act, Japanese immigrants filled the demand for laborers in the Western states. The Gentleman's Agreement of 1907 between the United States and Japan restricted the entry of Japanese laborers into the country. Japanese immigrants were subjected to virulent racism, violent attacks, and discrimination fueled by the recycled fear of the so-called "Yellow Peril." Western states enacted alien land laws that prohibited Asian immigrants from owning or leasing lands. In 1921, Washington enacted a law that prohibited immigrants from leasing or owning land unless they had declared their intent to become citizens, but federal laws prohibited Japanese immigrants from becoming naturalized citizens. The alien land law was challenged on the ground that it violated the due process and equal protection clauses of the Fourteenth Amendment and the 1911 treaty between the United States and Japan. In *Terrace v. Thompson* (1923), the Taft Court upheld the constitutionality of the law. Justice Pierce Butler found no discriminatory purpose in the law because states could use the racial classification created by Congress in the exercise of its plenary power over immigration and naturalization. The decision limited the option of Issei farmers from pursuing their livelihood and deprived them of the right to own property. Aoki (1998) found that the racialized alien land laws were important precursors to Japanese internment.

The Racial Prerequisite Cases

The Naturalization Act of 1870 established that being a white person was the prerequisite to become a naturalized citizen, but, in its zeal to restrict Asian immigration, Congress failed to statutorily define who was white. Federal courts were asked to determine racial identity and who was white by law without any guidance in the text or the legislative history of the 1870 law. Haney-López's (1996) seminal study of fifty-two racial prerequisite cases revealed that race was not a natural category—it was a category that was socially constructed and the law played an important role in constructing race. In the first racial prerequisite case, a Chinese immigrant claimed that he was white based on the indefinite description of the class of white persons in the 1870 law. In *In re Ah Yup* (1878), a federal circuit court rejected Ah Yup's claim that he was white based on the "common understanding" of who was white and so-called scientific definitions of race.

The Taft Court decided two racial prerequisite cases within a three-month period: *Ozawa v. United States* (1922) and *United States v. Thind* (1923). Justice George Sutherland wrote the unanimous decisions in both cases. Sutherland, who was born in England and raised in Utah, was active in Republican politics during the rise of anti-Chinese hostility in the West. He served two terms in the US Senate prior to his appointment to the court in 1917 by President Harding. Takao Ozawa was chosen to serve as the plaintiff in a test case to acquire the right of naturalization for the Japanese community (Carbado 2009). Ozawa argued that he was a free white person within the meaning of the 1790 naturalization law because its sole purpose was to exclude the African race and Indians, his skin color was white, and he was assimilable. In *Ozawa*, Sutherland explained that the framers intended to confer citizenship "upon that class of persons whom the fathers knew as white" and, if they had intended the "brown or yellow races" to be included in the law, "the language of the act would have been so varied as to include them within its privileges." Sutherland rejected the application of a skin color test to determine whether Ozawa was white, because skin color "differs greatly among persons of the same race" and a color test alone "would result in a confused overlapping of races and a gradual merging of one into the other, without any practical line of separation." Sutherland asserted that federal and state courts have "held that the words 'white person' were meant to indicate only a person of what is popularly known as the Caucasian race." He found that Ozawa was "clearly of a race who is not Caucasian."

Bhagat Singh Thind was a Sikh who was born in the Indian state of Punjab. After his service in the US Army during WWI, Thind successfully petitioned to become a naturalized citizen. The federal government appealed the decision on the ground that Thind was not white under the Naturalization Act of 1870 and the Immigration Act of 1917 barred immigrants from any country adjacent to the continent of Asia. To prove that he was white, Thind relied on ethnological studies that classified people who lived in the north and northwest states of India as belonging to the Aryan or Caucasian race. In *Thind*, Justice Sutherland rejected the use of scientific racial classification schemes to determine who was white because they "are in irreconcilable disagreement as to what constitutes a proper racial division." He singled out the "Aryan theory as a racial basis" as being "discredited by most, if not all, modern writers on the subject of ethnology" and the word "Caucasian" was "in scarcely better repute." When Sutherland expanded on the racial differences between "Hindus" and "Europeans," he found that the "physical group characteristics of the Hindus render them readily distinguishable from the various groups of persons in this country commonly recognized as white." He pointed out that children of European parentage "quickly merge into the mass of our population," but "it cannot be doubted that the children born in this country of Hindu parents would retain indefinitely the clear evidence of their ancestry." Sutherland was careful to point out that "it is very far from our thought to suggest the slightest question of racial superiority or inferiority. What we suggest is merely racial difference, and it is of such character and extent that the great body of our people instinctively recognize it and reject the thought of assimilation." Sutherland concluded that Thind did not belong to the body of people commonly known as white, and it "was not likely that Congress would be willing to accept as citizens a class of persons whom it rejects as immigrants."

The outcomes in the immigration and naturalization cases reveal that the court consistently exercised its power to advance the policy goals of the ruling regime of white supremacy. Congress was given a blank check by the court to further its racist immigration agenda by means of the plenary power doctrine to exclude and expel nonwhite immigrants. The court advanced its own race-based immigration agenda when it had to determine racial identity for naturalization purposes. The court invented racial identity tests that were based on racist assumptions to restrict the boundary of race to whites and others. Congress did not remove racial restrictions to naturalization until 1952 when it passed the McCarran Act.

Table 3.3. Fuller, White, and Taft Courts Asian Exclusion Cases, 1888–1930

Case	Vote	Outcome
Chae Chan Ping v. United States (1889) (Chinese Exclusion Case) F	8–0	Upheld the constitutionality of the Scott Act, which prohibited Chinese immigrants from reentering the country (C)
Fong Yue Ting v. United States (1893) F	5–3	Upheld § 6 of the Geary Act, which required Chinese immigrants to carry certificates of residence to prove their legal status (C)
Wong Wing v. United States (1896) F	9–0	Held that § 4 of the Geary Act was invalid because it subjected Chinese immigrants to imprisonment and deportation without due process rights (L)

Case	Vote	Outcome
United States v. Wong Kim Ark (1898) F	6–2	Held that a child of Chinese immigrants born in the United States was a citizen under the Fourteenth Amendment (L)
Ozawa v. United States (1922) T	9–0	Held that a Japanese immigrant was not eligible for naturalization because he was not white within the meaning of the 1790 and 1870 naturalization laws (C)
United States v. Bhagat Thind (1923) T	8–0	Held that a Punjabi immigrant was not eligible for naturalization because he was not white within the meaning of the Naturalization Act of 1870 and the Immigration Act of 1917 (C)
Terrace v. Thompson (1923) T	6–2	Upheld a Washington state law that prevented Japanese immigrants from owning or leasing land for agricultural purposes (C)
Porterfield v. Webb (1923) T	6–2	Upheld California's alien land law on the authority of *Terrace* (C)
Frick v. Webb (1923) T	6–2	Held that a Japanese immigrant could not purchase stock in an agribusiness company under California's alien land law (C)
Webb v. O'Brien (1923) T	6–2	Held that a Japanese immigrant had no right to enter into a sharecropping contract under California's alien land law (C)
Toyota v. United States (1925) T	8–1	Held that a Japanese WWI veteran was not eligible for naturalization because he was not white (C)
Cockrill v. California (1925) T	9–0	Upheld the conviction of a Japanese immigrant and a white agent who entered into an agreement to purchase farm land to evade the restrictions of California's alien land law (C)

Source: Created by the author.

Note: F for Fuller Court, W for White Court, and T for Taft Court. C for conservative outcomes, and L for liberal outcomes.

Disenfranchisement

From the late 1880s to the early 1900s, Southern Democrats took actions that undermined the political equality guarantees of the Fifteenth Amendment. In 1891, Senate Democrats filibustered the Lodge Bill of 1890, which would have required federal supervision over all phases of registration and voting in national elections (Kousser 1974, 29–30). The Democratic controlled Congress passed the Civil Rights Repeal Act of 1894, which repealed sections of the Enforcement Acts intended to protect black voting rights (Carr 1947, 46). Waning congressional support for civil rights and adverse voting rights decisions discouraged the Department of Justice from enforcing the remaining laws vigorously except for sporadic attempts (46–47). Southern legislatures enacted a variety of disenfranchisement schemes to maintain white political control: the white primary, grandfather clauses, literacy tests, restrictive registration laws, poll taxes, property requirements, residency requirements, and gerrymandering. Extralegal means included ballot box stuffing, election fraud, and corruption. Racial terrorism, lynching, murder, and intimidation were used to enforce black disenfranchisement.

In 1901, Alabama held a constitutional convention that resulted in a constitution that was explicitly designed to disenfranchise black voters. Persons who registered before January 1, 1903, who were almost all white men, remained voters for life unless disqualified by certain crimes, but after January 1, 1903, persons attempting to register to vote were subjected to residency requirements, literacy tests, understanding tests, good character tests, poll taxes, property requirements, and employment requirements. In 1900, there were 181,471 black eligible voters but only 3,000 were registered after the new provisions took effect in 1903 (Pildes 2000, 303–4). When black men attempted to register to vote for the 1902 election, they faced rejection and humiliation from white registrars. Jackson Giles, the leader of the Colored Men's Suffrage Association of Alabama, filed a class action lawsuit against the board of registrars that was secretly funded by Booker T. Washington (Meier 1957, 221–22). The federal circuit court dismissed the case for lack of jurisdiction. On appeal, attorney Wilford Smith, an aide to Washington, argued on behalf of the class that circuit courts sitting in equity have jurisdiction to enforce and protect the civil rights of citizens guaranteed by the Fourteenth and Fifteenth Amendments against "fraud and conspiracy and cunning and chicanery."

In *Giles v. Harris* (1903), Chief Justice Fuller assigned the majority opinion to the court's newcomer, Oliver Wendell Holmes, Jr. Born and raised in Boston, Massachusetts, Holmes was wounded several times while serving in the Union army during the Civil War. He taught law at Harvard and, prior to his appointment to the court, Holmes served on the Massachusetts Supreme Judicial Court. Justice Holmes found that the case was properly before the court, but he ruled that it should be dismissed because the court could not order the names of black plaintiffs to be placed on fraudulent registration lists. Holmes understood that the white registrars "accepted their office for the purpose of carrying out the scheme." He explained that there was no remedy for the black plaintiffs in a court of equity because it could not be enforced. Holmes asserted that the white population intended to keep blacks from voting and it would take "something more than ordering the plaintiff's name to be inscribed upon the lists of 1902." Holmes made it clear that the court was "not prepared to supervise the voting in that State by officers of the court," and black voters should seek relief from the state or Congress.

In his dissent, Justice Brewer argued that the federal circuit court had jurisdiction in the case and Giles's legal rights were violated by the white registrars. Justice Harlan's dissent focused on the procedural and jurisdictional questions raised in the case, but he believed that it was "competent for the courts to give relief in such cases as this." The *Giles* decision was an astonishing act of judicial abdication and indifference to the political equality rights of black citizens. Holmes never explained to the 5,000 black plaintiffs who were denied the right to register to vote how they could obtain relief from the Alabama legislature when the state was responsible for disenfranchising them in the first place.

The Waite Court's *Ex parte Siebold* (1880) and *Ex parte Yarbrough* (1884) decisions adopted a broad view of congressional power to protect black voting rights in national elections under the Elections Clause. In *James v. Bowman* (1903), the Fuller Court restricted the power of Congress to protect and enforce black voting rights in national elections under the Fifteenth Amendment. Two white men were indicted in federal court for bribery and intimidation to prevent blacks from voting in the 1898 Kentucky congressional election. One of the defendants challenged his indictment on the ground that § 5507 of the Revised Statutes (formerly § 5 of the Enforcement Act of May 31, 1870) was unconstitutional because it did not authorize Congress to punish the actions of private individuals who interfered with black voting in national elections. Writing for the majority, Justice Brewer cited *United States v. Reese* (1876) to declare § 5507 unconstitutional on the ground that the Fifteenth Amendment was limited to official action. Brewer asserted that congressional power to punish bribery was limited "to elections in which the nation is directly interested, or in which some mandate of the National Constitution is disobeyed." Brewer failed to mention the *Siebold* and *Yarbrough* precedents in his opinion. Justices Harlan and Brown dissented without opinions.

Southern states adopted escape clauses to prevent the disenfranchisement of poor whites who were affected by the administration of poll taxes, property requirements, literacy tests, and understanding tests. In 1910, Oklahoma approved a constitutional amendment that required voters to take a literacy test on any section of the state constitution prior to registration. Voters were exempted if they could prove that their grandfathers could vote under any form of government prior to January 1, 1866. The grandfather clause allowed illiterate white males to vote but it deprived black males of their right to vote, because the Fifteenth Amendment was not ratified until 1870. In 1911, federal prosecutors charged two Oklahoma election officials with conspiracy to deprive black citizens of their voting rights as secured by the Fifteenth Amendment. In the organization's first case before the court, NAACP president Moorfield Storey argued that the undoubted purpose and effect of Oklahoma's grandfather clause was to discriminate against black voters.

In *Guinn v. United States* (1915), the White Court ruled that Oklahoma's grandfather clause unconstitutionally infringed the rights of black voters under the Fifteenth Amendment. Writing for the unanimous court, Chief Justice White explained that the Fifteenth Amendment did not take away the power of state governments to regulate elections, but it did restrict the power of the state to deny or abridge the right of citizens to vote on account of race. When White examined the purpose of the grandfather clause, he found that there was no room for any serious doubt that the January 1, 1866, date preceded the ratification of the Fifteenth Amendment, and it was adopted as the "controlling and dominant test of the right of suffrage." The landmark precedent, *Guinn v. United States*, was the first decision to strike down a state law under the Fifteenth Amendment.

The white primary was the most effective electoral scheme used to disenfranchise black voters in the South. Its use applied to the Democratic Party's direct primary elections, which barred participation by black voters. Under one-party Democratic rule in the South, the winner in the primary election was guaranteed to be the winner in the general election. When Houston Democratic Party officials adopted a white primary rule for the February 1921 election, black leaders mobilized against the scheme and brought a test case to invalidate the white primary on Fifteenth Amendment grounds. In *Love v. Griffith* (1924), the court ruled that the case was moot because the election had taken place. In a campaign finance violation case unrelated to black voting rights, the court ruled in *Newberry v. United States* (1921) that primaries were not elections for office, and they were beyond the scope of congressional regulation.

The *Newberry* decision emboldened the Texas legislature to enact a more restrictive white primary law in 1923. The law provided that all qualified voters who were members of the Democratic Party were eligible to participate in any Democratic Party primary election in the state except black voters. The NAACP challenged the constitutionality of the revised white primary law on Fourteenth and Fifteenth grounds. In *Nixon v. Herndon* (1927), the Taft Court declared that the white primary law was unconstitutional on equal protection grounds. Writing for the unanimous court, Justice Holmes found that it was "too clear for extended argument that color cannot be made the basis of a statutory classification affecting the right set up in this case." The court's failure to address the Fifteenth Amendment issue allowed Texas Democratic Party officials to circumvent the ruling by excluding blacks from voting in primary elections based on party rules.

As shown in the table 3.4, the Fuller Court decided all voting rights cases in favor of black disenfranchisement. The intervention of the Department

Table 3.4. Fuller, White, and Taft Courts Disenfranchisement Cases, 1888–1930

Case	Vote	Outcome
Mills v. Green (1895) F	8–0	Dismissed a lawsuit to block South Carolina from holding a constitutional convention to disenfranchise blacks (C)
Giles v. Harris (1903) F	6–3	Held that courts of equity lacked enforcement power to remedy Alabama's massive black disenfranchisement scheme (C)
James v. Bowman (1903) F	6–2	Held that § 5507 of the Revised Statutes was invalid because the Fifteenth Amendment did not authorize Congress to punish private individuals who prevented blacks from voting in national elections (C)
Giles v. Teasley (1904) F	8–1	Dismissed a follow-up case to *Giles v. Harris* brought by black plaintiffs on procedural grounds (C)
Jones v. Montague (1904) F	9–0	Dismissed a challenge to disenfranchisement schemes directed at black voters in Virginia on procedural grounds (C)
Guinn v. United States (1915) W	8–0	Held that Oklahoma's grandfather clause was unconstitutional on Fifteenth Amendment grounds (L)

continued on next page

Table 3.4. Continued

Case	Vote	Outcome
Myers v. Anderson (1915) W	8–0	Held that Maryland's 1908 law that fixed the qualifications of voters in Annapolis's municipal elections violated the Fifteenth Amendment (L)
United States v. Mosley (1915) W	7–1	Held that § 19 of the Criminal Code, which provided for the punishment of conspiracy to injure and oppress the rights of black citizens to have their votes counted in a congressional election, could be applied to state election officials (L)
Love v. Griffith (1924) T	9–0	Dismissed a case on mootness grounds brought by black Texas voters who challenged the validity of a white primary election (C)
Nixon v. Herndon (1927) T	9–0	Held that the white primary violated the equal protection clause of the Fourteenth Amendment (L)

Source: Created by the author.

Note: F for Fuller Court, W for White Court, and T for Taft Court. C for conservative outcomes, and L for liberal outcomes.

of Justice and the expert advocacy of the NAACP influenced the favorable outcomes in the voting rights cases decided by the White and Taft Courts. The *Guinn* and *Herndon* decisions sent important signals to the NAACP that the doors of an ultraconservative court were not permanently closed to the pursuit of political equality.

Jury Discrimination

The landmark case *Strauder v. West Virginia* (1880), established that racial discrimination in the selection of juries violated the equal protection clause of the Fourteenth Amendment. In *Neal v. Delaware* (1881), the court held that the exclusion of blacks from juries may raise a prima facie case of purposeful discrimination. What would constitute sufficient evidence for a trial court to make that determination proved to be an insurmountable obstacle for poor black criminal defendants who had the burden of proving deliberate and systematic exclusion based on race. The problem of racial discrimination in the selection of juries in the South was difficult to resolve because of black disenfranchisement—only qualified registered voters were eligible to serve on juries.

Cornelius Jones, a black lawyer and community activist who served one term in the Mississippi legislature, brought a test case to challenge discriminatory voting and jury selection schemes. In *Williams v. Mississippi* (1898), Jones sought to quash Henry Williams's murder indictment by an all-white grand jury indirectly by attacking the constitutionality of Mississippi's restrictive voting and jury selection provisions. The state's 1890 constitutional convention produced a constitution that disenfranchised blacks on a massive scale. The constitution prescribed the payment of poll taxes, and voters were required to take literacy and understanding tests. Strict residency requirements were placed on voters, and the list of disqualifying crimes was broadened. The state code gave jury commissioners considerable discretion to select prospective jurors from discriminatory voter registration lists. None of the constitutional or statutory provisions explicitly mentioned race, but their intent was crystal clear.

In *Williams v. Mississippi* (1898), Jones argued that the restrictive voting provisions and jury selection procedures were enacted with a bad purpose and they were discriminatory in their actual administration. Writing for a unanimous court, Justice Joseph McKenna relied on the Mississippi Supreme Court's finding that there was no denial of the equal protection of the laws arising from the state's constitution and laws. McKenna found "nothing direct and definite in this allegation either as to means or times as affecting the proceedings against the accused." He asserted that there was "an allegation of the purpose of the convention, to disfranchise citizens of the colored race, but with this we have no concern, unless the purpose is executed by the constitution or laws or by those who administer them. If it is done in the latter way, how or by what means should be shown." McKenna also rejected Jones's argument that the *Yick Wo v. Hopkins* (1886) standard should apply, because Jones only established that "evil was possible" under the provisions of the Mississippi constitution and statutes.

The landmark case *Williams v. Mississippi* was significant because the court required black murder defendants to show persuasive evidence that Southern officials purposefully excluded blacks from jury panels. The decision also sanctioned the massive disenfranchisement of blacks in Mississippi. The Fuller Court permitted black defendants to challenge their murder convictions only when the trial court refused to accept evidence that showed blacks were intentionally excluded from juries. As shown in table 3.5, all of the jury discrimination cases were decided by the Fuller Court. It is likely that the White and Taft courts exercised their discretionary power to not review

Table 3.5. Fuller, White, and Taft Courts Jury Discrimination Cases, 1888–1930

Case	Vote	Outcome
Gibson v. Mississippi (1896) F	8–0	Denied a black murder defendant's motion to move his case to federal court on the authority of *Neal v. Delaware* (C)
Smith v. Mississippi (1896) F	8–0	Denied a black murder defendant's motion to move his case to federal court for failure to show proof that the state intended to exclude blacks from the jury (C)
Murray v. Louisiana (1896) F	9–0	Denied a black murder defendant's motion to move his case to federal court on the authority of *Gibson* (C)
Williams v. Mississippi (1898) F	9–0	Held that a black murder defendant failed to prove that the state's constitutional and statutory jury selection provisions were facially discriminatory under the Fourteenth Amendment (C)
Carter v. Texas (1900) F	9–0	Held that a black murder defendant must be allowed to present witnesses and evidence to support his motion to quash based on the exclusion of blacks from the grand jury (L)
Tarrance v. Florida (1903) F	8–0	Held that a black murder defendant must offer independent proof that the county purposefully excluded blacks from juries (C)
Brownfield v. South Carolina (1903) F	8–0	Held that a black murder defendant failed to prove that blacks were excluded from the grand jury (C)
Rogers v. Alabama (1904) F	9–0	Held that a black murder defendant must be allowed to present evidence that blacks were excluded from jury lists (L)
Martin v. Texas (1906) F	9–0	Held that a black murder defendant failed to prove racial discrimination in the selection of juries (C)
Thomas v. Texas (1909) F	9–0	Held that a black murder defendant failed to prove that jury commissioners intentionally excluded blacks from grand and petit juries (C)
Franklin v. South Carolina (1910) F	7–0	Held that a black murder defendant failed to prove that the jury commissioners purposefully excluded blacks from juries (C)

Source: Created by the author.

Note: F for Fuller Court, W for White Court, and T for Taft Court. C for conservative outcomes, and L for liberal outcomes.

jury discrimination cases because black murder defendants could not meet the onerous burden of proof established in *Williams v. Mississippi*.

Peonage

Congress passed the Anti-Peonage Act of 1867 two years after the ratification of the Thirteenth Amendment. The statute prohibited the holding of any person to service or labor under the system of peonage in the United States and its territories. Despite the law, the condition of involuntary servitude persisted in the form of peonage throughout the South (Terrell 1907; Daniel 1973; Blackmon 2008). Blackmon (2008, 7) found that "by 1900, the South's judicial system had been wholly reconfigured to make one of its primary purposes the coercion of African Americans to comply with the social customs and labor demands of whites." Peonage laws were written in race-neutral language, but in practice peonage was rooted in racial subordination and economic exploitation. Peonage was enforced by threats, intimidation, and acts of extreme violence, and it endured because of massive black disenfranchisement, corruption, and acquiescence of local law enforcement, and because all-white juries would not convict white employers accused of peonage practices.

Clyatt v. United States (1905) was the first peonage case to reach the court. Samuel Clyatt was convicted and sentenced to four years in prison for the forced return of black laborers to work out a debt owed to him. Clyatt challenged his conviction on the ground that the federal peonage statute did not apply to individuals because states had the obligation to punish peonage. Writing for the 8–1 majority, Justice Brewer defined peonage as "a status or condition of compulsory service, based upon the indebtedness of the peon to the master. The basal fact is indebtedness." When Brewer applied the definition to the condition of the black laborers, he reversed Clyatt's conviction for lack of evidence, because the testimony did not show that the black laborers were ever in a condition of peonage. Dissenting in part, Justice Harlan asserted that "there was evidence tending to make a case within the statute." He went on to say that "it is going very far to hold in a case like this, disclosing barbarities of the worst kind against these negroes, that the trial court erred in sending the case to the jury."

Southern states enacted contract labor laws that operated like debt peonage statutes. Black laborers were fined and imprisoned if they failed to fulfill the terms of their labor contracts. Booker T. Washington and white anti-peonage reformers secretly supported and financed a test case that attacked Alabama's notorious peonage system (Schmidt 1982b, 676–80). Alonzo Bailey was found guilty of violating Alabama's contract labor law when he entered into a written contract for work as a farm laborer and secured a $15 advance payment that was not repaid after he stopped working. Justice Harlan, who was the senior associate justice on the court before Associate Justice Edward White was sworn in as Chief Justice, assigned the opinion to its newcomer, Charles Evans Hughes. In *Bailey v. Alabama* (1911), the White Court struck down Alabama's contract labor statute under the Thirteenth Amendment and the Peonage Act of 1867. Justice Hughes asserted at the outset that Bailey's race did not matter because the statute was written in race neutral terms and the record did not show that racial discrimination was at issue. Hughes found that the main objective of the statute was to punish employees for failing to perform their work and to prevent indebted employees from leaving their employer's service. Hughes explained that the intent of the Thirteenth Amendment could be defeated through the guise of contracts that held debtors to compulsory service. Writing for the dissenters, Justice Holmes asserted that the "Thirteenth Amendment does not outlaw contracts for labor." He expressed the view that, as long as the contract was fair and proper, the state had every reason to enforce it, and it did not make the laborer a slave.

Alabama enacted a private convict leasing law that permitted the release of a convict on the payment of a fine by a third-party surety to avoid the chain gang. Convicts were subjected to separate imprisonment if they failed to carry out the terms of their contracts. Federal indictments were brought against two sureties who held two black men in a state of peonage in violation of the Anti-Peonage Act of 1867. In *United States v. Reynolds* (1914), the White Court struck down Alabama's criminal surety law. Writing for the unanimous court, Justice Day found that "the convict is thus kept chained to an everturning wheel of servitude to discharge the obligation which he has incurred to his surety, who has entered into an undertaking with the State or paid money in his behalf." Because the "contract must be kept, under pain of re-arrest, and another similar proceeding for its violation, and perhaps another and another," Day concluded that the criminal surety system violated the Thirteenth Amendment and the anti-peonage law.

Unlike other institutional structures that supported the ruling regime of white supremacy, the court quickly dismantled state imposed legal arrangements associated with peonage that kept blacks in a condition of involuntary servitude in the South. Daniel (1972, 80) found that after *Bailey*

Table 3.6. Fuller, White, and Taft Courts Peonage Cases, 1888–1930

Case	Vote	Outcome
Clyatt v. United States (1905) F	8–1	Reversed the conviction of a white employer accused of violating the Peonage Act based on the lack of evidence that the black laborers were ever in a condition of peonage (C)
Hodges v. United States (1906) F	7–2	Held that the federal government lacked jurisdiction under the Thirteenth Amendment to prosecute whites convicted of using violence to force blacks off jobs (C)
Bailey v. Alabama (1911) W	5–2	Held that an Alabama criminal statute that punished workers for failure to perform labor contracts violated the Thirteenth Amendment and the Peonage Act (L)
United States v. Reynolds (1914) W	8–0	Held that Alabama's criminal surety law violated the Thirteenth Amendment and the Peonage Act (L)

Source: Created by the author.

Note: F for Fuller Court, W for White Court, and T for Taft Court. C for conservative outcomes, and L for liberal outcomes.

and *Reynolds* were decided, complaints of peonage dropped off abruptly in Alabama, "but they continued to pour in to the justice department from neighboring Georgia and Florida." Their peonage statutes were invalidated by the Stone Court.

Fair Administration of Justice

A notorious Tennessee lynching case forced an unprecedented response from the Supreme Court to preserve the administration of justice. In 1906, a young white woman, Nevada Taylor, reported that she was raped as she walked home from work in Chattanooga, Tennessee (Curriden and Phillips 1999). Although Taylor stated that she never saw her attacker, the local newspaper reported that she had been raped by a "negro brute." Despite his claims of innocence, Sheriff Joseph Shipp arrested Ed Johnson for the assault. In a mob-dominated trial, the jury found Johnson guilty and sentenced him to death by hanging. After Johnson's state court appeals were rejected, his lawyers filed a federal habeas corpus petition that alleged that the state trial proceedings illegally excluded blacks from the juries and denied his request for a change in venue in violation of his constitutional rights. His petition was denied by the federal circuit court but a brief stay of execution was granted to allow an appeal to Justice Harlan, the Sixth Circuit Justice. Harlan granted the appeal and the full court ordered that all proceedings against Johnson be stayed pending the appeal. After the Chattanooga newspaper published a full account of the court's actions, a mob broke into the jail and took Johnson to the county bridge where he was hanged. When it appeared that Johnson was alive after a few minutes, the mob opened fire and Johnson's body dropped to the bridge. The mob put a second round of bullets into Johnson's body, which tore it apart. One leader of the mob pinned a note to Johnson's body which read, "To Justice Harlan. Come get your nigger now" (Curriden and Phillips 1999, 208–14). No one was arrested for the lynching nor was it investigated by Hamilton County officials.

A Justice Department investigation revealed that Sheriff Shipp, his deputies and leaders of the mob were involved in a conspiracy to lynch Johnson and the department filed a contempt of the Supreme Court charge against them. In *United States v. Shipp* (1906), the court unanimously decided that the case should go to trial under its original jurisdiction, and a special master was appointed to oversee the criminal trial. In *United States v. Shipp* (1909), the Fuller Court found Shipp, one of his deputies, and four leaders of the lynch mob guilty of contempt. During the conference deliberations, Curriden and Phillips (1999, 329) found that the justices differed on the importance of the case. Fuller and Holmes "contended that the case was exclusively about enforcing the integrity of the Supreme Court," but Harlan "wanted to use the case to send a message to the country that lynch law should not be tolerated and that local law enforcement should do everything within its power to prevent mob rule."

Writing for the 5–3 majority, Chief Justice Fuller emphasized the vigilante nature of Johnson's lynching and pointed out that "the persons who hung and shot this man were so impatient for his blood that they utterly disregarded the act of Congress as well as the order of this court." Fuller explained that Shipp and his accomplices had a duty to protect Johnson until his case was closed and their actions made a mockery of the administration of justice. Shipp and his accomplices received a minimal sentence, sixty to ninety days in a Washington, DC, jail, but they were released early for good behavior. Justice Rufus Peckham's dissent was joined by Justices White and McKenna. Peckham asserted that no evidence was presented to support the allegation that Sherrif Shipp was part of any conspiracy. Peckham believed that Shipp was an honored and respected citizen of Chattanooga. Under the circumstances of the case, "he was not called upon to sacrifice his life in a desperate and hopeless attempt to save his prisoner against all odds."

From 1898 until 1921, a series of race riots and antiblack pogroms broke out in several large cities and small towns in geographically diverse areas of the United States. One horrific massacre occurred in October 1919 in rural Phillips County, Arkansas. While black sharecroppers were meeting at a church to discuss economic exploitation by white planters, white law enforcement officials fired shots into the church, shots were returned, and the security guard was killed and the deputy wounded. After the local newspaper falsely reported that blacks were organizing to massacre whites, to seize their property, and to assume control of the government, hundreds of white men hunted down and killed scores of black people over the next three days (McWhirter 2011, 208–35). Sixty-five blacks were indicted and found guilty of crimes associated with the Elaine Massacre and were sentenced to prison terms up to twenty years, but no charges were brought against whites who murdered blacks. In a mob dominated trial that lasted less than an hour, twelve black men were convicted and sentenced to death for murdering five white men. The NAACP represented the defendants in two separate cases. The first group was not part of the appellate review process, and the habeas petitions of the second group were consolidated. In *Moore v. Dempsey* (1923), the NAACP argued on behalf of the six black defendants that the mob dominated trial violated their rights to due process under the Fourteenth Amendment.

Prior to *Moore*, state criminal proceedings were considered to be off limits from federal court review. *Moore* extended the reach of federal habeas corpus to criminal defendants seeking to challenge the constitutionality of their state court convictions. Writing for the 6–2 majority, Justice Holmes explained that the mob-dominated trial was a "mask," because the "counsel, jury and judge were swept to the fatal end by an irresistible wave of public passion" and state courts failed to correct the wrong. Holmes concluded that "it does not seem to us sufficient to allow a Judge of the United States to escape the duty of examining the facts for himself when if true as alleged they make the trial absolutely void." Justice James McReynolds, joined by George Sutherland in dissent, asserted that he was "unable to say that the District Judge, acquainted with local conditions, erred when he held that the petition for the *writ of habeas corpus* insufficient." McReynolds pointed out that "the fact that petitioners are poor and ignorant and black naturally arouses sympathy, but that does not release us from enforcing principles which are essential to the orderly operation of our federal system."

The federal judiciary became a key player in supervising the fairness of state criminal proceedings through the habeas corpus process because of the Taft Court's landmark decision, *Moore v. Dempsey*. The decision sent a strong signal to Southern state courts that "legal lynching" would not be upheld by the court. The NAACP's litigating efforts saved the lives of twelve black men from execution even though the case was difficult to litigate during its early operation (Francis 2014, 178).

Conclusion

The progressive era court's conservative policymaking in race cases did not occur in a vacuum. The Waite Court's restrictive interpretations of the Reconstruction amendments established the doctrinal framework for the progressive era court to advance the policy goals of the second phase of the ruling regime of white supremacy. The Fuller Court stands out for its ultraconservative policy choices that relegated blacks to a position of legal inferiority and second-class citizenship, and excluded nonwhite immigrants from the rights of American citizenship. During its twenty-two-year operation, the Fuller Court accomplished its anti–civil rights agenda by devising doctrines that made apartheid, race-based exclusion, disenfranchisement, and jury discrimination constitutional. The White and Taft Courts exercised their power to advance the policy goals of the white supremacist racial order, but both courts made limited concessions to the transformative egalitarian alliance in the areas of voting rights, peonage, housing segregation, and the fair administration of criminal proceedings. Although some of the White and Taft Courts' advances in civil rights were offset by subsequent restrictive decisions, the favorable civil rights decisions sent an important signal to the politically oppressed black community in the South that the institutional structures supporting the ruling regime of white supremacy were neither permanent nor impenetrable.

The outcomes of the fifty-three race cases examined in this chapter show that the progressive era court was a fully committed partner of the ruling regime of white supremacy—72 percent of the cases were decided in a conservative direction, and 28 percent were decided in a liberal direction in favor people of color and nonwhite immigrants. The extensive personnel changes that occurred on the court during this forty-two-year period failed to alter the direction of the court's ultraconservative racial policies. Two justices stood out for their sincerely held policy preferences with regard to racial equality: John Marshall Harlan and Charles Evans Hughes. When Hughes resigned from the court in 1916 to run for president, there was no advocate for racial equality on the court until he returned in 1930 in the strategic position of chief justice to influence outcomes in race cases.

Chapter 4

The Hughes, Stone, and Vinson Courts, 1930–1953

During the New Deal era, the transformative egalitarian alliance grew stronger due to impactful economic, political, and social changes that occurred in the United States. The Great Depression ended the sustained period of economic growth in the nation. A Democratic coalition successfully defeated Republicans at the polls and gave Franklin D. Roosevelt (FDR) landslide electoral victories in 1932, 1936, 1940, and 1944. The 1936 presidential election produced a historic break with black voters' affiliation with the Republican Party. Racial issues appeared on the national political agenda. The Great Depression hit blacks hard, but New Deal programs failed to give them the economic assistance they needed compared to the assistance whites received (Franklin 1974, 404–9). Race riots broke out in geographically diverse areas including Detroit, New York, Los Angeles, and Beaumont, Texas. After the Great Migration, blacks became an important voting bloc in Northern industrial cities. The forces of urbanization and industrialization accelerated the rise of black activism with regard to the formation of civil rights organizations and the use of a range of direct-action strategies to combat racial discrimination (Meier and Rudwick 2002, 307–62). FDR shaped the transformative egalitarian racial order by appointing New Dealers to the executive and judicial branches who were committed to advancing black civil rights (McMahon 2003). Southern Democrats remained a powerful force in Congress due to its seniority system.

The three courts that operated during the New Deal era—the Hughes Court (1930–1941), the Stone Court (1941–1946), and the Vinson Court (1946–1953)—are characterized as transitional courts, because they were bracketed on one side by the ultraconservative progressive era court and on the other side by the ultraliberal civil rights movement era court. With the important exception of wartime constraints on civil rights, the New Deal court repudiated the policy goals of the second phase of the white supremacist racial order. The old race jurisprudence was based on restrictive views of the Reconstruction amendments, and the ideology of caste and exclusion. The issue of race was a settled matter. The new race jurisprudence was based on broad interpretations of the Reconstruction amendments to dismantle the legal foundation of the ruling regime of white supremacy. Laws that curtailed the civil rights of racial minorities were viewed as constitutionally suspect. NAACP attorneys took advantage of the new race jurisprudence by devising litigation strategies to dismantle the institutional structures supporting the white supremacist regime. In this chapter, I appraise the New Deal court's policymaking role in race cases based on the predominant racial policy dichotomy of the era—racial discrimination versus equal rights under law. For people of color, there was new hope that the inscription "Equal Justice under Law" that appeared on the frieze above the front entrance to the new Supreme Court building would become meaningful to them.

The Composition of the Hughes, Stone, and Vinson Courts

Serious health issues forced Chief Justice William Taft to retire from the court on February 3, 1930. President Herbert Hoover nominated 68-year-old Charles Evans Hughes to succeed Taft as the eleventh chief justice. Hughes accepted the nomination at the expense of his son's high-ranking job in the Department of Justice. Solicitor General Charles Evans Hughes, Jr., resigned after serving less than a year in the position. Although Hughes faced a difficult confirmation because of his representation of corporate and business interests as a prosperous Wall Street attorney, he was confirmed on February 13, 1930, by a 52–26 vote. Justice Edward Sanford died on the same day as William Taft on March 8, 1930. Hoover nominated Fourth Circuit judge John Parker to succeed Sanford. Parker's nomination generated opposition from the NAACP because of his racist North Carolina gubernatorial campaign in 1920, and organized labor denounced his approval of the use of the injunction and yellow dog contracts to resolve violence that stemmed from labor disputes (Watson 1963). Parker's nomination was defeated by a 39–41 vote. Hoover's second choice, Owen Roberts, was unanimously confirmed by the Senate on May 20, 1930. Until 1937, Chief Justice Hughes presided over a court comprised of four conservative ideologues, Willis Van Devanter, James McReynolds, George Sutherland, and Pierce Butler; and three left-leaning justices, Louis Brandeis, Benjamin Cardozo, and Harlan Stone. Justice Oliver Wendell Holmes, Jr., served two terms on the Hughes Court prior to his retirement in 1932 at the age of 91.

Congress enacted FDR's economic relief policies that expanded national power in areas of industrial production, agriculture, oversight of prices and wages, and employer-employee relationships. A closely divided court struck down key components of FDR's New Deal plan with the swing votes of Chief Justice Hughes and Owen Roberts. Fed up with the court's excessive interference with his economic agenda, FDR submitted a plan to Congress in February 1937 to change the policy direction of the court in his favor by altering its composition if vacancies did not occur naturally. The court packing plan permitted the appointment of an additional justice for every sitting justice who was seventy years old or older. When the proposed bill was presented, six justices were over the age of seventy, which meant that the size of the court would increase to fifteen. Less than two months after FDR's court packing plan was submitted to Congress, Chief Justice Hughes and Roberts voted with the left leaning justices to uphold the Wagner Act and a minimum wage law for women. The ideological balance of power on the court had shifted in FDR's favor without congressional approval of his plan.

Between 1937 and 1941, FDR made nine appointments to the court. His most controversial nomination was Democratic senator Hugo Black of Alabama to succeed Van Devanter, who retired in June 1937. Black was an ardent New Dealer, but he was disliked by Southern members of Congress because he was a liberal (Leuchtenburg 1973, 5–8). A series of explosive articles published in mid-September by a Pittsburgh newspaper exposed Black's membership in the Ku Klux Klan. The controversy and criticism surrounding FDR's nomination of a Klansman to the court was embarrassing and serious. Amid significant pressure, Black admitted to belonging to the Klan prior to his election to the Senate in a nationwide radio address. In his speech, Black denounced the Klan's activities without mentioning its name, and he cautioned against racial and religious hatred (Leuchtenburg 1973, 18–19). Black's speech was good enough to quell the controversy surrounding his appointment, and he was confirmed on September 17, 1937, by a 63–16 vote.

When Sutherland, Brandeis, and McReynolds retired, and after the deaths of Cardozo and Butler, FDR appointed their successors: Stanley Reed (1938), William Douglas (1939), Felix Frankfurter (1939), Frank Murphy

(1940), and James Byrnes (1941). When Hughes retired from the Court in 1941, FDR appointed Harlan Stone to become the twelfth chief justice. Prior to his 1925 appointment to the court, Stone served as the dean of Columbia University's law school and attorney general in the Coolidge administration. Robert Jackson, who served in FDR's administration as solicitor general and attorney general, was appointed to fill Stone's seat. In 1942, James Byrnes submitted his resignation after serving sixteen months on the court. Wiley Rutledge was appointed in 1943 to succeed Byrnes.

Harry Truman became president after FDR's death on April 12, 1944. When Owen Roberts retired from the court in 1945, Truman appointed Harold Burton, former mayor of Cleveland and US senator, to succeed Roberts. The following year, Chief Justice Stone died from a massive stroke at the age of 73. Truman nominated his friend, Frederick (Fred) Vinson of Kentucky, to become the thirteenth chief justice. Vinson was Truman's secretary of the treasury and he had served in Congress and on the DC Circuit Court. Vinson was confirmed by the Senate on June 20, 1946, by a voice vote. Within a three-month period in 1949, the Vinson Court lost two of its most liberal members: Frank Murphy died of a heart attack at the age of 59, and Wiley Rutledge died from a massive stroke at the age of 55. Truman appointed Tom Clark and Sherman Minton to fill the vacancies.

The New Jurisprudential Regime

In 1929, Chief Justice Taft successfully lobbied Congress to authorize funds for a separate building to house the Supreme Court, but he would not live to see its completion. The "Marble Palace" opened in 1935 when the court was in a period of transition. Legal formalism, apartheid, exclusion, hostility toward the use of the police powers for social reform, and the elevation of the right to contract as a fundamental right were the hallmarks of the old, conservative jurisprudence. Legal realism, deference to national regulatory power, and a strong commitment to protect civil liberties and civil rights were the hallmarks of the new, liberal jurisprudence. Higginbotham and Smith (1992, 1101) found that "it was during the Hughes era that courageous civil rights lawyers, working in isolation or under the auspices of organizations such as the NAACP, confronted the Supreme Court with cases challenging racism in the courts and the electoral process, as well as challenging racial segregation in public schools, facilities, and transportation." The Hughes Court justices signaled that they were ready to take a new jurisprudential approach in a footnote in a commerce clause case, *United States v. Carolene*

Products Company (1938). Justice Harlan Stone outlined this approach in Footnote Four, which would become the most consequential footnote in American constitutional law:

> There may be narrower scope for operation of the presumption of constitutionality when legislation appears on its face to be within a specific prohibition of the Constitution, such as those of the first ten amendments, which are deemed equally specific when held to be embraced within the Fourteenth. . . .
>
> It is unnecessary to consider now whether legislation which restricts those political processes which can ordinarily be expected to bring about repeal of undesirable legislation, is to be subjected to more exacting judicial scrutiny under the general prohibitions of the Fourteenth Amendment than are most other types of legislation. On restrictions upon the right to vote, see *Nixon v. Herndon* (1927); *Nixon v. Condon* (1932). . . .
>
> Nor need we enquire whether similar considerations enter into the review of statutes directed at particular religious . . . or racial minorities: whether prejudice against discrete and insular minorities may be a special condition, which tends seriously to curtail the operation of those political processes ordinarily to be relied upon to protect minorities, and which may call for a correspondingly more searching judicial inquiry.

Justice Stone's former law clerk, Louis Lusky, described the origin and spirit of the footnote in a *Columbia Law Review* article. Lusky (1982, 1094–95) explained that after the balance of power had shifted on the court in 1937, Stone and his like-minded colleagues wanted "to guide the Court in the path of its duty as they perceived it"—that the "liberties enshrined in the Bill of Rights deserved as full constitutional protection as did liberty of contract." The *Carolene Products* case gave Stone the opportunity to address the imbalance over the pre-1937 court's aggressive use of the due process clause to protect business liberties. Chief Justice Hughes suggested changes to the footnote, which appeared in the first paragraph—that the rights enshrined in the Bill of Rights deserved more attention because they were mentioned in the text of the Constitution. Stone wrote the second and third paragraphs, which embraced the principles of equality and the integrity of the democratic process and indicated that the court would apply a "more searching judicial inquiry" against unrestrained majoritarian tyranny that violated the constitutional rights of racial minorities. Over time, the conceptual underpinnings of paragraphs two and three of Footnote Four would be applied by the justices to dismantle the institutional structures supporting the white supremacist racial order.

Disenfranchisement

The NAACP renewed its litigation strategy to invalidate the use of the white primary in Southern elections. After the Taft Court declared that the Texas white primary law was unconstitutional on Fourteenth Amendment grounds in *Nixon v. Herndon* (1927), the NAACP brought a second lawsuit that challenged a new Texas statute that gave the state executive committee of the Democratic Party the power to limit participation in primaries to white Democrats. In *Nixon v. Condon* (1932), the Hughes Court struck down the white primary scheme on the authority of *Herndon*. In response to the *Condon* decision, Texas Democrats adopted a new resolution at the State Democratic Convention that allowed only white citizens who were qualified to vote to be members of the Democratic Party and participate in primaries. A group of local black leaders challenged the resolution without the assistance of the NAACP. In *Grovey v. Townsend* (1935), the Hughes Court unanimously ruled that it was constitutional for a political party to restrict voting to whites in primaries as long as state action was not a requirement for the restriction. The *Grovey* decision was a major setback for the NAACP's legal strategy, and it took five years before the organization received the legal break it needed to invalidate the use of the white primary. That break would come in the form of a federal election fraud case unrelated to race in *United States v. Classic* (1941). In *Classic*, the Hughes Court ruled that election officials who willfully altered and falsely counted and certified ballots in primary elections were acts under color of law that deprived voters of their constitutional rights. The decision did not mention *Grovey*, but it was obvious that the *Classic* ruling undermined *Grovey*'s state action rationale.

The white primary met its constitutional demise in a class action lawsuit brought by the NAACP that challenged the refusal of Texas election officials to allow blacks to vote in the 1940 Democratic party primary. In the landmark voting rights case, *Smith v. Allwright* (1944), the Stone Court ruled that the white primary violated the Fifteenth Amendment. Writing for the 8–1 majority, Justice Stanley Reed asserted that the *Classic* decision erased any doubt as to whether primaries were part of elections. Reed declared that "the right to vote in such a primary for the nomination of candidates without discrimination by the State, like the right to vote in a general election, is a right secured by the Constitution. By the terms of the Fifteenth Amendment that right may not be abridged by any State on account of race." The Stone Court declared that the Fifteenth Amendment protected voting rights from state and private infringement, and it overruled the nine-year-old *Grovey* decision to send a clear message to Southern states that the Constitution "grants to all citizens a right to participate in the choice of elected officials without restriction by any State because of race."

The outcome in *Smith v. Allwright* changed the trajectory of black registration rates in Texas and throughout the South (Matthews and Prothro 1966, 17–18; Hine 1979, 238). Hine's (1979, 237) classic study revealed that the white primary symbolized black Texans' political powerlessness, second-class citizenship, and caste-like position, but *Allwright* meant that "with the vote blacks could defend themselves, their property, and their futures by electing those politicians most responsive to their needs." As shown in table 4.1, the New Deal court fulfilled its commitment to protecting the

Table 4.1. Hughes, Stone, and Vinson Courts Disenfranchisement Cases, 1930–1953

Case	Vote	Outcome
Nixon v. Condon (1932) H	5–4	Held that a Texas law that gave the state executive committee of the Democratic Party the power to exclude blacks from voting in primary elections was unconstitutional under the Fourteenth Amendment (L)
Grovey v. Townsend (1935) H	9–0	Held that political parties were private voluntary associations that had the right to limit their membership to whites in primary elections (C)
Lane v. Wilson (1939) H	6–2	Held that a modified version of Oklahoma's grandfather clause was unconstitutional on Fifteenth Amendment grounds (L)
Smith v. Allwright (1944) S	8–1	Held that the white primary was unconstitutional on Fifteenth Amendment grounds (L)
Terry v. Adams (1953) V	8–1	Held that an all-white voluntary association that excluded blacks from voting in Democratic Party elections violated the Fifteenth Amendment (L)

Source: Created by the author.

Note: H for Hughes Court, S for Stone Court, and V for Vinson Court. C for conservative outcomes, and L for liberal outcomes.

right to vote, but it would be left up to Congress to completely dismantle the institution of disenfranchisement.

Fair Administration of Justice

The New Deal court accepted criminal cases for review that exposed stark racial injustices with regard to police brutality, the use of excessive force, coerced confessions, and inadequate legal counsel. Selective incorporation of the criminal procedure provisions in the Bill of Rights did not gain momentum until the civil rights movement era. States had constitutional provisions similar to the ones in the national Bill of Rights that protected the rights of criminal defendants, but they were conservatively interpreted by Southern state courts when the rights of black criminal defendants were at stake.

The Right to Counsel

The Scottsboro cases invoked a variety of controversial themes with regard to the American criminal justice system: pending mob violence when white women accuse black men of rape, communist subversion, virulent racism, and the racial injustices of the Southern legal system. The Scottsboro saga began in 1931 when nine poor black youths between the ages of twelve and nineteen were riding on a freight train through Alabama on their way to Memphis (Carter 1969). Seven white youths and two white women in their twenties, Victoria Price and Ruby Bates, were also hitching a ride on the train. A fight broke out between the white and black youths and all but one of the white youths were thrown off the train. When the train reached Paint Rock, Alabama, the sheriff and a large posse arrested the black youths and loaded them on the back of a truck to take them to jail in Scottsboro. While the arrests were taking place, Bates and Price told the sheriff that the black youths had raped them. When word of the rape spread, the national guard was called to protect the Scottsboro defendants from mob violence in Scottsboro. The defendants—Ozie Powell, Olen Montgomery, Clarence Norris, Haywood Patterson, Willie Roberson, Charlie Weems, Eugene Williams, Andy Wright, and Roy Wright—pleaded not guilty to the rape charges. The defense attorneys who represented them were incompetent, inexperienced, and unprepared, and they failed to investigate the case. Price and Bates gave conflicting testimony on the witness stand, and statements from two physicians who examined the women found no evidence of a physical assault. The defendants' attorneys did not present a defense during the three sham trials, which occurred six days after arraignment and completed on the same day. The Scottsboro defendants were found guilty of rape by all-white juries and sentenced to death. The Alabama Supreme Court affirmed the death sentences with the exception of 12-year-old Roy Wright's death sentence. The International Labor Defense, the legal arm of the Communist Party, represented the Scottsboro defendants on appeal.

In *Powell v. Alabama* (1932), the Scottsboro defendants claimed that the state's denial of their right to counsel for effective consultation and opportunity of preparation for trial denied them due process and equal protection of the laws. The Hughes Court reversed the lower court's judgment. Chief Justice Hughes assigned the majority opinion to Justice George Sutherland, one of the far-right conservatives on the court. Sutherland found that during the most critical period from the time of their arraignment until the beginning of trial when consultation, investigation, and preparation were vitally important, the Scottsboro defendants did not have counsel in any real sense. Sutherland asserted that the facts—the defendants' illiteracy, their youthfulness, public hostility, separation from families and friends, and their lives being in jeopardy—made the assistance of counsel a necessity. Sutherland concluded that "the right to have counsel appointed when necessary is a logical corollary from the constitutional right to be heard by counsel."

In the landmark case, *Powell v. Alabama*, the court held for the first time that appointment of counsel by state courts was essential to due process of law in capital cases where the lack of representation would result in an unfair trial. Without the Hughes Court intervention in *Powell*, the Scottsboro defendants' death sentences would have been carried out. The outcome in *Powell* subjected some of the Scottsboro defendants to numerous trials, retrials, and convictions. In 2013, the Alabama legislature passed a formal resolution exonerating all of the Scottsboro defendants and posthumous pardons were granted to Haywood Patterson, Charlie Weems, and Andy Wright.

Coerced Confessions and Use of Excessive Force

Methods of police brutality and state sanctioned torture were used instrumentally to enforce the regime of white supremacy. In 1929, President Herbert Hoover established the Wickersham Commission to investigate lawlessness in law enforcement. The commission found that police brutality was a nationwide problem and third-degree practices—methods of violence that cause physical suffering—were particularly harsh against blacks and other races (National Commission on Law Observance and Enforcement 1931, 158–59). The court addressed the constitutionality of "compulsion by torture to extort a confession" for the first time in the notorious case *Brown v. Mississippi* (1936). When a white planter was found beaten to death in his home in Kemper County, Mississippi, three black tenant farmers were accused of the murder. A deputy sheriff accompanied by a mob of white men went to Yank Ellington's home and requested that he accompany them to the victim's house. Although Ellington denied that he had anything to do with the murder, the deputy put a rope around his neck and hung him from the limb of a tree twice to obtain a confession. When the attempted lynching failed to produce a confession, the mob tied Ellington to a tree and whipped him. A day or two later, the deputy arrested Ellington, and while they were on the way to the jail in Meridian, the deputy stopped and severely whipped Ellington again while stating that he would not stop until he confessed. After that beating, Ellington agreed to confess to the murder. When Ed Brown and Henry Shields were arrested, the deputy and his accomplices beat them across their backs with a leather strap with buckles until their backs were severely cut into pieces. The men confessed after the deputy told them that the whipping would continue unless they confessed to the crime.

Counsel was appointed for the defendants a day prior to the mob dominated trial. The defendants were found guilty of murder by an all-white jury and sentenced to death by hanging based on their coerced confessions. The Mississippi Supreme Court ruled that failure to exclude the coerced confessions did not deprive the defendants of life or liberty without due process of law. Judge Virgil Griffiths wrote a strong dissent that not only excoriated the sham trial but provided the framework for the Hughes Court to reverse the decision. Chief Justice Hughes wrote the brief unanimous decision, which rejected the state's federalism defense that there were no provisions in the Constitution that prohibited the state from admitting coerced confessions into evidence. Hughes found that the conviction and sentence were void for lack of the essential elements of due process. Asserting that "it would be difficult to conceive of methods more revolting to the sense of justice than those taken to procure the confessions of these petitioners," Hughes declared that the "rack and torture chamber may not be substituted for the witness stand."

In 1939, a white sharecropper family was brutally murdered and the house set on fire to conceal the crime in the rural town of Hugo, Oklahoma

(Williams 1998, 113–21). Two white convicts who were permitted to leave the state prison for unsupervised release visits were arrested and confessed to the murders. After newspapers criticized the governor and the prison warden for neglect of duty, the governor's aide ordered the release of the suspects and the "search would begin for the real culprit" (114). William Lyons, a 21-year-old black sharecropper, was later arrested for the murders. During the interrogation, Lyons was beaten, kicked repeatedly, and threatened by police officers who told him that he would be killed if he did not confess to the crime. Eleven days after the arrest, Lyons confessed after a night of being tortured and having a pan of charred bones of the deceased child killed in the fire placed on his lap. The officers continued to beat and threaten Lyons and fourteen hours after the first confession, Lyons signed a second confession statement. During the trial, police officers admitted to beating Lyons, and the judge threw out the first confession but not the second one. Lyons was found guilty by an all-white jury and sentenced to life in prison based on his second confession.

The coerced confession case attracted the attention of the NAACP, and Thurgood Marshall represented Lyons during the trial and appellate proceedings. Marshall challenged Lyons' conviction on the ground that the second confession violated his due process rights because it was involuntary and coerced. In *Lyons v. Oklahoma* (1944), Marshall lost his first case before the court. In a 6–3 decision, Justice Stanley Reed found that Lyons' second confession was voluntary because it was "separated from the early morning statement by a full twelve hours." Reed asserted that the "Fourteenth Amendment does not protect one who has admitted guilt because of forbidden inducements against the use at trial of his subsequent confessions under all possible circumstances." Justice Frank Murphy dissented on the ground that "the whole confession technique used here constituted one single, continuing transaction. To conclude that the brutality inflicted at the time of the first confession suddenly lost all of its effect in the short space of twelve hours is to close one's eyes to the realities of human nature."

In 1939, Attorney General Frank Murphy established a civil liberties unit in the Justice Department to investigate and prosecute civil rights violations. The unit was later renamed the Civil Rights Section (Carr 1947, 24–32; McMahon 2003, 144–46). Prior to 1940, federal civil rights prosecutions in the South were limited to election corruption and peonage cases. The Civil Rights Section turned to § 20 (currently 18 U.S.C. § 242) of the federal criminal code, which was one of the few remaining civil rights statutes enacted to protect federal civil rights. Section 20 was derived from

§ 2 of the Civil Rights Act of 1866 that provided for the punishment of any person who, under color of law, deprived any person of any right secured or protected by the Constitution or federal laws on account of race or color. Section 20 made it a crime for any person acting under color of law, statute, ordinance, regulation, or custom to willfully deprive a person of a right or privilege secured or protected by the Constitution or federal laws.

The Justice Department's civil rights enforcement theory was tested in *Screws v. United States* (1945)—a case Justice William Douglas described as "a shocking and revolting episode in law enforcement." In 1943, Sheriff Claude Screws of Baker County, Georgia, and two deputies arrested Robert Hall, a young leader in the black community, under the pretext of stealing a tire. Screws knew Hall, and prior to the arrest they had an altercation involving the possession of a pistol lawfully owned by Hall. The officers beat Hall for fifteen to thirty minutes with their fists and a two-pound blackjack in plain sight of residents in the courthouse square. The beating crushed Hall's skull and left a wide pool of blood on the ground. Hall was then dragged feet first through the yard and thrown into jail. An ambulance took Hall to the hospital, where he died without regaining consciousness. Sheriff Screws claimed that Hall, who was handcuffed, reached for a gun and had used insulting language against him as he alighted from the car. After Georgia officials refused to prosecute Screws and his deputies, a federal grand jury indicted them under § 20. Screws and his deputies were found guilty of willfully depriving Hall of his life without due process of law, and they were sentenced to three years in prison and had to pay a $1,000 fine. The defendants challenged the constitutionality of § 20 on the ground that the law contained broad and fluid definitions of due process that provided no ascertainable standard of guilt.

The outcome in *Screws v. United States* highlighted the ideological differences among the Stone Court justices. Writing for the 5–4 plurality, Justice Douglas found that the law enforcement officers "acted under color of law in making the arrest of Robert Hall and in assaulting him." When Douglas interpreted the word "willfully" as used in criminal statutes, he found that it generally meant an act done with a bad purpose. Applying this interpretation to § 20, Douglas asserted that the statute required a finding of specific intent to deprive a person of a constitutional right. Because the question of intent was not submitted to the jury with proper instructions, Douglas reversed the lower court decision and ruled that the law enforcement officers should be granted a new trial. Justice Murphy was highly critical of Douglas's reasoning in his dissent. Murphy explained that too often "unpopular minorities, such as Negroes, are unable to find effective refuge from the cruelties of bigoted and ruthless authority." Murphy asserted that when "states are unwilling for some reason to prosecute such crimes, the federal government must step in unless constitutional guarantees are to become atrophied." Justice Wiley Rutledge voted with the plurality to avoid a stalemate in the case and Justices Owen Roberts, Felix Frankfurter, and Robert Jackson argued in a separate dissent that Douglas's interpretation of § 20 would allow the national government to take over the administration of criminal justice from the states.

Screws' intent requirement made it more difficult for federal prosecutors to win convictions in cases involving excessive use of force. When Screws and his deputies were retried in federal court, they were acquitted. Following the police killing of George Floyd and the Black Lives Matter protests that ensued in 2020, considerable pressure was placed on Congress to enact measures to address the problem. In 2021, the House of Representatives passed H.R. 1280: George Floyd Justice in Policing Act. Among other changes, the proposed legislation amends § 242 (§ 20) in the following ways: it strikes out "willfully" and inserts "knowing or recklessly," it prohibits the use of chokeholds by police officers, it alters qualified immunity available to law enforcement officers, and calls for independent investigations and the use of a special prosecutor in cases involving the use of deadly force. The bill was defeated in the Senate. It was reintroduced in the 118th Congress in 2024, but the bill remains stalled in the House of Representatives.

Table 4.2. Hughes, Stone, and Vinson Courts Administration of Justice Cases, 1930–1953

Case	Vote	Outcome
Powell v. Alabama (1932) H	7–2	Held that the right to counsel in a capital case was a fundamental right guaranteed by the due process clause of the Fourteenth Amendment (L)
Brown v. Mississippi (1936) H	9–0	Held that black defendants' confessions obtained by brutality and torture violated the due process clause (L)
Chambers v. Florida (1940) H	8–0	Held that the use of repeated questioning over a period of several days to secure a murder conviction violated the due process clause (L)

continued on next page

Table 4.2. Continued.

Case	Vote	Outcome
White v. Texas (1940) H	9–0	Reversed the death sentence of a black man who was convicted of rape based on a coerced confession (L)
Ward v. Texas (1942) S	9–0	Held that a black man's murder confession obtained during questioning for three days while being beaten, whipped, and burned violated the due process clause (L)
Lyons v. Oklahoma (1944) S	6–3	Upheld the life sentence of a black man convicted of murdering a white family on the ground that his second confession was not coerced (C)
Ashcraft v. Tennessee (1944) S	6–3	Held that a black teenager's murder confession that was obtained by repeated questioning for three days under powerful electric lights violated his due process rights (L)
Screws v. United States (1945) S	9–0	Required federal prosecutors to prove specific intent in the use of excessive force cases (C)
Louisiana ex rel. Francis v. Resweber (1947) V	5–4	Held that the Eighth Amendment's cruel and unusual punishments provision and the Fifth Amendment's double jeopardy provision were not violated when a new death warrant was issued after mechanical difficulty failed to result in the death of a black teenager (C)
Haley v. Ohio (1948) V	5–4	Held that a black teenager's murder conviction that was obtained by a coerced confession violated the due process clause (L)
Harris v. South Carolina (1949) V	5–4	Held that an illiterate black man's due process rights were violated when he was held incommunicado, questioned for three days for periods as long as twelve hours, and was not told of his murder charges, which all led to his conviction (L)

Source: Created by the author.

Note: H for Hughes Court, S for Stone Court, and V for Vinson Court. C for conservative outcomes, and L for liberal outcomes.

Jury Discrimination

The Hughes Court restored jury discrimination cases to its docket, and all of them were decided in a liberal direction except one. The decisions did not break new legal ground, but they reaffirmed the principle established in *Strauder v. West Virginia* (1880) and *Neal v. Delaware* (1881) that systematic and intentional exclusion of blacks from jury service violated the equal protection clause. In *Aldridge v. United States* (1931), the Hughes Court displayed greater sensitivity to the effects of racial discrimination during the voir dire in a case that involved a black man sentenced to death for the murder of a white police officer. Alfred Aldridge's attorney was not permitted by the trial court to ask white jurors whether they had any racial prejudice against blacks. In an 8–1 decision, Chief Justice Hughes found that fairness demands that the practice of permitting questions about racial prejudice during the voir dire should be allowed. He explained that if jurors were found to be impartial, then no harm would be done in permitting the questions, but if any one of them were racially biased, then a gross injustice would result and the risk would be most grave in death penalty cases.

The Hughes Court decided two additional Scottsboro cases that addressed the use of all-white juries in the retrials of Haywood Patterson and Clarence Norris. When Alabama attempted to retry Patterson a third time for rape, his attorney moved to quash the indictment on the ground that blacks were excluded from juries in violation of the equal protection clause. The motion was denied, and Patterson was convicted and sentenced to death. The state supreme court refused to grant Patterson a new trial, and it did not rule on the merits of the jury discrimination claim. In *Patterson v. Alabama* (1935), Chief Justice Hughes pointed out that Clarence Norris and Haywood Patterson were convicted under the same indictment, and both cases were similar, but the state supreme court failed to reach the merits of Patterson's case. Hughes asserted that under the court's appellate jurisdiction, the Supreme Court has the power "not only to correct error in the judgment under review but to make such disposition of the case, as justice requires. And in determining what justice does require, the Court is bound to consider any change, either in fact or in law, which has supervened since the judgment was entered." Hughes vacated the judgment and the Alabama Supreme Court reversed Patterson's guilty verdict. In *Norris v. Alabama* (1935), the Hughes Court addressed the merits of Norris's claim that the systematic exclusion of blacks from jury service violated the equal protection clause. Although blacks were qualified for jury service when Norris was retried for rape, none had served on a jury for more than a generation in Jackson County, where he was indicted, and witnesses testified that blacks had never served on a jury within their memory in Morgan County, where Norris was tried. Chief Justice Hughes wrote the unanimous decision that reversed the judgment of the lower court based on prima facie evidence that

Table 4.3. Hughes, Stone, and Vinson Courts Jury Discrimination Cases, 1930–1953

Case	Vote	Outcome
Aldridge v. United States (1931) H	8–1	Held that defense questions about racial prejudice during the voir dire were permitted in a death penalty case (L)
Patterson v. Alabama (1935) H	8–0	Held that the court had jurisdiction over a judgment from a state court not only to correct error but to make such disposition of the case as justice requires (L)
Norris v. Alabama (1935) H	8–0	Held that the systematic and arbitrary exclusion of blacks from jury service violated the equal protection clause (L)
Hollins v. Oklahoma (1935) H	9–0	Reversed the conviction of a black man sentenced to death for the rape of a white woman because blacks were excluded from jury service (L)
Hale v. Kentucky (1938) H	8–0	Reversed a black man's murder conviction because blacks were systematically and arbitrarily excluded from jury service (L)
Pierre v. Louisiana (1939) H	8–0	Held that the same principles that prohibited racial discrimination in the selection of petit juries apply to the selection of grand juries (L)
Smith v. Texas (1940) H	9–0	Reversed a black man's rape conviction because blacks were intentionally and systematically excluded from grand jury service (L)
Hill v. Texas (1942) S	9–0	Reversed a black man's rape conviction based on prima facie evidence of racial discrimination in the selection of grand juries (L)
Akins v. Texas (1945) S	6–3	Held that a black murder defendant failed to establish that jury commissioners intentionally limited the number of blacks on the panel (C)
Patton v. Mississippi (1947) V	9–0	Reversed a black man's murder conviction by an all-white petit jury because blacks had not served on grand or petit juries for thirty years (L)
Cassell v. Texas (1950) V	7–1	Reversed a black man's murder conviction based on statements made by jury commissioners that they did not know any eligible black jurymen (L)

Case	Vote	Outcome
Avery v. Georgia (1953) V	8–0	Reversed a black man's rape conviction based on the jury commissioners' practice of discriminating in the drawing of prospective jurors' names from a box (L)

Source: Created by the author.

Note: H for Hughes Court, S for Stone Court, and V for Vinson Court. C for conservative outcomes, and L for liberal outcomes.

the "long-continued, unvarying, and wholesale exclusion" of blacks from jury service denied Norris equal protection of the laws.

Japanese Exclusion and Incarceration

The United States entry into World War II tested the strength of the Stone Court's commitment to Footnote Four's corrective to apply a more searching judicial scrutiny to laws that violate the constitutional rights of racial minorities. After the Japanese military launched an aerial attack on the American naval station at Pearl Harbor, Hawaii, on December 7, 1941, Congress declared war on Japan the next day. FDR invoked the Alien Enemies Act of 1798, which allowed for the arrest and detainment of Japanese Americans and citizens of the enemy nation deemed to be dangerous to the safety of the United States. Amid growing fears that the West Coast might be invaded by Japan, FDR issued Executive Order No. 9066, which authorized the military commander of the Western Defense Command, Lt. General John DeWitt, to issue and implement emergency war orders for the Pacific Coast states. On March 27, 1942, General DeWitt issued a curfew order that required all persons of Japanese ancestry to remain in their residences between the hours of 8 p.m. and 6 a.m. Gordon Hirabayashi, a Japanese American student, was tried, convicted, and sentenced to three months in prison for violating the curfew order. Hirabayashi challenged his conviction on the ground that Congress unconstitutionally delegated its legislative powers to the military commander. He argued that the imposition of the curfew on the Japanese community, which consisted of Japanese American citizens and Japanese immigrants who were prevented from becoming citizens, constituted racial discrimination in violation of the Fifth Amendment.

In *Hirabayashi v. United States* (1943), Chief Justice Harlan Stone wrote the unanimous decision that upheld the curfew order and Hirabayashi's conviction. After examining the background of the executive order, the military orders, and subsequent legislation, Stone reached the conclusion that it was within the constitutional power of Congress and the president to order the curfew as an emergency war measure and there was no unlawful delegation of legislative power. Stone characterized the curfew order as a defense measure taken for the purpose of safeguarding the military area from the danger of sabotage and espionage from disloyal members of the Japanese community. In response to Hirabayashi's claim that the curfew order racially discriminated against the Japanese community, Stone asserted that "distinctions between citizens solely because of their ancestry are by their very nature odious to a free people whose institutions are founded upon the doctrine of equality." Nonetheless, Stone carved out a national security exception to prohibitions on racial discrimination by the government during times of war "based upon the recognition of facts and circumstances which indicate that a group of one national extraction may menace that safety more than others."

Korematsu v. United States (1944) addressed the constitutionality of Lt. General DeWitt's Civilian Exclusion Order No. 34 that directed the exclusion of all persons of Japanese ancestry from the Pacific coast states after May 9, 1942. DeWitt's order was based on his racist assessment of the so-called "Yellow Peril" threat (Commission on Wartime Relocation and Internment of Civilians 1982, 82). Fred Korematsu, a twenty-three-year-old Japanese American from Oakland, was arrested, convicted, and sentenced to a five-year probationary sentence for violating the curfew order and failing to report to an Assembly Center where he would be held until sent to a concentration camp. Korematsu challenged his conviction on the ground that the exclusion order and incarceration were unconstitutional. Justice Black wrote the 6–3 majority opinion that upheld the constitutionality of the exclusion order and Korematsu's conviction. To determine whether Korematsu's civil rights were violated under the Fifth Amendment, Black established a strict scrutiny standard of review to apply to laws that discriminate against racial groups—"It should be noted, to begin with, that all legal restrictions which curtail the civil rights of a single racial group are immediately suspect. That is not to say that all such restrictions are unconstitutional. It is to say that courts must subject them to the most rigid scrutiny. Pressing public necessity may sometimes justify the existence of such restrictions; racial antagonism never can."

Justice Black upheld the exclusion order on national security grounds because it had "a definite and close relationship to the prevention of espionage and sabotage" and the military had the authority to determine "who should, and who should not, remain in the threatened areas." Black deferred to DeWitt's judgment that there were disloyal members of the Japanese community, and it was impossible "to bring about an immediate segregation of the disloyal from the loyal." Black explained that "the power to exclude includes the power to do it by force if necessary. And any forcible measure must necessarily entail some degree of detention or restraint whatever method of removal is selected." Without addressing the constitutionality of indefinite incarceration, the majority affirmed Korematsu's conviction.

Justices Owen Roberts, Frank Murphy, and Robert Jackson wrote scathing dissenting opinions that condemned the exclusion and incarceration of the Japanese community. The dissenters agreed that the curfew order was different from the exclusion order, the exclusion of the Japanese community was based on racism, they pointed out that guilt was personal and not inheritable, and there was no evidence that Fred Korematsu was disloyal. Justice Roberts emphasized that the "two conflicting orders, one which commanded him to stay and the other which commanded him to go, were nothing but a cleverly devised trap to accomplish the real purpose of the military authority, which was to lock him up in a concentration camp." Justice Murphy explained that "there should be limits to military discretion, especially when martial law has not been declared." Murphy found that the government failed to show that the exclusion order was reasonably related to an immediate, imminent, and impending public danger, and he criticized DeWitt's final report on the evacuation as racist. Justice Jackson pointed out that "had Korematsu been one of four—the others being, say, a German alien enemy, an Italian alien enemy, and a citizen of American-born ancestors, convicted of treason but out on parole—only Korematsu's presence would have violated the order." Jackson believed that courts were limited in their determination of whether a military order has a reasonable basis in necessity without evidence. Jackson explained that by upholding the exclusion order, "the Court for all time has validated the principle of racial discrimination in criminal procedure and of transplanting American citizens."

When the human rights of a racial group were pitted against national security and military necessity justifications during World War II, the Stone Court exercised its power to support the wartime policies of the executive and Congress. The national government's policies were rooted in offensive, racist stereotypes and biased, unsubstantiated reports about the Japanese community's threat to the national security of the nation. The court disregarded the "more searching judicial scrutiny" guarantee in Footnote Four when it allowed unrestrained majoritarian tyranny to violate the constitutional rights of the Japanese community. The landmark *Korematsu* decision sanctioned the exclusion and indefinite incarceration of approximately 126,000 members of the Japanese community without any evidence of their disloyalty or engagement in sabotage or espionage activities. The War Relocation Authority did not close the internment camps until 1946. Upon their resettlement to the West Coast, the Japanese community was confronted with lost homes and possessions, deaths of family members, illnesses, severe economic hardships, and psychological pain and suffering from relocation, incarceration, and virulent racism (Commission on Wartime Relocation and Internment of Civilians 1982, 240–43).

Ball (1991, 184) found that some of the justices engaged in unethical actions to support FDR's wartime policies while the cases were before the court: "At least four of the justices had some contact with government officials involved in the development and implementation of the Japanese exclusion policy and should have recused themselves. Frankfurter had frequent contacts with John J. McCloy of Secretary of War Henry Stimson's staff. Stone acted in concert with War Department officials. Justices Douglas and Black evidently were social acquaintances of General DeWitt." Irons (1983, 320–45) found that the justices manipulated the timing of the *Korematsu* and *Ex parte Endo* (1944) decisions and Justice Frankfurter informed the War Department about their status. Irons's research (186–218) on the Japanese exclusion cases revealed that the federal government suppressed evidence and presented tainted evidence to support its military necessity justification. As a result of his findings, Fred Korematsu, Gordon Hirabayashi, and Minoru Yasui filed coram nobis petitions in federal court to vacate their original criminal convictions on the basis of misconduct by lawyers in the Justice and War Departments. The legal strategy worked, which resulted in the nullification of their convictions.

An organized redress movement persuaded Congress to establish a commission to review the wartime exclusion and indefinite detention of the Japanese community and to issue a report of its findings and recommendations (Commission on Wartime Relocation and Internment of Civilians 1982, 455–67). The commission found no documented acts of espionage, sabotage, or fifth column activity committed by members of the Japanese community; nor did it find any support for the military necessity justification for Executive Order 9066. The commission found that the Japanese community suffered enormous material and immaterial damages due to the federal government's actions. The commission recommended the establishment of a fund to provide survivors with monetary compensation and the giving of a national apology for the grave injustices done to the Japanese community. President Ronald Reagan signed the Civil Liberties Act of 1988 into law to "right a grave wrong" for the exclusion and incarceration of members of the Japanese community. The legislation authorized $20,000 reparation payments to each of the 60,000 Japanese survivors.

Table 4.4. Hughes, Stone, and Vinson Courts Japanese Exclusion Cases, 1930–1953

Case	Vote	Outcome
Hirabayashi v. United States (1943) S	9–0	Upheld the constitutionality of a curfew order that confined the Japanese community to their homes on the basis of the war power (C)
Yasui v. United States (1943) S	9–0	Upheld the conviction of a Japanese American attorney who violated the curfew order (C)
Korematsu v. United States (1944) S	6–3	Upheld the conviction of a Japanese American who violated the military exclusion order on the basis of the war power to meet national security threats (C)
Ex parte Endo (1944) S	9–0	Granted the unconditional release of a Japanese American on the ground that the War Relocation Authority, a civilian agency, could not detain concededly loyal and law-abiding American citizens (L)
Oyama v. California (1948) V	6–3	Held that California's Alien Land Law violated the equal protection clause (L)
Takahashi v. Fish & Game Commission (1948) V	7–2	Held that a California law that barred commercial fishing licenses to Japanese immigrants violated the Fourteenth Amendment (L)

Source: Created by the author.

Note: H for Hughes Court, S for Stone Court, and V for Vinson Court. C for conservative outcomes, and L for liberal outcomes.

Apartheid

During the New Deal era, apartheid was under constant attack in lawsuits brought by the NAACP. The court took an incremental approach to the problem by chipping away at the application of the separate but equal principle in transportation, housing, and higher public education cases. By 1953, the court had reached a critical juncture in its equal protection jurisprudence and it could no longer put off the decision whether to overrule *Plessy*'s separate but equal constitutional mandate. The court's choice would have a profound impact on American constitutional democracy.

TRANSPORTATION

Segregated transportation was one of the most despised forms of apartheid because of its publicly insulting character (Du Bois 1948, 243; Barnes 1983, 17–19). On trains, the segregated section was filthy, foul-smelling, had extremely dirty toilets and lacked the basic conveniences that were found in the white section. Blacks were often subjected to insulting and abusive treatment by railroad officials. Terminal stations were segregated, and restrooms or food service may not have been available to blacks. On streetcars and buses, blacks were assigned to the least comfortable rear seats, and they had to give up their seats to white passengers when they became crowded. Segregated transportation was a symbol of racial superiority for whites, but it was a constant reminder of racial hierarchy for blacks.

Twenty-seven years after Justice Hughes applied the substantial equality of treatment standard to segregated trains in *McCabe v. Atchison, Topeka & Santa Fe Railway Co.* (1914), Chief Justice Hughes applied the principle to a case that lacked *McCabe*'s procedural defects. In 1937, Arthur Mitchell, a black member of the US House of Representatives from Chicago, paid a first-class, roundtrip fare for a trip from Chicago to Hot Springs, Arkansas. When Representative Mitchell transferred to the train headed for Hot Springs, the conductor refused to accept his payment for the Pullman sleeper coach and ordered him to leave the first-class section of the train. Mitchell filed a complaint with the Interstate Commerce Commission, but it was dismissed after a finding that there was comparatively little black traffic for the luxury cars to warrant the running of extra cars or the construction of partitions. Two months prior to his retirement, Chief Justice Hughes wrote the unanimous decision in *Mitchell v. United States* (1941). Hughes found that Mitchell's treatment by the railroad "was manifestly a discrimination against him in the course of his interstate journey and admittedly that discrimination was based solely upon the fact that he was a Negro." Citing *McCabe*, Hughes found that "the denial to appellant of equality of accommodations because of his race would be an invasion of a fundamental individual right which is guaranteed against state action by the Fourteenth Amendment." He rejected the comparative volume of traffic argument because "it is the individual, we said, who is entitled to the equal protection of the laws,—not merely a group of individuals, or a body of persons according to their numbers." Hughes found that the Interstate Commerce Act "expressly extends its prohibitions to the subjecting of 'any particular person' to unreasonable discriminations." For the first time, the court held that the Interstate Commerce Act's antidiscrimination provision and the equal protection clause required the same standard of equality of treatment for blacks and whites in transportation.

In a case that predated the more famous Rosa Parks bus incident by eleven years, Irene Morgan was arrested in 1944 when she refused to move to the rear seat for a white passenger on a crowded Greyhound bus in Gloucester County, Virginia, that was en route to Baltimore, Maryland. Morgan was charged and convicted of violating a Virginia law that required the separation of black and white passengers on interstate and intrastate motor carriers. In *Morgan v. Virginia* (1946), the court struck down the Virginia law on commerce clause grounds. Justice Reed applied the undue burden test to the segregation statute and found several burdens on interstate commerce: black passengers traveling interstate were subjected to multiple seat changes

Table 4.5. Hughes, Stone, and Vinson Courts Transportation and Housing Cases, 1930–1953

Case	Vote	Outcome
Hansberry v. Lee (1940) H	9–0	Reversed a restrictive covenant enforcement judgment against a black family because the signatories had dual and potentially conflicting interests (L)
Mitchell v. United States (1941) H	8–0	Held that segregated railway travel violated the Interstate Commerce Act (L)
Morgan v. Virginia (1946) S	6–1	Held that a state statute that required segregated motor vehicle travel was an undue burden on interstate commerce (L)

continued on next page

Table 4.5. Continued.

Case	Vote	Outcome
Bob-Lo Excursion Company v. Michigan (1948) V	7–2	Held that a state public accommodations law that prohibited segregation on public carriers as applied to steamboats traveling on international waters did not violate the commerce clause (L)
Shelley v. Kraemer (1948) V	6–0	Held that judicial enforcement of restrictive covenants constituted state action and violated the Fourteenth Amendment (L)
Hurd v. Hodge (1948) V	6–0	Held that judicial enforcement of restrictive covenants in Washington, DC, violated the CRA of 1866 (L)
Henderson v. United States (1950) V	8–0	Held that segregated railway dining cars violated the Interstate Commerce Act (L)
Barrows v. Jackson (1953) V	6–1	Held that judicial enforcement of a restrictive covenant to recover damages from a white signatory for breach of the agreement violated the Fourteenth Amendment (L)
District of Columbia v. John R. Thompson Co. (1953) V	8–0	Held that the 1872 and 1873 District of Columbia antidiscrimination laws prohibited restaurants from denying service to blacks (L)

Source: Created by the author.

Note: H for Hughes Court, S for Stone Court, and V for Vinson Court. C for conservative outcomes, and L for liberal outcomes.

on a single trip that interfered with their comfort and freedom of choice in selecting accommodations, states had different laws on segregated transportation and they were subject to different interpretations as to whether they applied to interstate passengers, and states had different definitions of race for the purposes of racial separation on common carriers. After considering the competing interests at stake, Reed applied greater weight to national uniformity in regulations for interstate travel to justify striking down the law.

HOUSING

The use of restrictive covenants remained a problem in Northern cities after the second phase of the Great Migration. The Federal Housing Administration's underwriting manual adopted explicit racist guidelines to encourage their use

(Rothstein 2017, 82–89). When the NAACP renewed its legal campaign to invalidate the use of restrictive covenants in the mid-1940s, the organization advanced a novel legal theory—that the enforcement of restrictive covenants in court constituted state action (Vose 1955, 112–19). The NAACP applied the enforcement theory in three test cases brought in St. Louis, Detroit, and Washington, DC. In all three cases, white property owners sued blacks to enforce private agreements that restricted the sale of homes to whites only.

In the lead case, *Shelley v. Kraemer* (1948), the Vinson Court struck down the use of restrictive covenants under the Fourteenth Amendment. Writing for the unanimous court, Chief Justice Vinson found that state action was invoked when white property owners sought judicial enforcement of the restrictive covenants in state courts. Citing *Buchanan v. Warley* (1917) and the Civil Rights Act of 1866, Vinson asserted that the Fourteenth Amendment protected the civil rights of blacks from discriminatory state action to acquire, own, and dispose of property. Vinson found that "but for the active intervention of the state courts, supported by the full panoply of state power, petitioners would have been free to occupy the properties in question without restraint." Vinson cited his majority opinion in *Oyama v. California* (1948), which held that a state law that denied equal enjoyment of property rights to a class of Japanese citizens based on race or ancestry was unconstitutional under the equal protection clause. In *Hurd v. Hodge* (1948), the court ruled that judicial enforcement of restrictive covenants in the District of Columbia violated § 1 of the Civil Rights Act of 1866. Vinson asserted that the phrase "in every State and Territory" covered the District of Columbia, and the close relationship between § 1 of the 1866 law and the Fourteenth Amendment "leaves no doubt that judicial enforcement of the restrictive covenants by the courts of the District of Columbia is prohibited by the Civil Rights Act." Vinson added that it would be inconsistent with national public policy to permit federal courts to enforce restrictive covenants but deny state courts that authority. The landmark *Shelley* case curtailed the use of state and federal courts as instruments to enforce racial discrimination in housing. The court took the bold step to circumvent the state action problem by redefining the relationship between public and private racial discrimination.

As shown in table 4.5, the outcomes in the transportation and housing cases indicated the willingness of the justices to break new legal ground to find workable solutions to the evils of apartheid. It would be left up to Congress to address the widespread problem of racial discrimination in the areas of interstate travel and housing.

Public Higher Education

Charles Hamilton Houston, the NAACP's first general counsel, was the architect of the organization's legal strategy to attack racial segregation in the area of public education (McNeil 1983, 133–44). To further black economic advancement, Houston targeted higher education, because Southern and border states did not have many graduate and professional programs set aside for black students. In 1936, Houston hired attorney Thurgood Marshall to assist in the organization's litigation activities. In 1940, Marshall founded the NAACP's Legal Defense Fund (LDF) and became its first director-counsel. A Missouri case became the NAACP's first line of attack against segregated higher education (Endersby and Horner 2016). Missouri law required segregated public schools, but there was no express provision that required segregated higher education. In 1921, the Missouri legislature enacted a law that established a separate university for black residents, Lincoln University. A provision in the law created an out-of-state tuition scholarship program for black students who wanted to pursue professional degrees that were not offered at Lincoln University. Lloyd Gaines, a recent Lincoln University graduate, was chosen to serve as the plaintiff in the NAACP's test case. When Gaines applied to the University of Missouri School of Law in 1935, the board of curators directed the university's registrar to deny his admission after lengthy delays in processing his application and litigation by the NAACP.

In *Missouri ex rel. Gaines v. Canada* (1938), Chief Justice Hughes found that the university's refusal to admit Gaines violated the equal protection clause. Hughes asserted that the issue "is not as to what sort of opportunities other States provide, or whether they are as good as those in Missouri, but as to what opportunities Missouri itself furnishes to white students and denies to negroes solely upon the ground of color." Citing *McCabe v. Atchinson, Topeka & Santa Fe Railway Company* (1914), Hughes explained that it did not matter that there was limited demand for legal education for blacks in Missouri, because the constitutional right does not depend on the number of persons discriminated against. He asserted that Gaines' right "was a personal one. It was as an individual that he was entitled to the equal protection of the laws, and the State was bound to furnish him within its borders facilities for legal education substantially equal to those which the State there afforded for persons of the white race." The court held that Gaines was entitled to admission to the law school at the University of Missouri "in the absence of other and proper provision for his legal training within the state."

Justice James McReynolds' vitriolic dissent was joined by Pierce Butler. McReynolds asserted that the decision may cause the state to "abandon her law school and thereby disadvantage her white citizens without improving petitioner's opportunities for legal instruction; or she may break down the settled practice concerning separate schools and thereby, as indicated by experience, damnify both races." McReynolds clearly understood the implications of the *Gaines* decision—the application of the substantial equality of treatment principle would eventually bring about the demise of state mandated segregation as long as the costs of providing separate but equal facilities would become an unbearable financial burden on the state. The costs associated with financing dual degree programs forced Missouri to abandon its exclusionary admissions policy in 1950 (Endersby and Horner 2016, 192–200, 248–61).

In the landmark *Gaines* case, Chief Justice Hughes applied the substantial equality of treatment principle to weaken *Plessy*'s grip on racial segregation. The costs associated with the *Gaines* litigation took a major financial toll on the NAACP because it had run out of funds. A decade had passed before the NAACP could bring another higher education case to the court. In a case that was very similar to *Gaines*, *Sipuel v. Board of Regents of the University of Oklahoma* (1948), the Vinson Court ruled in a per curiam decision that Ada Sipuel must be admitted to Oklahoma's all-white law school. Two years later, the Vinson Court decided two higher education cases on the same day: *Sweatt v. Painter* (1950) and *McLaurin v. Oklahoma State Regents* (1950). In both cases, the court applied *McCabe*'s substantial equality of treatment principle to strike down state segregation laws that authorized all-white universities to exclude blacks.

After a state trial court ruled that the University of Texas denied Heman Sweatt the equal protection of the laws when the university refused to admit him to the law school, the court continued the case for six months to allow the state to create a substantially equal law school for blacks. In *Sweatt v. Painter* (1950), Chief Justice Vinson found that the makeshift law school was substandard in several areas: the number and quality of its faculty, the low number of volumes in its library, the lack of a full-time librarian, and the law school's lack of accreditation. When Vinson considered the qualities of law schools that were incapable of objective measurement, such as faculty reputation, position and influence of the alumni, traditions and prestige, he found that it was "difficult to believe that one who had a free choice between these law schools would consider the question close."

George McLaurin, who was in his sixties, agreed to serve as a plaintiff in the Oklahoma case to fend off charges from white supremacists that the only thing blacks were trying to do was to get social equality and to intermarry (Kluger 2004, 265). The federal district court struck down Oklahoma's segregation statute and ruled that the state had a constitutional duty to provide McLaurin with the education he sought. In response, the Oklahoma legislature amended its laws to permit the admission of blacks to graduate programs, but internal segregation practices were required. After McLaurin was admitted, he was assigned to segregated seating in the classroom, library, and cafeteria. In *McLaurin*, Chief Justice Vinson found that the restrictions administered by the state "sets McLaurin apart from the other students. The result is that appellant is handicapped in his pursuit of effective graduate instruction. Such restrictions impair and inhibit his ability to study, to engage in discussions and exchange views with other students, and, in general, to learn his profession." Vinson concluded that the university's internal segregation requirements deprived McLaurin of "his personal and present right to the equal protection of the laws."

As shown in Table 4.6, the NAACP launched a successful legal strategy that struck down exclusionary admission practices based on race in public

Table 4.6. Hughes, Stone, and Vinson Courts Higher Education Cases, 1930–1953

Case	Vote	Outcome
Missouri ex rel. Gaines v. Canada (1938) H	6–2	Held that the state's failure to provide legal education for black students that was substantially equal to legal education provided to white students violated the equal protection clause (L)
Sipuel v. Board of Regents of the University of Oklahoma (1948) V	9–0	Held that the state's law school must admit blacks under *Gaines* (L)
Fisher v. Hurst (1948) V	7–2	Rejected the NAACP's mandamus petition to compel the University of Oklahoma to comply with the court's previous mandate to admit Sipuel-Fisher to its law school (C)
McLaurin v. Oklahoma State Regents (1950) V	9–0	Held that internal racial segregation practices in graduate education violated the equal protection clause (L)
Sweatt v. Painter (1950) V	9–0	Held that a makeshift law school for black students was not substantially equal to the law school for whites (L)

Source: Created by the author.

Note: H for Hughes Court, S for Stone Court, and V for Vinson Court. C for conservative outcomes, and L for liberal outcomes.

higher education. The NAACP's ultimate goal was to have *Plessy* overruled, but the Vinson Court was either unwilling or not ready to make that policy choice in *Sweatt* and *McLaurin*. Thurgood Marshall understood that the separate but equal doctrine was on shaky constitutional ground and as the LDF's director-counsel, he had to devise yet another legal strategy to force the court to overturn *Plessy*.

THE PATH TO BROWN

After World War II, Mexican Americans waged political and legal attacks against segregation and discrimination in the area of public education (Strum 2010). In 1944, Gonzalo and Felicitas Mendez attempted to enroll their children in the Westminster School in Orange County, California, but school officials informed them that they had to attend a segregated public school located in another school district. Gonzalo Mendez brought a class action lawsuit on behalf of citizen children of Mexican or Latin descent who were similarly affected by the school districts' segregation policies. The lawsuit alleged that the districts' segregation policies unconstitutionally discriminated against them on the basis of ancestry. In *Mendez v. Westminster School District* (1946), the federal district court found that the laws relating to California's public education system forbid distinctions among students based on race or ancestry and that the actions taken by school officials constituted state action and violated the equal protection clause. In 1947, the Ninth Circuit affirmed the lower court's ruling. Because of the *Mendez* litigation, California became the first state to formally end de jure school segregation. The historically significant *Mendez* decision predated the *Brown* decision by seven years.

Approximately three weeks after *McLaurin* and *Sweatt* were decided, Thurgood Marshall convened a two-day conference of attorneys and NAACP officials in New York to plan a legal strategy to have the courts declare racial segregation unconstitutional in elementary and secondary education (Kluger 2004, 309–10). By 1951, the NAACP found black plaintiffs who were willing to bring lawsuits to challenge school segregation in South Carolina, Kansas, Virginia, Delaware, and Washington, DC. The Vinson Court accepted the five cases for review, consolidated the state cases under the name of the Kansas case, *Brown v. Board of Education*, and scheduled oral arguments on December 9, 1952. The federal government submitted an amicus curiae brief that took the position that segregation imposed or supported by law was per se unconstitutional and the separate but equal doctrine should be overruled.

During conference deliberations, the justices were divided on the question whether racial segregation in public schools should be declared unconstitutional (Kluger 2004, 606–35). As a delay tactic to give the justices more time to work out their differences, Justice Felix Frankfurter drafted five questions that asked the parties to research the history and purpose of the Fourteenth Amendment to determine whether Congress intended state legislatures to abolish segregated schools. On June 8, 1953, the Vinson Court issued a miscellaneous order that restored the cases to the docket for reargument at the beginning of the October 1953 term. The order requested that the parties discuss their findings in their legal briefs and oral arguments. Prior to the beginning of the October 1953 term, Chief Justice Fred Vinson died of a heart attack at the age of sixty-three on September 8, 1953.

Conclusion

From 1801 until 1930, Supreme Court policymaking in race cases advanced the policy goals of the predominant white supremacist racial orders to a significant degree. The Great Depression and other political and social forces strengthened the transformative egalitarian racial alliance. The three courts that operated during the New Deal era—the Hughes, Stone, and Vinson Courts—responded favorably to the egalitarian goals of the new political coalition. The shift in the court's response to demands for equal rights under law was truly remarkable and transformative. Of the forty-eight race cases examined in this chapter, 19 percent were decided in a conservative direction and 81 percent were decided in a liberal direction in favor of the rights of people of color. The decisive break in the court's exercise of power to advance the policies of the ruling regime of white supremacy was clearly linked to the return of Charles Evans Hughes to the court in 1930 as chief justice. Because he sincerely believed in racial equality, Chief Justice Hughes applied his leadership skills to guide the court down a path to protect the civil rights of blacks (O'Brian 1950, 48–49; Higginbotham and Smith 1992, 1107).

Before FDR made a single appointment to the court, the Hughes Court had amassed an impressive record in correcting racial injustices in the criminal justice system (the Scottsboro Cases and coerced confessions), it restored jury discrimination cases to the court's docket, and its voting decisions paved the way for the demise of the white primary. In 1938, Hughes was given the unique opportunity to continue what he started in

1914—to bring about the demise of the separate but equal doctrine by requiring substantial equality of treatment in equal protection cases. As a result, the house of cards built by constitutionally sanctioned apartheid began to fall in the areas of transportation, housing, and public higher education. The Hughes Court's placement of Footnote Four in the *Carolene Products* decision brought about jurisprudential regime change. The footnote expressed the justices' intention to move the court in a liberal policy direction in the areas of civil liberties and civil rights, and it would subject racial classifications in laws to a more searching judicial inquiry. With the exception of the notorious Japanese exclusion cases, the Stone and Vinson Court justices remained on the policymaking path toward equal rights under law, but they were more ideologically divided.

At the time of Chief Justice Vinson's death in 1953, the school segregation cases had been restored to the court's docket. The newly elected Republican president and former World War II general Dwight D. Eisenhower would appoint Vinson's successor. There was considerable speculation on and off the court about who would succeed Vinson. The stakes were extraordinarily high for the LDF, for black citizens, and for American constitutional democracy. The new chief justice would have the responsibility of presiding over a court as it faced the most important race case in fifty-eight years.

Chapter 5

The Warren Court, 1953–1969

The Warren Court operated during an era of consequential political, social, and constitutional change. Three presidents were elected to office: Dwight Eisenhower (1953–1961), John Kennedy (1961–1963), and Lyndon Johnson (1963–1969). During the Kennedy administration, the Cuban Missile Crisis brought the United States and the Soviet Union to the brink of nuclear war. On November 22, 1963, the nation experienced its fourth presidential assassination when John Kennedy was fatally shot while riding in a motorcade in Dallas, Texas. His brother, Robert Kennedy, was assassinated on June 6, 1968, while campaigning for the presidency in Los Angeles. The escalation of the Vietnam War during the Johnson administration sparked widespread student protests, the anti-war movement, and war casualties that climbed over 35,000. Despite the social turbulence of the 1960s, two amendments were added to the Constitution in 1961 and 1964 that addressed political inequality—the Twenty-Third Amendment granted citizens residing in the District of Columbia the right to vote for president and vice president, and the Twenty-Fourth Amendment abolished the payment of poll taxes in federal elections.

King and Smith (2005, 82) asserted that a convergence of litigating, lobbying, militant protest actions, Cold War pressures, and actions taken by key political actors and institutions brought the transformative egalitarian racial order to predominance during the post–World War II years. Groups excluded from the centers of power in the American political system demanded that the democratic values of freedom, equality, and first-class citizenship rights be granted to all Americans regardless of their race or skin color. Johnson's ambitious Great Society domestic policy agenda resulted in legislation

127

that addressed poverty, inequities in healthcare for the elderly, and indigent and educational inequities. Congress enacted the most impactful civil rights legislation since Reconstruction: the Civil Rights Act of 1964, the Voting Rights Act of 1965, and the Fair Housing Act of 1968. Over time, these civil rights laws would transform the legal landscape of race and rights in the United States. The civil rights movement's most prominent leader, Rev. Martin Luther King, Jr., was assassinated on April 4, 1968, in Memphis, Tennessee, while there to support a strike by black sanitation workers.

During the civil rights movement era, the executive, Congress, and the Warren Court exercised their powers as allies to institute racial regime change in the United States. This chapter examines the Warren Court's policy response to the demands of the transformative egalitarian alliance to dismantle the remaining institutional structures supporting the regime of white supremacy. The era-defining racial policy dichotomy used to appraise whether the New Deal court advanced the policy goals of the rival racial orders—racial discrimination versus equal rights under law—was applied to the Warren Court's resolution of policy conflicts in the issue areas of apartheid, civil rights protests, disenfranchisement, jury discrimination, federal civil rights enforcement, and housing discrimination. As shown in this chapter, Warren Court decisions mark the high point in the development of a positive racial policy agenda by the Supreme Court.

The Composition of the Warren Court

When Chief Justice Fred Vinson died on September 8, 1953, President Eisenhower was pressured to find a successor quickly, because the Supreme Court's October 1953 term was about to commence and the school segregation cases were on its docket. On October 2, 1953, Eisenhower gave Earl Warren a recess appointment to fill Vinson's seat for supporting his 1952 presidential campaign. Warren was formally nominated to the position on January 11, 1954, and confirmed by the Senate on March 1 by a unanimous voice vote to become the fourteenth chief justice. Warren was a former prosecutor and state attorney general prior to becoming the governor of California. Although Warren was a progressive Republican, his gubernatorial record on race consisted of his active participation in the exclusion and incarceration of the Japanese community during World War II. A leading weekly black newspaper, the *Pittsburgh Courier*, asked the 1952 Republican Party presidential candidates about their views on civil rights.

The newspaper reported that Eisenhower's response was complete ignorance on the subject, but Warren's response was described as the first presidential candidate to advocate for a full civil rights program, and he insisted upon one law for all men (Kluger 2004, 667).

Eisenhower made four additional appointments to the court. John Marshall Harlan II, the grandson of Justice John Marshall Harlan, was appointed to succeed Robert Jackson after his death in October 1954. Harlan, who was confirmed by a 71–11 vote, was a conservative justice who did not share his grandfather's reputation as a defender of racial equality. Eisenhower made his second recess appointment in 1956 after Sherman Minton retired from the court. The appointment of William Brennan, Jr., defied expectations, because he was a left-leaning Democratic judge on the New Jersey Supreme Court. He was confirmed by a voice vote in March 1957. After Stanley Reed retired in February 1957, Eighth Circuit judge Charles Whittaker was unanimously confirmed to fill the vacancy. Eisenhower's third recess appointment was given to Sixth Circuit judge Potter Stewart to succeed Harold Burton after his retirement in October 1958. Stewart was confirmed by a 70–17 vote in May 1955. Opposition to the Harlan and Stewart nominations came from Southern senators, who believed that they would support civil rights.

In April 1962, President Kennedy nominated his deputy attorney general, Byron White, to succeed Charles Whittaker, who resigned from the court due to his severe physical and mental breakdown. When Felix Frankfurter retired in August 1962, Kennedy appointed his secretary of labor, Arthur Goldberg, as his successor. President Johnson persuaded Goldberg to resign from the court in 1965 to become the US ambassador to the United Nations. The vacancy gave Johnson the opportunity to appoint his friend and advisor Abe Fortas to the court. Johnson had to create another vacancy because he wanted to appoint his solicitor general, Thurgood Marshall, to the Supreme Court. To carry out his plan, Johnson appointed sitting justice Tom Clark's son, Ramsey Clark, to become the attorney general. As expected, Justice Clark retired from the court to prevent conflicts of interests. Marshall had amassed a stellar legal career prior to his nomination to the court. Marshall argued thirty-two cases before the court and won twenty-nine of them, and he served on the Second Circuit Court of Appeals. The chair of the Senate Judiciary Committee, James Eastland, and other white supremacists on the committee sought to derail Marshall's nomination by portraying him as a communist and as being prejudiced against whites and by attacking him for his responses to arcane questions with regard to the history of the Fourteenth Amendment and constitutional interpretation. After the contentious confirmation hearing and delay, the Senate Judiciary Committee voted to confirm Marshall by an 11–5 vote. Johnson persuaded twenty Southern senators who were facing reelection to miss the vote for Marshall as a safety-valve strategy to guarantee his confirmation (Williams 1998, 337–38). The Senate voted to confirm Marshall by a 69–11 vote. On August 30, 1967, Thurgood Marshall became the first African American to serve on the Supreme Court.

Two Hughes Court holdovers, Justices Hugo Black and William Douglas, served on the Warren Court throughout its tenure. Like Chief Justice Hughes, Chief Justice Warren applied his leadership skills to move the court in a more liberal policy direction on race that comported with his personal preferences and those of like-minded justices. Warren also addressed the discriminatory practices that took place inside the Supreme Court building. Schwartz (1983, 127) found that when Chief Justice Warren arrived, "the Supreme Court had a separate washroom for Negroes. One of the first things he did was to end discrimination taking place in the Court building itself."

The Constitutional Demise of Apartheid

After the Vinson Court declared segregated higher education and railway dining cars unconstitutional, the NAACP intensified its litigation campaign to persuade the court to take the next steps to declare racial segregation in undergraduate, secondary, and elementary education and segregation as practiced by interstate carriers unconstitutional. Several Vinson Court justices were divided on the question whether to overturn *Plessy*'s separate but equal principle, and it was unclear how Warren's presence on the court would affect the justices' decisional behavior in the cases.

EDUCATION

A recess appointed chief justice who had never held a judicial position and had served less than three months on the court presided over the conference, which took place after the December 1953 rearguments on the school segregation cases. According to Kluger's (2004, 686–712) account, Chief Justice Warren stated his position that public school segregation could not be permitted because the separate but equal doctrine rested upon a belief in black inferiority and he could not determine how it could be sustained on an alternative theory. Four justices agreed with Warren's position: Black, Douglas, Burton, and Minton. The positions taken by Clark, Frankfurter, Jackson, and Reed were either conflicted or were opposed to overturning *Plessy*. By late March 1954, the justices voted on the outcome in the cases, and all except Stanley Reed agreed to declare segregated public schools unconstitutional. Rather than assign the opinion to one of the senior liberal justices, Warren assigned the opinion to himself. He wanted a unanimous decision, and he applied his personal, political, and leadership skills to obtain one (Kluger 2004, 713–18).

Warren circulated his opinion on May 7, and on May 10 he obtained Justice Jackson's approval while he was recovering in the hospital from a serious heart attack. By May 12, Warren had obtained Reed's approval by pressing the need for unanimity and asking him to put aside his dissent for the good of the country (Kluger 2004, 701–2). As a condition of support, Reed sought a pledge from Warren that the implementation of the decision would occur gradually. During the May 15 conference, the justices voted to approve Warren's opinion. In his memoirs, Warren wrote that he believed President Eisenhower attempted to influence the outcome in the cases shortly before the decision was announced. Warren and John Davis, the attorney for the Southern states, were invited to attend a White House dinner. During the dinner, Warren recalled that Eisenhower made every effort to tell him that Davis was a "great man." After the dinner, Eisenhower took Warren by the arm as they walked into another room and told him, "These are not bad people. All they are concerned about is to see that their sweet little girls are not required to sit in school alongside some big overgrown Negroes" (Warren 1977, 291).

On May 17, 1954, Chief Justice Warren announced the decisions in *Brown v. Board of Education* (1954) (*Brown I*) and *Bolling v. Sharpe* (1954). Both decisions were unanimous and there were no concurring opinions. In *Brown*, Warren acknowledged that the findings submitted by the parties about the intended effects of the Fourteenth Amendment on racial segregation in public schools yielded inconclusive results. Warren then turned to the common legal question presented in the cases—whether black children who had been denied admission to public schools attended by white children were deprived of the equal protection of the laws. Warren found that prior precedents that applied the separate but equal principle to public education were not helpful in resolving the legal question. Warren had to "look instead to the effect of segregation itself on public education" and "consider public education in the light of its full development and its present place in American life throughout the Nation." Warren asserted that education was the most important function of state and local governments, it was the very foundation of good citizenship, and it was required in the performance of the nation's most basic public responsibilities, including service in the armed forces. If the state provides for education, then it "is a right which must be made available to all on equal terms."

Warren then asked, "Does segregation of children in public schools solely on the basis of race, even though the physical facilities and other 'tangible' factors may be equal, deprive the children of the minority group of equal educational opportunities?" His succinct response was, "We believe that it does." Warren explained that the harm caused by separating black children "generates a feeling of inferiority as to their status in the community that may affect their hearts and minds in a way unlikely ever to be undone." In Footnote Eleven, Warren cited contemporary social science studies to support the contention that segregated public schools had a detrimental effect on black children's motivation to learn and deprived them of some of the benefits they would receive in integrated schools. Warren concluded that separate but equal has no place in the field of public education because "separate educational facilities are inherently unequal." The court held in *Brown* that segregated public schools deprived black children of the equal protection of the laws.

Warren acknowledged that *Bolling v. Sharpe*, the companion case, presented a legal problem for the court because "the Fifth Amendment, which is applicable in the District of Columbia, does not contain an equal protection clause as does the Fourteenth Amendment which applies only to the states." To resolve the problem, Warren interpreted the Fifth Amendment as containing the concept of equal protection of the laws: "But the concepts of equal protection and due process, both stemming from our American ideal of fairness, are not mutually exclusive. The 'equal protection of the laws' is a more explicit safeguard of prohibited unfairness than 'due process of law,' and, therefore, we do not imply that the two are always interchangeable phrases. But, as this Court has recognized, discrimination may be so unjustifiable as to be violative of due process." Citing *Hirabayashi v. United States* (1943) and *Korematsu v. United States* (1944), Warren asserted that "classifications based solely upon race must be scrutinized with particular care, since they are contrary to our traditions and hence constitutionally suspect." Warren explained that the definition of liberty in the due process clause "extends to the full range of conduct which the individual is free to pursue, and it cannot be restricted except for a proper governmental objective." Finding no proper governmental objective for segregated schools, Warren concluded that racial segregation in the District of Columbia's public schools imposed "a burden that constitutes an arbitrary deprivation of their liberty in violation of the Due Process Clause." He asserted that it would be unthinkable to rule that the Constitution prohibited the states from maintaining racially segregated schools but not impose the same duty on the federal government.

Brown v. Board of Education and *Bolling v. Sharpe* were the most significant human rights decisions of the twentieth century, because they dismantled the main institutional structure supporting the old white supremacist racial order—apartheid. Apartheid was practiced throughout the nation, but the repressive system was more pronounced in the Southern states. The decisions were important catalysts for democratic regime change in the United States because they exposed how apartheid was incompatible with the values of liberal democracy. The decisions silenced communist critics who challenged the view that American democracy was a superior form of government with regard to race (Dudziak 2000, 107–12). The *Brown* and *Bolling* decisions established that the Constitution would no longer provide a safe haven for governmental actions predicated on white supremacist ideology and caste.

Chief Justice Warren's sincerely held policy preferences with regard to racial equality were shaped by the experiences of his close friend, Edgar "Pat" Patterson. Patterson was a black state capitol police officer who became Warren's driver when he was elected governor. Patterson had frequent conversations with Warren about his experiences growing up in segregated New Orleans and his experience with racial segregation in Sacramento (Cray 1997, 105, 225–26). Because of their friendship, Warren became sensitized to the effects of racial segregation on blacks. Warren (1977, 289–90) wrote in his memoirs that "one effect of the *Brown* decision was to show blacks that they need no longer be supplicants for equal rights dispensed at the white man's whim; the Supreme Court had decreed that they were fully entitled to such rights according to the laws of the land. This inevitably led to ever more insistent individual and class action demands by the black community."

The cases were restored to the court's 1954 docket for reargument to obtain the parties' views on the formulation of desegregation decrees. The Legal Defense Fund pressed for an immediate start to the desegregation process with specified beginning and end dates. The Southern states did not want the court to tell them how to desegregate, and they pressed for delay in the implementation of *Brown*. The federal government took the compromise position that the court should be flexible in setting a time-table for desegregation and the federal district courts should oversee the desegregation process. In *Brown v. Board of Education* (1955) (*Brown II*), Chief Justice Warren wrote the unanimous decision, which explained how the school desegregation process should proceed. The cases were remanded to the courts where the lawsuits originated because of their proximity to the varied local conditions. School authorities would have "the responsibility for elucidating, assessing, and solving these problems" and "courts will have to consider whether the action of school authorities constitutes good faith implementation of the governing constitutional principles." Warren explained that "in fashioning and effectuating the decrees, the courts will be guided by equitable principles" that call for flexibility in shaping remedies and giving weight to public and private considerations. He required segregated school districts to "make a prompt and reasonable start toward full compliance" with *Brown I* and "to admit to public schools on a racially nondiscriminatory basis with all deliberate speed the parties to these cases." Warren later admitted that it was a mistake to qualify desegregation enforcement by including Justice Felix Frankfurter's "all deliberate speed" language in *Brown II* (Schwartz 1983, 123–24).

Southern white supremacists immediately denounced the *Brown* decisions and pledged not to comply with any desegregation decrees. Several schemes were used to resist *Brown*'s mandate to desegregate: racial violence, mob agitation, state interposition resolutions, school closures, inaction, and delay (Peltason 1961; Canon and Johnson 1998). Governor Orval Faubus and the Arkansas legislature took the position that they had no duty to obey the *Brown* ruling, and in 1956, Faubus ordered the Arkansas National Guard to forcibly prevent nine black students from attending Little Rock's Central High School. After the crisis became an international embarrassment, a reluctant President Eisenhower ordered troops from the Army's 101st Airborne Division to escort the students into Central High. The court convened a special term to decide whether the actions of the governor and the state legislature to nullify *Brown*'s mandate were constitutional. In *Cooper v. Aaron* (1958), the court unanimously ruled in a per curiam decision signed by all justices that "the constitutional rights of children not to be discriminated against in school admissions on grounds of race or color declared by this Court in the *Brown* case can neither be nullified openly and directly by state legislators or state executive or judicial officers, nor nullified indirectly by them through evasive schemes for segregation." The court reminded the governor and legislature that Article VI made the Constitution the supreme law of the land and *Marbury v. Madison* (1803) declared that "it is emphatically the province and duty of the judicial department to say what the law is."

Virginia responded to *Brown*'s mandate to desegregate by instituting a policy of statewide massive resistance. The Prince Edward County school board decided to close its public schools when faced with an order to desegregate from the Fourth Circuit. A private foundation operated private schools for white children, who were eligible for county and state tuition grants, but black children lacked access to formal education from 1959 to 1963. In *Griffin v. County School Board of Prince Edward County* (1964), Justice Hugo Black found that the closure of the schools denied black students the equal protection of the laws. Black asserted that the "time for mere 'deliberate speed' has run out, and that phrase can no longer justify denying these Prince Edward County school children their constitutional rights to an education equal to that afforded by the public schools in other parts of Virginia."

The federal government became a partner in the school desegregation process when Congress enacted the Elementary and Secondary Education Act of 1965. The law allowed federal financial assistance to go to school districts to address educational inequalities that were linked to race and poverty, and it required the Department of Health, Education, and Welfare to adopt guidelines that compelled school districts to make progress toward desegregation. By 1968, the court had reached its breaking point with schemes designed to thwart compliance with *Brown*. In *Green v. County School Board of New Kent County* (1968), the court ruled that the freedom of choice plan adopted by the school board was unconstitutional. Writing for a unanimous court, Justice William Brennan reminded the school board that thirteen years had elapsed since *Brown II* mandated school districts to formulate desegregation plans "to convert to a unitary system in which racial discrimination would be eliminated root and branch." Delay would no longer be tolerated, and the school board had to formulate a plan that promised realistically to work immediately. The case outcomes presented in table 5.1 indicate that the Warren Court never wavered in its commitment to the correctness of the *Brown* decisions.

Table 5.1. Warren Court School Desegregation Cases, 1953–1969

Case	Vote	Outcome
Brown v. Board of Education (1954)	9–0	Held that racial segregation in public schools was unconstitutional under the equal protection clause (L)
Bolling v. Sharpe (1954)	9–0	Held that racial segregation in public schools in the District of Columbia was unconstitutional under the due process clause of the Fifth Amendment (L)
Brown v. Board of Education (1955)	9–0	Explained how the school desegregation implementation process should proceed (L)
Pennsylvania v. Board of Directors of City Trusts (1957)	9–0	Held that restricting admission to a school for poor male white orphans under the terms of a will that was effectuated by a trust operated by city officials violated the equal protection clause (L)
Cooper v. Aaron (1958)	9–0	Held that state officials could not nullify *Brown*'s mandate to desegregate under the supremacy clause of the Constitution (L)
Goss v. Board of Education of Knoxville (1963)	9–0	Held that a school transfer plan designed to maintain segregation violated the equal protection clause (L)
Griffin v. County School Board of Prince Edward County (1964)	7–2	Held that Prince Edward County could no longer evade *Brown*'s mandate by keeping its public schools closed (L)
Green v. County School Board of New Kent County (1968)	9–0	Held that school districts must present desegregation plans that promised realistically to work immediately (L)
Raney v. Board of Education (1968)	9–0	Held that the school district's freedom of choice plan was inadequate under the authority of *Green* (L)
Monroe v. Board of Commissioners of Jackson (1968)	9–0	Held that the free transfer plan was inadequate to desegregate schools under the authority of *Green* (L)
United States v. Montgomery County Board of Education (1969)	8–0	Upheld the trial court's plan in relation to hiring and placement of faculty based on the board's recalcitrance in desegregating its schools (L)

Source: Created by the author.

Note: C for conservative outcomes, and L for liberal outcomes.

PUBLIC EQUALITY

Segregated public spaces were a constant reminder of racial inferiority and caste for people of color. In a series of per curiam orders, the Warren Court extended *Brown*'s mandate to desegregate to public places: a privately owned amphitheater located in a park, beaches, golf courses, city busses, boxing matches, and courtrooms. The decisions foreclosed any possibility that racial segregation would survive outside of the public education context. The principle of public equality—equal access to public places without regard to race or color—was essential to the enjoyment of the privileges of first-class citizenship. The court applied the public equality principle in *Boynton v. Virginia* (1960) and *Burton v. Wilmington Parking Authority* (1961) to make certain that privately owned facilities located in public places would not refuse service to people of color. In both cases, the dissenters questioned whether state action was present. Congress found the solution to the state action problem when it enacted the historic antidiscrimination law—Title II of the Civil Rights Act of 1964—under its constitutional authority to regulate interstate commerce. Title II prohibited discrimination on account of race, color, religion, or national origin in any place of public accommodation. Purely private clubs were exempt from Title II's coverage.

The constitutionality of Title II was quickly challenged in *Heart of Atlanta Motel v. United States* (1964) and *Katzenbach v. McClung* (1964). In *Heart of Atlanta Motel*, the court unanimously held that Congress had ample authority under the commerce clause to enact Title II. Justice Tom Clark explained that the *Civil Rights Cases* (1883) had no precedential value in determining the constitutionality of Title II. Clark placed considerable weight on congressional hearings, reports, and debates in both houses that revealed that racial discrimination in travel was a nationwide problem. He found that it "had become so acute as to require the listing of available lodging for Negroes in a special guidebook which was itself 'dramatic testimony to the difficulties' Negroes encounter in travel." Clark asserted that Congress could "prohibit racial discrimination by motels serving travelers, however 'local' their operations may appear," as long as the means chosen were reasonably adapted to the end permitted by the Constitution.

In *Katzenbach v. McClung*, the owner of a Birmingham restaurant that served only white customers argued that his business operated locally and the connection between food that moved in interstate commerce and the congressional finding that racial discrimination affected interstate commerce was tenuous at best. The court unanimously ruled that Title II applied to restaurants. Relying on congressional findings, Justice Clark asserted that blacks were prevented from buying food while making interstate trips except for those places that operated in substandard conditions in isolated areas. Clark concluded that Congress had the power to regulate local activities if there were a close and substantial relation between local activities and interstate commerce.

In the landmark case *Heart of Atlanta Motel v. United States*, the Warren Court repudiated the principle of social equality embraced by the Waite Court in the *Civil Rights Cases* and replaced it with the principle of public equality. The decision vindicated Justice John Marshall Harlan's position that access to public places invoked legal and civil rights, not social rights. The outcomes in table 5.2 show that racial segregation was antithetical to the public equality principle underlying the Fourteenth Amendment.

Table 5.2. Warren Court Public Equality Cases, 1953–1969

Case	Vote	Outcome
Muir v. Louisville Park Theatrical Association (1954)	order	Held that a privately owned, segregated amphitheater located in a public park was unconstitutional (L)
Mayor and City Council of Baltimore v. Dawson (1955)	order	Held that segregated public beaches and bathhouses were unconstitutional (L)
Holmes v. City of Atlanta (1955)	order	Held that segregated municipal golf courses were unconstitutional (L)
Gayle v. Browder (1956)	order	Held that Montgomery's segregated city bus policy was unconstitutional (L)
Derrington v. Plummer (1957)	cert. denied	Held that a private cafeteria located in the basement of a new county courthouse could not deny service to blacks (L)
New Orleans City Park Improvement Association v. Detiege (1958)	order	Held that segregated golf facilities located in a public park violated the Constitution (L)
State Athletic Commission v. Dorsey (1959)	order	Held that a state law banning interracial boxing matches was unconstitutional (L)
Boynton v. Virginia (1960)	7–2	Held that the Interstate Commerce Act prohibited a privately operated bus terminal restaurant that served interstate passengers from discriminating on the basis of race (L)

Case	Vote	Outcome
Burton v. Wilmington Parking Authority (1961)	6–3	Held that a privately operated restaurant located in a public parking garage could not refuse service to blacks under the equal protection clause (L)
Turner v. City of Memphis (1962)	8–0	Held that a privately operated restaurant located in a municipal airport could not refuse service to blacks (L)
Watson v. City of Memphis (1963)	9–0	Held that segregated public parks and recreational facilities violated the equal protection clause (L)
Johnson v. Virginia (1963)	order	Held that courtroom segregation violated the equal protection clause (L)
Wright v. Georgia (1963)	9–0	Reversed the breach of peace convictions of six young blacks for peacefully playing basketball in a whites-only public park for lack of evidence (L)
Heart of Atlanta Motel v. United States (1964)	9–0	Upheld the constitutionality of Title II of the 1964 CRA under the commerce clause (L)
Katzenbach v. McClung (1964)	9–0	Held that Title II extends to local restaurants where a substantial portion of its food had moved in interstate commerce (L)
Evans v. Newton (1966)	6–3	Held that private trustees who operated an all-white park to effectuate the terms of a will violated the equal protection clause (L)
Newman v. Piggie Park Enterprises (1968)	8–0	Held that Title II applied to drive-in restaurants (L)
Lee, Commissioner of Corrections v. Washington (1968)	8–0	Held that racial segregation in prisons violated the equal protection clause (L)
Daniel v. Paul (1969)	7–1	Held that Title II applied to an amusement park (L)

Source: Created by the author.

Note: C for conservative outcomes, and L for liberal outcomes.

Interracial Intimate Relationships and Marriage

Under the system of apartheid, states restricted interracial intimate relationships and marriage between whites and persons of color to maintain the "purity of the races" and whiteness as a separate racial category. Originally, state laws prohibited marriages between whites and blacks but eventually they were extended to marriages between whites and members of the American Indian, Asian, and Hindu communities. By the mid-1960s, the Warren Court signaled that it was ready to dismantle the last vestige of apartheid—laws that prohibited interracial relationships and marriage. In *McLaughlin v. Florida* (1964), the court struck down a Florida law that made it a crime for blacks and whites to habitually occupy the same room at night to prevent breaches of the basic concepts of sexual decency. Justice Byron White asserted that the equal application theory formulated in *Pace v. Alabama* (1883) represented "a limited view of the Equal Protection Clause which has not withstood analysis in the subsequent decisions of this Court." He added that judiciary inquiry under the equal protection clause "does not end with a showing of equal application among the members of the class defined by the legislation." White found that the stated purpose of the criminal law failed to satisfy strict scrutiny's heavy burden of justification.

In 1958, Richard Loving, a 24-year-old white man, and Mildred Jeter, an 18-year-old woman who self-identified as being part black and part Rappahannock Indian, were married in Washington, DC. When the Lovings returned to their home in Caroline County, Virginia, they were arrested and later convicted of violating Virginia's Racial Integrity Act of 1924, which prohibited whites and blacks from leaving the state to marry with the intention of returning. The trial judge suspended their one-year sentences on the condition that they leave the state and not return together for twenty-five years. In 1963, the Lovings contacted the ACLU for legal assistance, and their attorneys filed a motion to vacate their convictions on the ground that the state's ban on interracial marriages was unconstitutional.

In *Loving v. Virginia* (1967), the court ruled that Virginia's statutory ban on interracial marriage violated the Fourteenth Amendment. Writing for the unanimous court, Chief Justice Warren asserted that the state's police power to regulate marriage did not extend to the application of invidious racial classifications that punished equally both whites and blacks in interracial marriages. Warren examined the history of the Racial Integrity Act and found that it was "passed during the period of extreme nativism which followed the end of the First World War"; and since that time, only sixteen states maintained their interracial marriage bans. Warren explained that "the clear and central purpose of the Fourteenth Amendment was to eliminate all official state sources of invidious racial discrimination in the States. . . . The fact that Virginia prohibits only interracial marriages involving white persons demonstrates that the racial classifications must stand on their own justification, as measures designed to maintain White Supremacy." Warren also found that the interracial marriage ban deprived the Lovings of their liberty without due process of law. Warren asserted that prior precedents recognized marriage as one of the "basic civil rights of man" that was "fundamental to our very existence and survival." Warren explained that to deny this fundamental freedom based on an unsupportable racial classification that directly subverts the principle of equality "is surely to deprive all the State's citizens of liberty without due process of law." Warren concluded that "under our Constitution, the freedom to marry, or not marry, a person of another race resides with the individual and cannot be infringed by the State."

The landmark *Loving v. Virginia* decision recognized for the first time that people of color, as first-class citizens, had the constitutional freedom to marry without state-imposed restrictions based on pseudoscientific, master race theories and white supremacist ideology. The regulation of intimate personal relationships and marriage was no longer relegated to the private sphere of state government when Fourteenth Amendment equal protection and due process rights were infringed.

Civil Rights Protests

Historical accounts recognize the Montgomery bus boycott as the watershed event that sparked the civil rights movement (Morris 1984; Holt 2021). On December 1, 1955, Montgomery civil rights activist and NAACP member Rosa Parks refused an order by the bus driver to move from the middle section of the bus where black passengers were permitted to sit to relinquish her seat to a white man after the bus became crowded. Parks's arrest for violating a city bus segregation ordinance evolved into a 381-day bus boycott and a direct-action movement. While Parks's criminal case was pending in state courts, recent law school graduate Fred Gray filed a class action lawsuit against the mayor of Montgomery in federal district court on February 1, 1956, with the support of the Montgomery Improvement Association and the NAACP to challenge the constitutionality of the city bus segregation policy. Four black women volunteered to serve as plaintiffs in the case: Aurelia Browder, Susie McDonald, and two teenagers, Claudette Colvin and Mary Louise Smith. In *Gayle v. Browder* (1956), the Warren Court unanimously affirmed the lower court ruling that the segregation ordinance was unconstitutional.

During the civil rights movement, blacks participated in sit-ins, nonviolent mass protests, and economic boycotts to resist the regime of white supremacy. Civil rights organizations such as the NAACP, the Southern Christian Leadership Conference, the Congress for Racial Equality, and the Student

Nonviolent Coordinating Committee played important roles in organizing and mobilizing participants. The LDF continued its litigation strategy to achieve racial equality in the courts, and it won important cases that helped shaped the movement's objectives. The protests and mass demonstrations resulted in many arrests and convictions across the South. Civil rights protesters challenged their convictions on First and Fourteenth Amendment grounds.

Sit-Ins

Most of the protest cases decided by the Warren Court involved sit-ins—a peaceful and orderly tactic used by protesters to challenge segregation policies of businesses that served the public. In the South, white-owned businesses would hire blacks and permit them to shop in their stores, but the color line began at lunch counters and restaurants. Some retail stores with lunch counter service permitted blacks to purchase food and eat while standing up in a separate area. Other eating establishments allowed blacks to purchase food from take-out windows only. Growing up in an environment inspired by civil rights activism, four black students from North Carolina Agricultural and Technical State University in Greensboro—Joseph McNeil, Franklin McCain, David Richmond and Ezell Blair—devised a plan to protest Woolworth's segregated lunch counter policy (Chafe 1980, 79–83). On February 1, 1960, the students sat down at the lunch counter to order food after they purchased items. The store refused to serve the students, but they remained at the lunch counter until it closed. The number of protesters at the store grew each day, and by the end of the week, hundreds of students from surrounding black colleges had joined lunch counter sit-ins. The Greensboro sit-in received extensive local and national media coverage, and organized protests and boycotts of stores with segregation policies quickly spread to other Southern cities. Six months after the initial sit-in, Woolworth's abandoned its segregated lunch counter policy.

Sit-in protesters were met with racist insults, threats, and acts of physical violence committed by the police and angry white mobs to force them to end their campaign for racial justice. They were arrested and convicted of trespass and breach of peace laws when they failed to leave the businesses when requested. In the first sit-in case, *Garner v. Louisiana* (1961), Southern University students were convicted of disturbing the peace while participating in a peaceful lunch counter sit-in. The statute defined disturbance of the peace as "the doing of specified violent, boisterous or disruptive acts in such a manner as to unreasonably disturb or alarm the public." The students challenged their convictions on the ground that the statute violated their

First and Fourteenth Amendments' due process rights. Citing *Thompson v. City of Louisville* (1960), the court found that the students' due process rights were violated because there was no evidence to support the charges.

Ten days prior to the enactment of Title II of the Civil Rights Act of 1964, the court decided five sit-in cases. The lead case, *Bell v. Maryland* (1964), highlighted the ideological divisions among the justices with regard to the state action problem. In *Bell*, twelve black students were convicted of violating a criminal trespass law for participating in a sit-in at a downtown Baltimore restaurant. The LDF argued on behalf of the students that a privately owned restaurant could not invoke the full legal machinery of the state to impose criminal sanctions on blacks to enforce segregation policies. The restaurant owner argued that the trespass law was neutral, no state action was present and private property owners had the right to choose their guests and decide who should remain on their premises even though their choices were based on racism. After the Maryland Court of Appeals affirmed the students' convictions but prior to the Supreme Court's ruling, the state and the City of Baltimore enacted public accommodation laws that made it illegal for restaurants to deny service to any person because of race. The statutory developments gave Justice Brennan the break he needed to avoid the state action issue. Brennan reversed the students' convictions based on the state's common law rule of abatement, which prohibited the prosecution of conduct that was no longer criminal. Justice Arthur Goldberg's concurrence, joined by Justices Warren and Douglas, added that the denial of access to public places on the basis of race was contrary to *Brown*'s public equality principle. Justice Black, joined by Justices Harlan and White in dissent, argued that the Fourteenth Amendment did not prohibit the application of a state's trespass laws to enforce the rights of private property owners from choosing their own customers.

The 121-page *Bell* decision produced strong, emotional divisions among the justices that centered on the tension between protecting civil rights and property rights. The case highlighted the justices' strategic maneuvering to obtain their preferred policy outcome. Conference deliberations indicated that Justice Black's property rights position initially commanded a majority (Schwartz 1985, 143–90; Schmidt 2018, 308–14). Justice Brennan's position ultimately prevailed because of three factors: delay that occurred due to requests for additional briefings from the solicitor general, Brennan's insistence in his draft dissent that the court should avoid deciding the constitutional issue because of the pending public accommodations bill in Congress, and last-minute vote switching by the justices. Chief Justice Warren initially circulated a draft dissent that was prepared for one of the companion cases, *Barr v. City of Columbia* (1964)—a lunch counter sit-in case. Schwartz (1985, 147) pointed out that Warren's dissent "was an atypically emotional opinion, demonstrating the Chief Justice's depth of feelings against a practice that to him was just as repugnant as school segregation." Schwartz (1985, 164–72) reprinted Warren's dissent in his compilation of the unpublished opinions of the Warren Court. Warren (in Schwartz 1985, 169) asserted that the whites-only lunch counter policy

> was founded on a right to compel Negroes to stand up to buy
> their food solely for the reason that they were Negroes. The store
> might as well have offered to feed only Negroes who would crawl
> in on their hands and knees, or, as in other caste systems, who
> would purchase food under conditions that would not cause their
> shadow to fall on the food of whites. It saddens me deeply to
> think that this Court, which has so far advanced the notion of
> racial dignity of all men before the law, would sanction the right
> so publicly first to shame and then to punish one who merely
> seeks that which any white man takes for granted.

Warren's dissent in *Barr* was withdrawn, and he did not write separately in the *Bell* case.

The enactment of Title II resolved the constitutional conflict presented in the sit-in cases. In *Hamm v. City of Rock Hill* (1964), the court vacated the trespass convictions of sit-in protesters on the ground that their still-pending convictions were abated by Title II. As shown in table 5.3, the

Table 5.3. Warren Court Sit-In Cases, 1953–1969

Case	Vote	Outcome
Thompson v. City of Louisville (1960)	9–0	Held that the conviction of a black man for loitering and disorderly conduct without evidentiary support violated the due process clause (L)
Garner v. Louisiana (1961)	9–0	Reversed sit-in protesters' disturbance of the peace convictions because there was no evidence of any crime committed (L)
Taylor v. Louisiana (1962)	7–1	Reversed sit-in protesters' breach of peace convictions on the authority of *Garner* (L)
Peterson v. City of Greenville (1963)	9–0	Reversed sit-in protesters' trespass convictions on equal protection grounds because a city ordinance required segregated eating facilities (L)

Case	Vote	Outcome
Gober v. Birmingham (1963)	8–1	Reversed and vacated sit-in protesters' criminal trespass convictions on the authority of *Peterson* (L)
Lombard v. Louisiana (1963)	8–1	Reversed sit-in protesters' trespass convictions because the segregated eating facilities requirement was not based on any ordinance (L)
Shuttlesworth v. City of Birmingham (1963)	8–1	Reversed the convictions of two black civil rights leaders for aiding and abetting criminal trespass when they told students to participate in lunch counter sit-ins because no crime was committed (L)
Bouie v. City of Columbia (1964)	6–3	Reversed the sit-in protesters' criminal trespass convictions because they were punished for conduct that was not criminal at the time (L)
Griffin v. Maryland (1964)	6–3	Reversed the sit-in protesters' criminal trespass convictions because the deputy sheriff who arrested them was an employee of the amusement park and acted under state authority (L)
Barr v. City of Columbia (1964)	9–0 6–3	Reversed the sit-in protesters' convictions for violating a misdemeanor statute on state action grounds (L)
Robinson v. Florida (1964)	9–0	Reversed the sit-in protesters' breach of peace and criminal trespass convictions on due process and equal protection grounds (L)
Bell v. Maryland (1964)	6–3	Vacated sit-in protesters' convictions because they were abated by recently enacted city and state public accommodations laws (L)
Hamm v. Rock Hill (1964)	5–4	Vacated sit-in protesters' trespass convictions because they were abated by the passage of Title II (L)
Brown v. Louisiana (1966)	5–4	Reversed sit-in protesters' breach of peace convictions on the authority of *Garner* (L)

Source: Created by the author.

Note: C for conservative outcomes and L for liberal outcomes.

outcomes in the sit-in cases supported the court's commitment to *Brown*'s public equality principle. A few years later, the sit-in cases disappeared from the court's docket.

Civil Rights Demonstrations

Unlike sit-ins, mass demonstrations occurred in public spaces such as streets, sidewalks, and government property. During the civil rights movement, thousands of demonstrators were convicted of violating breach of peace, trespass, and antipicketing ordinances and statutes. The civil rights demonstrators argued that their convictions violated the free speech and assembly protections guaranteed by the First and Fourteenth Amendments. In *Edwards v. South Carolina* (1963), the court reversed the breach of peace convictions of 187 black high school and college students who peacefully assembled on the state capitol grounds to express their dissatisfaction with racial discrimination. Justice Potter Stewart found that the students were convicted of an offense that was so generalized that the South Carolina Supreme Court found that it was "incapable of exact definition." Stewart asserted that the "Fourteenth Amendment does not permit a State to make criminal the peaceful expression of unpopular views."

Rev. B. Elton Cox was convicted of breach of peace, obstructing public passages, and courthouse picketing after he led a demonstration of approximately two thousand Southern University students to the Baton Rouge courthouse to protest racial segregation. He was sentenced to twenty-one months in jail and fined $5,700. The court decided Cox's appeal in two separate opinions. In *Cox v. Louisiana* (1965) (*Cox I*), Justice Arthur Goldberg found that the facts in *Cox* were strikingly similar to the facts in *Edwards*, because both breach of peace statutes were unconstitutionally broad in scope and the lower court interpreted the statute to "allow persons to be punished merely for peacefully expressing unpopular views." With regard to the obstructing public passages conviction, Goldberg found that city officials applied a statute that precluded all street assemblies and parades with "completely uncontrolled discretion" that permitted officials to act as a censor. In *Cox v. Louisiana* (1965) (*Cox II*), the justices were divided over Cox's conviction of violating a statute prohibiting picketing near a courthouse with the intent to obstruct justice. Justice Goldberg upheld the constitutionality of the statute because it was narrowly drawn but the record indicated that the police permitted the demonstration to take place across the street from the courthouse. Goldberg concluded that to convict Cox under the statute would subject him to a type of entrapment.

In his *Cox II* dissent, Justice Black expressed his dissatisfaction with the use of street protests to advance group causes. Black's antiprotest views prevailed in *Adderley v. Florida* (1966), which involved a civil rights demonstration of two-hundred Florida A&M University students that took place at the Leon County jail in Tallahassee. Thirty-two students were convicted of violating a Florida statute that prohibited trespass "with a malicious and mischievous intent." Justice Black did not find any evidence that the sheriff objected to the political views of the protesters or that large groups were permitted to gather on the jailhouse grounds for any purpose. Black explained that as long as the state was even-handed in its enforcement of trespass statutes on state owned property, the state had the power to regulate its use without violating the First Amendment. Writing for the dissenters, Justice Douglas forcefully asserted that the First Amendment protected the students' right to protest and petition for the redress of grievances on the jailhouse grounds when conventional methods of petitioning may be shut off to them. *Adderley* represented a significant break in the line of decisions that strengthened the First Amendment right to demonstrate peacefully in public places.

In 1963, Martin Luther King, Jr., took his nonviolent, direct-action campaign to Birmingham, where an entrenched white power structure was determined to keep blacks in an inferior political, social, and economic position. When members of the Southern Christian Leadership Conference applied for permits for a planned peaceful demonstration on April 14, 1963, Birmingham's public safety commissioner Eugene "Bull" Connor refused to issue them. Connor was granted an ex parte temporary injunction prohibiting King and his followers from holding the civil rights demonstration. Based on their beliefs that the injunction was unjust, undemocratic, and unconstitutional, the Good Friday demonstration proceeded, and its leaders were arrested, jailed, and fined. While King was in jail, he wrote his impactful "Letter from a Birmingham Jail," which explained why the nonviolent direct-action campaign against racial injustice was necessary. In *Walker v. City of Birmingham* (1967), a divided court upheld the validity of the injunction. Justice Stewart placed greater weight on the state's interest in having court orders obeyed and the city's interest in regulating the use of its streets over the civil rights leaders' First Amendment rights. Chief Justice Warren, along with Brennan, Douglas, and Fortas dissented on the ground that the ordinance gave city officials considerable discretion to deny permits to organizations whose views they disliked.

A few weeks after King was assassinated, the court reconsidered its disapproval of nonviolent demonstrations in a case arising out of the Good Friday Birmingham march. Rev. Fred Shuttlesworth's appeal of his 1963 conviction for leading the demonstration without obtaining a permit was held up in the Alabama court system for years. In *Shuttlesworth v. City of Birmingham* (1969), the court unanimously reversed Shuttlesworth's conviction. Justice Stewart found that the parade ordinance was unconstitutional on three grounds: it granted the city commission unbridled discretion to issue parade permits, it was a prior restraint on free speech, and the city's action was enforced in a racially discriminatory manner.

As shown in table 5.4, the Warren Court refused to uphold mass arrests and convictions of civil rights demonstrators who publicly protested against the regime of white supremacy in most cases. The protest decisions

Table 5.4. Warren Court Civil Rights Demonstrations Cases, 1953–1969

Case	Vote	Outcome
Edwards v. South Carolina (1963)	8–1	Reversed the breach of peace convictions of 187 students who protested peacefully on state capitol grounds because the offense was too generalized (L)
Cox v. Louisiana (*Cox I*) (1965)	9–0	Reversed a civil rights leader's breach of peace and obstructing public passages conviction for leading a mass student demonstration near a courthouse to protest segregation on overbreadth grounds (L)
Cox v. Louisiana (*Cox II*) (1965)	5–4	Reversed a civil rights leader's conviction of violating a statute prohibiting picketing near a courthouse with the intent to obstruct justice because the police allowed the demonstration (L)
Adderley v. Florida (1966)	5–4	Upheld students' trespass with malicious and mischievous intent convictions who assembled on the driveway of a county jail to protest segregation (C)
Walker v. City of Birmingham (1967)	5–4	Affirmed civil rights leaders' criminal contempt of court convictions for violating an injunction prohibiting marches (C)
Cameron v. Johnson (1968)	7–2	affirmed the convictions of picketers who violated Mississippi's antipicketing law by blocking access to the courthouse (C)
Shuttlesworth v. City of Birmingham (1969)	8–0	Reversed the conviction of a civil rights leader who failed to obtain a permit from the city commission when he led a peaceful civil rights march on public streets and sidewalks on First Amendment grounds (L)

Case	Vote	Outcome
Gregory v. Chicago (1969)	9–0	Reversed the convictions of peaceful civil rights demonstrators who were arrested for disorderly conduct when they marched to the mayor's home to protest public school segregation on First Amendment grounds (L)

Source: Created by the author.

Note: C for conservative outcomes and L for liberal outcomes.

revealed how First Amendment freedoms were essential to the attainment of racial equality during the civil rights movement (Kalven 1965; Karst 1975).

POLITICAL SPEECH

The Warren Court exercised its power to protect the free speech rights of persons who expressed their dissatisfaction with the regime of white supremacy and the Vietnam War. After King was arrested and charged with felony perjury in 1960 for allegedly signing fraudulent tax returns, his supporters organized the Committee to Defend Martin Luther King to raise funds for his defense. A jury later acquitted King of the bogus tax charges. On March 29, 1960, the group placed a paid, full-page editorial advertisement in the *New York Times* entitled "Heed Their Rising Voices" to show that King's arrest was politically motivated. The ad described how students were engaged in nonviolent demonstrations that were met with an unprecedented wave of terror, and it made an appeal for funds to support the student movement, the right to vote, and the legal defense of King. The ad included the names of persons who were well-known for their civil rights activities along with the names of four black Alabama ministers who endorsed the appeal for funds. The ad also contained several minor errors. Although the ad did not identify the names of public officials, Montgomery city commissioner Lester Sullivan contended that it referred to him, and he sued the newspaper and the four ministers on the ground that certain statements in the ad were libelous, false, and injurious to his reputation under Alabama libel law. The Alabama Supreme Court upheld a $500,000 libel judgment against the *New York Times* and the ministers.

In *New York Times v. Sullivan* (1964), the court threw out the libel judgments against the newspaper and the ministers in a landmark decision that protected political speech and freedom of the press. Writing for the unanimous court, Justice Brennan asserted that there was a "profound national commitment to the principle that debate on public issues should be uninhibited, robust, and wide-open." He rejected Sullivan's argument that the ad should forfeit its First Amendment protection based on the falsity of some of its statements. Brennan explained that Alabama's libel law was used by public officials who were opposed to the civil rights movement to deter critics "from voicing their criticisms, even though it is believed to be true and even though it is in fact true, because of doubt whether it can be proved in court or fear of the expense of having to do so." Brennan established a new standard, the actual malice test, to determine whether public officials could recover damages for libelous speech relating to their official conduct. The test required public officials to prove that defamatory falsehoods were made with a knowledge that the statements were false or with reckless disregard of whether they were false. Brennan did not find any evidence that the newspaper or the ministers were aware of the erroneous statements or that they recklessly disregarded the errors. The *New York Times v. Sullivan* decision revolutionized the approach to libel law under the First Amendment. The decision effectively blocked attempts to weaponize the threat of libel lawsuits to deter a robust exchange of views on public issues about race.

Blacks were vulnerable to political and legal attack and other forms of retribution when they expressed views that were considered "militant" by the establishment. Julian Bond, a twenty-five-year-old Student Nonviolent Coordinating Committee member from Atlanta, was elected to the Georgia House of Representatives after the Voting Rights Act of 1965 became law. Bond sued the Georgia House for violating his free speech rights when it voted to prevent him from taking office because of his anti-war and anti-draft views. In *Bond v. Floyd* (1966), Chief Justice Warren ruled in a unanimous decision that the Georgia legislature may not apply a stricter First Amendment standard to its legislators than to private citizens. Warren asserted that the "manifest function of the First Amendment in a representative government requires that legislators be given the widest latitude to express their views on issues of policy."

When Sidney Street, a black World War II veteran and Bronze Star recipient, heard about the assassination attempt on civil rights activist James Meredith in 1966, he removed an American flag from his drawer, went to a nearby street corner, and burned it in protest. Onlookers heard Street say, "We don't need no damn flag. Yes, that is my flag; I burned it. If they let that happen to Meredith, we don't need an American flag." Street was arrested and convicted of violating a New York flag burning statute. In *Street v. New York* (1969), Justice John Harlan found that Street could not constitutionally be punished under the statute for his verbal criticism of the flag. On the same day *Street* was decided, the court protected an eighteen-year-old black draftee from prosecution for making threatening comments about President Johnson in *Watts v. United States* (1969). The facts of the case indicated that during an anti-war rally held at the Washington Monument in 1966, an investigator for the Army Counter Intelligence Corps heard Watts make the following remarks before a small crowd of young protesters—"They always holler at us to get an education. And now I have already received my draft classification as 1-A and I have got to report for my physical this Monday coming. I am not going. If they ever make me carry a rifle the first man I want to get in my sights is L.B.J. They are not going to make me kill my black brothers." Watts was arrested the next day for making a true threat to kill President Johnson under Title 18 U.S.C. § 817, which prohibits any person from knowingly and willfully making any threat to take the life of or to inflict bodily harm upon the president. In *Watts*, the court ruled in a 5–4 per curiam decision that the government failed to prove that Watts' remarks constituted a true threat and that he intended to carry it into execution. The court interpreted his remarks as political hyperbole, which did not fit within the statutory language of § 817.

The Southern Assault on the NAACP

Southern states launched a counterattack against the NAACP's efforts to dismantle the institutional structures supporting the regime of white supremacy by weaponizing the power of the state legislature, the executive, and the judiciary to curtail the organization's civil rights and litigation activities (Murphy 1959). In 1956, Alabama's attorney general sued the NAACP for its failure to comply with a law that required out-of-state businesses to file its corporate charter and other business records prior to operating in the state. The state's objective was to publicly expose the names of NAACP members, which would place them in danger and make it difficult for the organization to recruit new members. When the NAACP refused to turn over its membership lists, the organization was held in contempt and fined $100,000. In *NAACP v. Alabama ex rel. Patterson* (1958), the court reversed the civil contempt judgment and fine imposed on the NAACP because the production order infringed on the group's associational rights that were protected by the First Amendment. Writing for the unanimous court, Justice Harlan asserted that "the freedom to engage in association for the advancement of beliefs and ideals is an inseparable aspect of the 'liberty' assured by the Due Process

Clause of the Fourteenth Amendment, which embraces freedom of speech." Alabama's attack on the NAACP backfired because it resulted in a landmark decision that protected the fundamental right of associational privacy for all persons under the First and Fourteenth Amendments.

The *Patterson* decision did not deter Southern states from instituting other schemes to obtain the NAACP's membership lists. In *Shelton v. Tucker* (1960), the court struck down an Arkansas law that compelled public school and college teachers to file annual affidavits that listed all organizations they belonged to or regularly contributed to for the preceding five years. Under the guise of investigating communist infiltration, Southern state legislative committees demanded that the NAACP turn over its membership lists. In *Gibson v. Florida Legislative Investigation Committee* (1963), the court reversed the conviction of the president of a local branch of the NAACP because the legislative investigation intruded upon the organization's First and Fourteenth Amendment's associational rights. The record failed to show a substantial connection between the local NAACP branch and communist activities to inquire into the membership of the association.

Several Southern states attempted to curtail the NAACP's school desegregation litigation by resorting to laws that regulated unethical and nonprofessional conduct by attorneys. Virginia enacted five statutes regulating the solicitation of legal business in the state, including a "running and capping" law that prohibited persons from acting as agents to solicit business on behalf of an attorney. In *NAACP v. Button* (1963), the court struck down the running and capping law. Justice Brennan explained that litigation was important to achieving the NAACP's objectives because "it is thus a form of political expression. Groups which find themselves unable to achieve their objectives through the ballot frequently turn to the courts." He pointed out that "litigation may well be the sole practicable avenue open to a minority to petition for redress of grievances." Brennan found that the law was written in such a way that any person who advised another of their legal rights had committed a crime and "a statute broadly curtailing group activity leading to litigation may easily become a weapon of oppression." Writing for the dissenters, Justice Harlan criticized the NAACP's litigating strategy and tactics for departing from the ethical rules of professional conduct. Because conduct was involved, Harlan believed that the government could impose reasonable regulations on litigation activity without violating protected free speech rights.

The *Button* decision was significant because the Warren Court gave its constitutional stamp of approval to cause lawyering (Scheingold and Sarat 2004, 4). Hilbink (2002, 100) asserted that the decision whittled away at the traditional ideology of law and politics as separate spheres, and it acknowledged "an alternative ideal that saw lawyers as explicitly political actors, lawsuits as political action, and courts as political forums." The outcomes in table 5.5 show that the court protected the NAACP's right of

Table 5.5. Warren Court NAACP Litigation Cases, 1953–1969

Case	Vote	Outcome
NAACP v. Alabama ex rel. Patterson (1958)	9–0	Held that the contempt of court fine imposed on the NAACP for its refusal to turn over its membership lists infringed on the organization's right to associational privacy (L)
Bates v. Little Rock (1960)	9–0	Reversed the convictions of NAACP record keepers who refused to submit membership lists to city officials on freedom of association grounds (L)
Shelton v. Tucker (1960)	5–4	Held that a state law that required public school and college teachers to file annual affidavits listing every organization to which they belonged or regularly contributed deprived them of their associational rights (L)
Louisiana ex rel. Gremillion v. NAACP (1961)	9–0	Held that Louisiana could not enforce statutes that required the NAACP to file annual membership lists and declarations that none of their officers were members of subversive organizations (L)
Gibson v. Florida Legislative Investigation Committee (1963)	5–4	Held that a state legislative committee could not compel the president of a local branch of the NAACP to submit the branch's membership list on freedom of association grounds (L)
NAACP v. Button (1963)	6–3	Held that a state may not use its laws to regulate the legal profession to infringe on the associational rights of the NAACP and its members (L)
NAACP v. Alabama ex rel. Flowers (1964)	9–0	Reversed a lower court judgment that permanently enjoined the NAACP from operating in the state for failure to comply with Alabama's corporate regulations and qualification laws on freedom of association grounds (L)

Source: Created by the author.

Note: C for conservative outcomes and L for liberal outcomes.

associational privacy, and the organization's right to use litigation as a tool to achieve its policy objectives.

Federal Protection of Voting Rights

During the early phase of the civil rights movement, blacks pressured President Eisenhower and Congress to enact legislation to address voting discrimination in the South. The legislative response came in the form of two weak voting rights laws. The Civil Rights Act of 1957 was the first voting rights law passed since Reconstruction. The law created the US Commission on Civil Rights and the Civil Rights Division in the Department of Justice. The act authorized the attorney general to obtain federal court injunctions to secure and protect black voting rights. The Civil Rights Act of 1960 authorized court-appointed referees to help blacks register to vote, and it required federal election officers to retain and preserve all voting related records and to produce them to the attorney general on demand. The election records were used by the Justice Department to establish evidence of discriminatory voting practices. Stringent voting rights protections were removed from the bills to appease Southern senators.

After the demise of the white primary, Southern states resisted any additional erosion of their political power. In 1957, the Alabama legislature enacted a redistricting law that redrew the city of Tuskegee's boundary from a square to a twenty-eight-sided figure. The gerrymander converted Tuskegee from an all-black city to an all-white city. In *Gomillion v. Lightfoot* (1960), the court found that the broad power of a state to fix the boundaries of its municipalities is limited by the Fifteenth Amendment. Justice Felix Frankfurter explained that to reach the opposite conclusion would sanction the state's impairment of voting rights as long as "it was cloaked in the garb of the realignment of political subdivisions." Four years later, the court was less receptive to a racial gerrymandering challenge in a Northern redistricting case. In *Wright v. Rockefeller* (1964), the court upheld a New York congressional redistricting law that concentrated blacks and Puerto Ricans into the eighteenth congressional district and excluded them from the predominantly white seventeenth district. Justice Black found that the minority challengers failed to show evidence of discriminatory intent, which was required to prove an unconstitutional racial gerrymander.

Civil rights groups launched voting rights campaigns in the South. One prominent example took place in 1964 when the Student Nonviolent Coordinating Committee organized the Freedom Summer campaign in Mississippi, where black and white college students traveled from across the country to assist in black voter registration. Approximately 17,000 black Mississippians filled out voter registration forms, but only 1,600 were permitted to register (Carson 1981, 117). In 1965, the Southern Christian Leadership Conference targeted Selma, Alabama, because of its entrenched resistance to black voting. The March 7, 1965, "Bloody Sunday" fifty-four-mile march from Selma to the state capital in Montgomery was the watershed event that triggered the enactment of strong voting rights legislation. As they left Selma, the marchers were met by numerous state troopers and an armed white mob that viciously attacked them with night sticks, bullwhips, and tear gas as they attempted to cross the Edmund Pettus Bridge. Among the marchers who were severely injured was the twenty-five-year-old chairman of the Student Nonviolent Coordinating Committee, John Lewis, and Amelia Boynton, who helped organized the march. Extensive media coverage of the domestic terrorist attack provoked public shock and outrage across the nation. President Johnson responded by instructing Attorney General Nicholas Katzenbach to draft a tough voting rights bill. On March 15, Johnson presented the proposed legislation in a televised address to a joint session of Congress. Both houses of Congress passed the legislation by overwhelming majorities.

After ninety-five years of Southern resistance to the Fifteenth Amendment, Johnson signed the historic Voting Rights Act into law on August 5, 1965. The law prohibited racially discriminatory voting practices in the United States, and the Department of Justice was given the authority to enforce the law. The Voting Rights Act contained three main provisions. Section 2, which applied nationwide and did not have an expiration date, prohibited state and local governments from denying or abridging the right to vote on account of race through qualifications, practices, or procedures. Section 4 established a coverage formula to identify state and local governments that required the use of any test or device as a condition for voter registration. Section 5 established a preclearance mechanism that required covered states and local governments to obtain permission from the US District Court in the District of Columbia or the attorney general before enacting or administering any change in voting qualification or prerequisite to voting, or standard, practice, or procedure that was different from that in force or effect on November 1, 1964.

South Carolina, one of the states covered by the law, immediately filed an original jurisdiction lawsuit to have the Voting Rights Act's key provisions declared unconstitutional on the ground that they exceeded the powers of Congress and encroached on the reserved powers of the state. In *South Carolina v. Katzenbach* (1966), Chief Justice Warren wrote the 8–1 decision that upheld all of the Voting Rights Act's contested provisions. At the outset, Warren recounted the history of voting rights discrimination in the United States. He explained that Congress was "confronted by an insidious and pervasive evil which had been perpetuated in certain parts of the country through unremitting and ingenious defiance of the Constitution." Congress concluded that "the unsuccessful remedies which it had prescribed in the past would have to be replaced by sterner and more elaborate measures in order to satisfy the clear commands of the Fifteenth Amendment." Warren asserted that the framers of the Fifteenth Amendment indicated that Congress would be chiefly responsible for implementing the rights created in § 1 and Congress had plenary power under § 2 to use any rational means to effectuate the constitutional prohibition of racial discrimination in voting. Warren found that "after enduring nearly a century of systematic resistance to the Fifteenth Amendment, Congress might well decide to shift the advantage of time and inertia from the perpetrators of the evil to its victims." He concluded that, "hopefully, millions of non-white Americans will now be able to participate for the first time on an equal basis in the government under which they live." Dissenting in part, Justice Black objected to the preclearance provision on federalism grounds because it made covered states "beg federal authorities to approve their policies" and it created the impression that they were "little more than conquered provinces."

In the landmark case *South Carolina v. Katzenbach*, the Warren Court exercised its power to uphold congressional authority to enact legislation designed to dismantle the institution of disenfranchisement that supported the ruling regime of white supremacy in the South. As shown in table 5.6, the Warren Court rejected a variety of schemes used to disenfranchise black voters, including the use of poll taxes in state elections.

Jury Discrimination

Two weeks before the *Brown* decision was announced, the Warren Court decided a jury discrimination case that shed important insights about how

Table 5.6. Warren Court Voting Rights Cases, 1953–1969

Case	Vote	Outcome
Lassiter v. Northampton County Board of Elections (1959)	9–0	Upheld North Carolina's literacy test for voter registration under the Fifteenth Amendment because it was applicable to all races (C)
Gomillion v. Lightfoot (1960)	9–0	Held that a racial gerrymander deprived blacks of their right to vote in violation the Fifteenth Amendment (L)
United States v. Raines (1960)	9–0	Upheld the constitutionality of the CRA of 1957 (L)
Wright v. Rockefeller (1964)	7–2	Held that evidence of intent was required to show that congressional districts were drawn to minimize the voting strength of minorities (C)
Anderson v. Martin (1964)	9–0	Held that a state law that required the race of the candidate to be placed on all ballots for all elections violated the equal protection clause (L)
Louisiana v. United States (1965)	9–0	Held that Louisiana's interpretation test violated the Fifteenth Amendment (L)
South Carolina v. Katzenbach (1966)	8–1	Upheld the constitutionality of the VRA of 1965 under the Fifteenth Amendment (L)
Harper v. Virginia Board of Elections (1966)	6–3	Held that the use of poll taxes in state elections violated the equal protection clause (L)
Katzenbach v. Morgan (1966)	7–2	Upheld the constitutionality of § 4(e) of the VRA, which prohibited the denial of the right to vote to non-English speaking citizens (L)
Allen v. State Board of Elections (1969)	7–2	Held that § 5's preclearance provision reached any state enactment that altered the election law of a covered state even in a minor way (L)
Gaston County v. United States (1969)	7–1	Held that North Carolina's attempt to have the literacy test reinstated violated § 4(a) of the VRA (L)

Source: Created by the author.

Note: C for conservative outcomes and L for liberal outcomes.

it would approach racial classifications under the equal protection clause. A murder in Edna, Texas, gave attorneys Gus Garcia, John Herrera, and James DeAnda the opportunity to bring a test case challenging Mexican American discrimination (Olivas 2006). In 1950, Pedro Hernandez was indicted for murder by an all-Anglo grand jury in Jackson County, Texas. His attorneys filed motions to quash the indictment and the jury panel on the ground that Mexican Americans were systematically excluded from service as jury commissioners, grand jurors, and petit jurors even though fully qualified Mexican American jurors resided in Jackson County. Hernandez's case challenged the conventional black-white binary approach to race cases (Perea 1997). Mexican Americans were legally classified as white under the Treaty of Guadalupe Hidalgo of 1848 and a federal district court case, *In re Rodriguez* (1897). In *Sanchez v. State* (1951), the Texas Court of Criminal Appeals ruled that "they were white people of Spanish descent." Hernandez's attorneys argued that widespread discrimination and segregation practices in Jackson County demonstrated that the Mexican American community was actually treated as a race, class, or group apart from other whites.

In *Hernandez v. Texas* (1954), Chief Justice Warren wrote the unanimous decision that rejected the black-white binary as the determinant of the class of persons protected by the equal protection clause. Warren made no attempt to define race; instead, he asserted that shifting community prejudices may set a class of persons apart for discriminatory treatment:

> Throughout our history differences in race and color have defined easily identifiable groups which have at times required the aid of the courts in securing equal treatment under the laws. But community prejudices are not static, and from time to time other differences from the community norm may define other groups which need the same protection. Whether such a group exists within a community is a question of fact. When the existence of a distinct class is demonstrated, and it is further shown that the laws, as written or as applied, single out that class for different treatment not based on some reasonable classification, the guarantees of the Constitution have been violated. The Fourteenth Amendment is not directed solely against discrimination due to a "two-class theory"—that is, based upon differences between "white" and Negro.

Warren found that the evidence presented in the case met the prima facie burden of proof required by *Norris v. Alabama* (1935): officials and citizens admitted that residents of the community distinguished between whites and Mexicans, children of Mexican descent were required to attend segregated schools, restaurants would not serve Mexican Americans, and the courthouse provided separate toilets for white men and Mexican and black men. The fact that Mexican Americans had been systematically excluded from jury service for the past twenty-five years "bespeaks discrimination, whether or not it was a conscious decision on the part of any individual commissioner." Warren concluded that Hernandez was entitled to "the right to be indicted and tried by jurors from which all members of his class are not systematically excluded—juries selected from among all qualified persons regardless of national origin or descent." *Hernandez* was an important landmark for Mexican American civil rights because the decision extended Fourteenth Amendment protection to Mexican Americans as a separate class.

The decision in *Swain v. Alabama* (1965) was a significant departure from a long line of cases that established that racial discrimination in jury selection violated the equal protection clause. In 1962, nineteen-year-old Robert Swain was arrested for the rape of a seventeen-year-old white female in Talladega County, Alabama. The judge denied his lawyer's motion to quash the indictment on the ground that blacks were systematically excluded from jury service throughout the county. The prosecutor then used peremptory strikes to remove blacks from the petit jury, and Swain was convicted and sentenced to death by an all-white jury. On appeal, the LDF argued that black males were severely underrepresented on grand jury venires and blacks had not served on a petit jury in the county since the 1950s.

The court ruled that Swain failed to produce evidence to establish prima facie discrimination in the selection of the grand and petit juries or that prosecutors used their peremptory strikes in a racially discriminatory manner. Writing for the 6–3 majority, Justice Bryon White found that it "was wholly obvious that Alabama had not totally excluded a racial group from either grand or petit jury panels," and he did not consider an average of six to eight blacks on panels "as constituting forbidden token inclusion within the meaning of the cases in this Court." White agreed with the state's contention that its use of peremptory strikes was fair and impartial and applied to qualified jurors "whether they be Negroes, Catholics, accountants or those with blue eyes." After an extensive examination of the history of the peremptory system, White asserted that to "subject the prosecutor's challenge in any particular case to the demands and traditional standards of the Equal Protection Clause would entail a radical change in the nature and operation of the challenge." The majority refused to "hold that the

Constitution requires an examination of the prosecutor's reasons for the exercise of his challenges in any given case." White acknowledged that the Fourteenth Amendment claim takes on added significance in instances where a prosecutor uses peremptory strikes resulting in all-white juries.

The *Swain* decision produced an ideological split among the liberal justices. Justices Brennan and Black voted with the majority and Justice Goldberg's dissent was joined by Chief Justice Warren and Douglas. Goldberg believed that Swain made out a strong prima facie case of jury discrimination and the majority's new burden of proof rule "will make it more difficult to put an end to discriminatory selection of juries on racial grounds." The landmark *Swain* decision placed a heavy burden of proof on defendants to show that prosecutors used peremptory challenges to systematically strike blacks from venires because they lacked access to the relevant evidence in jury cases. The decision effectively removed the discriminatory use of peremptory challenges from judicial scrutiny for two decades.

Table 5.7. Warren Court Jury Discrimination Cases, 1953–1969

Case	Vote	Outcome
Hernandez v. Texas (1954)	9–0	Held that the exclusion of Mexican Americans from jury service as a race, class, or group apart from other whites violated the equal protection clause (L)
Michel v. Louisiana (1955)	6–3	Held that no violation of due process occurred when three black men sentenced to death for rape had a reasonable opportunity to challenge the exclusion of blacks from the grand jury but failed to do so (C)
Reece v. Georgia (1955)	9–0	Held that a black man convicted of murder was not given the opportunity to challenge the systematic exclusion of blacks from jury service (L)
Eubanks v. Louisiana (1958)	9–0	Held that the exclusion of blacks from grand juries denied a black man convicted of murdering a white woman equal protection of the laws (L)
Arnold v. North Carolina (1964)	9–0	Held that two black men convicted of murder made out a prima facie case of the systematic exclusion of blacks from the grand jury (L)
Coleman v. Alabama (1964)	9–0	Held that a black man convicted of murder was entitled to show evidence of systematic exclusion of blacks from grand and petit juries (L)

Case	Vote	Outcome
Swain v. Alabama (1965)	6–3	Held that once a clear record of race-based jury exclusion has been shown, the burden of proof was placed on the defendant, not the state, to show peremptory abuse by prosecutors (C)
Whitus v. Georgia (1967)	9–0	Held that two black men convicted of murder made out a case of systematic exclusion of blacks from the grand jury (L)

Source: Created by the author.

Note: C for conservative outcomes and L for liberal outcomes.

Federal Civil Rights Enforcement

White supremacists committed brutal acts of racial terrorism to enforce the regime of white supremacy in the South. State prosecutors either refused to bring indictments against perpetrators of racial terrorism or all-white juries refused to convict them. The notorious murder of fourteen-year-old Emmett Till, which occurred in a small town in the Mississippi Delta in 1955, helped galvanized the civil rights movement. Till's murder was widely publicized, and it exposed the world to the extreme acts of racial violence and oppressive conditions experienced by Southern blacks. Till's murderers, who later confessed to the crime, were acquitted by an all-white jury. Increased pressure was placed on the Justice Department to take a more aggressive stance toward civil rights enforcement. Two related Reconstruction era laws were available to federal prosecutors to charge public officials and private persons who violated the federal civil rights of any person. Section 241 made it a crime for two or more persons to conspire to injure, threaten, or intimidate any person in the exercise or enjoyment of any right secured by the Constitution or federal laws. Section 242 imposed criminal penalties on any person acting under color of law to deprive any person of a federally protected right on account of race or color.

Civil rights leaders and workers were frequently targeted by white supremacist groups in the South. During the 1964 Freedom Summer voter registration campaign, the Klan executed three civil rights workers, Michael Schwerner, Andrew Goodman, and James Chaney, in the widely publicized "Mississippi Burning" case (Ball 2004). The dynamics of weak federal enforcement of civil rights shifted when the FBI was contacted after the civil rights workers failed to return to Meridian from a trip to investigate a church bombing. After six weeks of searching and receiving an informant's tip, their bodies were recovered at a construction site. State and local law enforcement officials failed to indict the Klan for the murders, but a federal grand jury indicted Deputy Sheriff Cecil Ray Price, two law enforcement officers, and fifteen Klan members under §§ 241 and 242. Federal District Judge Harold Cox, an ardent segregationist, dismissed most of the charges. In *United States v. Price* (1966), the court ruled that § 242 applied to law enforcement officials and the Klan. Writing for a unanimous court, Justice Abe Fortas explained that the deprivation of civil rights counts in the indictment applied to private persons who jointly engaged with state officials in the prohibited action, and they acted under color of law for the purposes of the statute. Fortas rejected Judge Cox's interpretation of § 241 that it only applied to "a narrow and relatively unimportant category of rights." Fortas found that § 241 embraced all rights and privileges secured by the Fourteenth Amendment and federal laws, and it covered conspiracies that involved state participation in murder.

On the same day *Price* was decided, the court addressed the scope of § 241 in *United States v. Guest* (1966). The Klan fired shots into a car driven by Lt. Col. Lemuel Penn, who was driving through Athens, Georgia, on his way home to Washington, DC, along with two Army Reserve passengers. Penn was killed immediately. After an FBI investigation found that the Klan perpetrated acts of terrorism against black residents of Athens, Herbert Guest and five other Klan members were charged with criminal conspiracy to deprive black citizens from using state facilities and engaging freely in interstate travel. The indictment specified the means used by the Klan to carry out the conspiracy against blacks: shootings, beatings, murder, cross burnings, damaging and destroying property, car pursuits, gun threats, and filing false police reports. Writing for the 8–1 majority, Justice Potter Stewart asserted that "we have made clear in *Price* that when § 241 speaks of 'any right or privilege secured . . . by the Constitution or laws of the United States,' it means precisely that." Stewart found that the conduct associated with the Klan's criminal acts and the murder of Penn were punishable under § 241. The decision established that the right to travel freely from one state to another was a fundamental right under the Constitution. The *Guest* decision also eroded the impact of the state action doctrine by allowing private conduct to be reached under the Fourteenth Amendment.

Fair Housing

Civil rights groups' demands for federal fair housing legislation were met when Congress passed the Fair Housing Act of 1968. The Warren Court did not decide any housing discrimination cases arising under the law. The recodified property rights provision of § 1 of the Civil Rights Act of 1866, § 1982, made it illegal to discriminate in the sale or rental of housing on the basis of race. The law was ineffective because lower courts had limited its reach to state action. In 1965, an interracial couple was prevented from buying a home in a new planned community in St. Louis County because of the real estate developer's policy not to sell homes or lots to blacks. The couple sued the real estate developer, but the lawsuit was dismissed on the ground that § 1982 did not reach private refusals to sell. In the landmark case *Jones v. Alfred H. Mayer Company* (1968), the court ruled for the first time that § 1982 applied to all racial discrimination, public and private, in the sale or rental of housing. Justice Stewart found that Congress had the power to prohibit all private and public racial discrimination in the sale and rental of property under the Thirteenth Amendment. The court overruled *Hodges v. United States* (1906), which held that Congress lacked the power to reach private acts of discrimination to enforce the Thirteenth Amendment. Justices Harlan and White disagreed with the majority's interpretation of § 1982. They argued that the recent passage of the Fair Housing Act of 1968 would make relief available to others who experienced housing discrimination. The *Jones* decision was consistent with the policy goals of the Radical Republicans during Reconstruction, and it provided people of color with a legal weapon to challenge private acts of racial discrimination in housing.

State and local governments resisted fair housing laws by resorting to forms of direct democracy to negate their objectives. Justice White wrote the majority opinion in two cases that rejected the use of initiatives and referenda that made it easier for majorities to restrict or repeal fair housing laws. In *Reitman v. Mulkey* (1967), the court ruled that a California initiative that repealed the state's housing antidiscrimination laws violated the equal protection clause because it created a constitutional right to discriminate. In *Hunter v. Erickson* (1969), the court struck down an Akron, Ohio, city charter amendment that made it mandatory for any fair housing ordinance to be first approved by a majority of voters before becoming effective. Justice White found that the amendment violated the equal protection clause because "the law's impact falls on the minority" even though it was written in neutral language. *Reitman* and *Hunter* were significant decisions, because they prohibited the state from imposing extra burdens on legislation benefitting racial minorities beyond those of the ordinary political process.

Conclusion

Scholars debate whether President Eisenhower actually made unflattering statements about Earl Warren such as that Warren's nomination was "the biggest damn-fool mistake I ever made" or that his biggest mistake was "the appointment of that dumb son-of-a-bitch Earl Warren." Whether personal or political, the feud that existed between the two leaders of the executive and judicial branches was over the policy direction of the country with regard to race and rights. As it happened, Eisenhower's most significant contribution to civil rights was the appointment of Warren to the position of chief justice. The Warren Court remained steadfast on the decisional path of equal rights under law that was initiated by the New Deal Court, but Chief Justice Warren's main policy goal was to dismantle, not weaken, the institutional structures supporting the regime of white supremacy and to repudiate its racist ideology. Warren Court policymaking was highly responsive to the racial equality demands of the civil rights movement, and its liberal record on race outmatched the 81 percent liberal record of the New Deal Court. Of the eighty-nine race cases examined in this chapter, 8 percent were decided in a conservative direction and 92 percent were decided in a liberal direction in favor of people of color or pro–civil rights claimants. This impressive record demonstrates that the court exercised its power to effectuate the democratic principles that guided the framers of the Reconstruction amendments—freedom, equality, and full citizenship rights.

The Warren Court's race decisions generated considerable antagonism from the ultraconservative John Birch Society and white supremacists (Bethune 2022). Despite calls for Warren's impeachment from oppositional forces, impeachment proceedings never materialized in Congress; nor did the court waver in its commitment to advancing the policy goals of the ruling regime of transformative egalitarianism. The decisions of the Warren Court produced jurisprudential regime change in other areas besides racial equality—freedom of speech, freedom of religion, political representation, and due process protections for criminal defendants. In their assessment of why the Warren Court matters today, Stone and Strauss (2020, 2) maintained that "the Constitution, as we know it today, is very much the work of the

Warren Court. It would be unthinkable to return to the world that existed before the Warren Court." During its sixteen-year tenure, the decisions of the Warren Court strengthened American constitutional democracy.

On March 31, 1968, President Johnson announced that he would not run for reelection, and a few months later, Chief Justice Warren announced his retirement from the court. These developments, their consequences, and unrelenting conservative resistance to egalitarian policies would negatively affect the ability of the transformative egalitarian alliance to solidify and expand its policy goals. They would also have a profound impact on the ideological direction of the court's race decisions in future cases.

Chapter 6

The Burger Court, 1969–1986

The civil rights laws enacted by Congress, the Warren Court's egalitarian decisions, the creation of federal civil rights agencies, and a commitment to civil rights enforcement brought the modern transformative egalitarian racial order to predominance (King and Smith 2005, 82–83). The egalitarian alliance expanded its policy goals to include women and members of the Latino, Asian, and Native American communities. Although the policies of the transformative egalitarian alliance were enshrined into federal law and case precedents, they remained vulnerable to attack by whites in the North and South who were opposed to the dismantling of the white supremacist racial order and the pace of racial and social change. As King and Smith (83) pointed out, the Republican Party became the chief beneficiary of the discontent with the policy agenda of the transformative egalitarian alliance. Three Republican presidents and one Democratic president occupied the White House from 1969 until 1986: Richard Nixon (1969–1974), Gerald Ford (1974–1977), Jimmy Carter (1977–1981), and Ronald Reagan (1981–1989). During his second term, Nixon resigned from office rather than face pending impeachment proceedings due to his involvement in illegal activities and abuse of power associated with the Watergate scandal. Gerald Ford's highly unpopular decision to pardon Nixon for his Watergate offenses cost him his first election bid to become president. President Jimmy Carter's term in office was beset by serious domestic and foreign policy events that contributed to his reelection loss in 1980, which paved the way for the Republican takeover of the Supreme Court.

During the Reagan presidency, the executive branch set out to execute an anti–civil rights policy agenda. In addition to the appointment of conservatives to head key civil rights positions in federal departments and agencies, the

Reagan administration attempted to influence the way the Supreme Court interpreted the Constitution. In a speech to the American Bar Association, Attorney General Edwin Meese argued that a jurisprudence of original intention was the only legitimate standard of interpretation. Meese's (1986, 464) embrace of originalism was based on his policy disagreements with the liberal Warren Court's "radical egalitarianism and expansive civil libertarianism." He believed that originalism "would produce defensible principles of government that would not be tainted by ideological predilection." Justice William Brennan (1986, 433) responded to Meese's views in a Georgetown University speech by pointing out that "our amended Constitution is the lodestar for our aspirations." Brennan (435) asserted that the doctrine of original intent was flawed because "it is little more than arrogance cloaked as humility. It is arrogant to pretend that from our vantage we can gauge accurately the intent of the Framers on application to specific, contemporary questions." Brennan (438) went on to say that "the ultimate question must be: What do the words of the text mean in our time?"

This chapter addresses the tensions between the policy goals of the second transformative egalitarian order and the emergence of a new racial order—the anti-transformative racial order. King and Smith (2005, 83) described the anti-transformative racial order as a modern descendant of the second white supremacist order, but its members reject the white supremacist label. The anti-transformative New Right alliance had a widely recognized but negative racial agenda and its actors and institutions opposed measures explicitly aimed at reducing inequalities. The Burger Court is characterized as a transitional court bracketed between the ultraliberal Warren Court and the conservative Rehnquist Court. The court was asked to decide policy conflicts that tested its commitment to liberal Warren Court precedents and transformative federal civil rights laws. The court took an active role in regulating legal policy in the areas of education, voting rights, employment discrimination, housing discrimination, jury discrimination, and capital punishment. The racial policy dichotomy used to appraise Burger Court policymaking is racial discrimination versus equal rights under law. Unlike the transitional New Deal Court that became more liberal in its policymaking, the transitional Burger Court drifted to the right over time and produced mixed outcomes in race cases.

The Composition of the Burger Court

Three months after President Johnson decided not to run for reelection in March 1968, seventy-seven-year-old Chief Justice Earl Warren announced his decision to retire at the end of the court's term contingent on the appointment of a qualified successor. Johnson nominated his friend and advisor, Associate Justice Abe Fortas, to succeed Warren. Fortas was subjected to vile anti-Semitic hostility and conservative criticism for his liberal voting record on civil rights (Johnson 2016, 110). Senate Judiciary committee hearings revealed that as a sitting justice, Fortas regularly attended White House staff meetings, he briefed Johnson on court deliberations, and he received a privately funded stipend of $15,000 for conducting a nine-week seminar at American University School of Law (111–16). After realizing Fortas's nomination would not move forward, Johnson withdrew the nomination a month prior to the presidential election. In an October 1968 campaign speech, Richard Nixon pledged that he would appoint "strict constructionists" to the court who would "see their duty as interpreting the law, rather than making law." Nixon nominated Warren Burger to become the fifteenth chief justice. Burger was born in St. Paul, Minnesota, and he obtained his law degree by taking night classes from St. Paul College of Law. He practiced law in St. Paul for twenty years until President Eisenhower appointed him to the position of assistant attorney general, and two years later, to the DC Circuit court. Nixon was impressed with Burger's conservative judicial philosophy, and he was easily confirmed by a 74–3 vote.

In May 1969, Fortas submitted his resignation after another judicial ethics scandal revealed that he took $20,000 for unspecified services from a charitable foundation that was under investigation by the Justice Department (Johnson 2016, 117–18). Nixon adopted a strategy to build Republican support in the South by appointing Southerners to the court to play on white fears of racial integration and civil rights enforcement, but he quickly realized that the Senate would not rubberstamp his nominations. In August 1969, Nixon nominated Fourth Circuit judge Clement Haynsworth to succeed Fortas but judicial ethics and conflicts of financial interest allegations derailed his nomination. The Senate rejected Nixon's next choice to fill the Fortas vacancy, Fifth Circuit judge G. Harrold Carswell. In addition to being described as intellectually unfit and incompetent to serve on the court, Carswell was a self-avowed proponent of white supremacy. Nixon's third choice to fill Fortas's seat was Eighth Circuit judge Harry Blackmun. A lifelong friend of Warren Burger, Blackmun was unanimously confirmed by the Senate in May 1970.

In September 1971, two vacancies were created six days apart by the retirements of Hugo Black and John Harlan. Both retirements were due to serious health issues. In October, Nixon nominated corporate attorney and former American Bar Association president Lewis Powell to fill Black's seat and Assistant Attorney General William Rehnquist to fill Harlan's seat. Powell was a moderate Southern Democrat who was easily confirmed by an 89–1 vote. Rehnquist's nomination generated considerable controversy after *Newsweek* magazine revealed a few days prior to his Senate confirmation vote that he wrote a memo in 1952 opposing school desegregation while serving as Justice Robert Jackson's law clerk. The memo stated that *Plessy v. Ferguson* (1896) was rightly decided and should be reaffirmed. Although the memo was written in the first person and had his initials on it, Rehnquist claimed that it expressed Jackson's tentative views about the school segregation cases. Despite the controversy, the Senate confirmed Rehnquist by a 68–26 vote.

In November 1975, the last remaining FDR appointee, William Douglas, retired from the court after suffering a stroke in December 1974. President Ford nominated Seventh Circuit judge John Paul Stevens to succeed Douglas who was unanimously confirmed by the Senate in December 1975. No vacancies occurred on the court during Jimmy Carter's one term in office. Potter Stewart's retirement in July 1981 gave President Reagan the opportunity to carry out his campaign pledge to appoint a woman to the court. Reagan nominated a long-time friend of William Rehnquist, Arizona Court of Appeals judge Sandra Day O'Connor. O'Connor was unanimously confirmed by the Senate and became the first woman to serve on the Supreme Court.

Racial Discrimination in Public and Private Spaces

The Burger Court addressed unresolved issues concerning the legality of racially discriminatory actions that occurred in public and private spaces. In some instances, the disagreements were about a question that vexed the Warren Court justices—whether state action existed for the purposes of the Fourteenth Amendment. In *Moose Lodge No. 107 v. Irvis* (1972), the court refused to apply the reasoning in *Burton v. Wilmington Parking Authority* (1961) to private segregated clubs. In 1968, the Democratic majority leader of the Pennsylvania legislature, K. Leroy Irvis, was an invited guest to a private club in Harrisburg. The Moose Lodge club refused to serve him in the dining room and bar on account of his race. Irvis sued the club, arguing that state action was present because the state's liquor board had issued a liquor license to the private club. Writing for the 6–3 majority, Justice Rehnquist found that the state was not significantly involved in the act of private discrimination. When Rehnquist compared Moose Lodge to the

Table 6.1. Burger Court Public and Private Discrimination Cases, 1969–1986

Case	Vote	Outcome
Adickes v. S. H. Kress (1970)	5–2	Held that a white Freedom School teacher who accompanied black students to a segregated lunch counter failed to prove that her civil rights were violated under § 1983 when she was arrested (C)
Evans v. Abney (1970)	5–2	Held that under the terms of a segregationist's will, a public park must be closed and the property reverted to the heirs because the park could no longer be operated on a segregated basis under the Fourteenth Amendment (C)
Palmer v. Thompson (1971)	5–4	Held that the closure of a city's swimming pools to avoid a desegregation order did not deny black plaintiffs the equal protection of the laws (C)
Moose Lodge No. 107 v. Irvis (1972)	6–3	Held that a state liquor license did not constitute state action to challenge a private club's refusal to admit blacks (C)
Tillman v. Wheaton-Haven Recreation Association (1973)	9–0	Held that a community association's racially discriminatory membership policy violated § 1982 because it was not a private club (L)
Palmore v. Sidote (1984)	9–0	Held that racial prejudice cannot be used to justify removing a white infant child from its white mother because the mother was married to a black man under the Fourteenth Amendment (L)

Source: Created by the author.

Note: C for conservative outcomes, and L for liberal outcomes.

Eagle Restaurant in *Burton*, he found that the club had no lease agreement, it was not open to the public, it was a private social club, and the liquor board played no part in establishing or enforcing the club's membership or guest policies. Justice Brennan, joined by Justice Marshall in dissent, asserted that the state's regulations were so closely interconnected with the club's bar that state involvement in racial discrimination was undoubtedly present. The court would later revisit the tension presented in cases that pitted the associational rights of private organizations to discriminate in their membership against the rights of minorities and women to have equal access to accommodations, facilities, and privileges in all business establishments, such as the Jaycees and Rotary Clubs. As shown in table 6.1, the Burger Court's response to claims of discrimination in public and private spaces produced mixed outcomes.

Education

The Burger Court's education agenda extended beyond determining whether school desegregation remedies were permissible. The court was asked to decide cases involving discriminatory private school admissions, the constitutionality of affirmative action in higher education, inequities in public school financing, whether undocumented children had a right to public education, and the right to English language instruction in public schools. The Burger Court became a key player in the regulation of education policy, and its decisions were consequential for children of color in the struggle to achieve equal educational opportunities in the United States.

SCHOOL DESEGREGATION REMEDIES

One of the main strategies used by state and local officials to thwart compliance with *Brown*'s mandate was delay. During its first term, the Burger Court ruled in *Alexander v. Holmes County Board of Education* (1969) that the "all deliberate speed" standard for desegregation was no longer constitutionally permissible and "the obligation of every school district is to terminate dual school systems at once." Deciding whether desegregation remedies were permissible in small, rural county school systems was easy compared to a larger, metropolitan school system that enrolled 84,000 students that attended 107 schools in the South. During the 1968–1969 school year, the demographic ratio of the Charlotte-Mecklenburg school system was 71 percent white and 29 percent black, and students attended racially identifiable schools. A federal district court approved a desegregation plan that required busing, zoning, pairing, and grouping techniques to desegregate the school system.

In the landmark case, *Swann v. Charlotte-Mecklenburg Board of Education* (1971), the court clarified the standard to apply in school desegregation cases. Writing for the unanimous court, Chief Justice Burger asserted that if school officials failed to eliminate all vestiges of state-imposed segregation as mandated by *Brown I*, then federal district court judges have broad equitable powers to remedy past wrongs under *Brown II*. The nature of the constitutional violation determined the scope of the remedy to desegregate a school system. Citing *Green v. County School Board of New Kent County* (1968), Burger explained that the "policy and practice with regard to faculty, staff, transportation, extracurricular activities, and facilities are among the most important indicia of a segregated system, and the first remedial responsibility of school authorities is to eliminate invidious racial distinctions in those respects." The court affirmed the federal district judge's remedial decree in its entirety with respect to the racial balance requirement, the presence of one-race schools, alteration of attendance zones, and the use of busing to transport students to desegregate the schools.

Pervasive racial segregation in public schools existed outside of the South and many non-Southern school districts refused to desegregate after *Brown* was decided (Douglas 2005). When school desegregation cases were filed in Northern and Western states in the early 1970s, federal district courts were confronted with the complexity of devising remedies to desegregate all-black inner city school districts that were surrounded by all-white suburban districts. The justices approached the problem by applying a de jure-de facto distinction to determine whether a constitutionally required remedy existed under the Fourteenth Amendment. Rothstein (2017, xii–vii) argued that the distinction was based on the myth that de facto segregation was the consequence of individual choices and well-meaning regulations rather than systematic federal, state, and local policies that explicitly segregated every metropolitan area in the United States. *Keyes v. School District No. 1* (1973) was the court's first non-Southern school desegregation case and the first tri-ethnic case that gave Latinos the right to attend desegregated schools. Justice Brennan found that the Denver school board took racially inspired actions to segregate the schools in the northeast area of the city, and a finding of segregative intent in one part of a school system was relevant to the school board's intent in the other parts. Having placed the burden of proof on the school board, Brennan ordered a district-wide remedy in *Keyes* after a finding on remand that the Denver school system operated as a dual school system.

The use of busing students to integrate public schools in Northern school desegregation districts generated considerable public and official resistance. Extensive media coverage of extreme antibusing opposition in cities like Boston made the Northern school desegregation process more difficult. In *Milliken v. Bradley* (1974), the question before the court was whether a federal district court may impose a multidistrict, area-wide remedy that included busing to desegregate Detroit's all-black public schools. Writing for the 5–4 majority, Chief Justice Burger did not find any evidence that the actions of the outlying school districts contributed to Detroit's segregated public schools. Burger explained that a metropolitan-wide remedy would require consolidation of fifty-four independent school districts and cause an array of problems in financing and operating a new school system. In his dissent, Justice Marshall criticized the majority's ruling as "taking a giant step backwards" after "20 years of small, often difficult steps" toward the "constitutional ideal of equal justice under law" to desegregate public education. Marshall asserted that Detroit's public schools would remain racially identifiable and school district lines would be "perceived as fences to separate the races."

Some states responded to antibusing opposition by enacting statewide ballot initiatives that prohibited the use of busing as a remedy to desegregate public schools. In *Washington v. Seattle School District No. 1* (1982), the court struck down a Washington state initiative because it was drawn for racial purposes to interfere with busing as a desegregation remedy. In *Crawford v. Board of Education of the City of Los Angeles* (1982), the court upheld a California antibusing initiative that prohibited state courts from ordering mandatory student reassignment and busing unless a federal court would be permitted to do so to remedy a de jure violation. In *Pasadena City Board of Education v. Spangler* (1976), the court narrowed the *Swann* ruling when it rejected a federal district court's desegregation order that no school in the district should have a majority of minority students after a finding of intentional segregation and white flight to the suburbs that resulted in all black schools. Justice Rehnquist asserted that the no majority requirement would have forced the school district to remedy resegregation in perpetuity. In *Dayton Board of Education v. Brinkman* (1979) and *Columbus Board of Education v. Penick* (1979), the Burger Court demonstrated its willingness to approve court-ordered, systemwide remedies based on findings by the lower courts that the school boards' actions had an unconstitutional segregative purpose and impact to warrant a systemwide remedy.

The outcomes in the school desegregation cases reveal that the court attempted to chart a path toward desegregation by regulating the remedial power of federal district courts. As shown in table 6.2, the *Milliken* decision was a turning point in the court's school desegregation jurisprudence. The court was more likely to circumscribe the remedial powers of federal judges in non-Southern cases, but districtwide remedies were permitted when minority plaintiffs could prove that the actions taken by school boards intended to perpetuate segregated schools.

Table 6.2. Burger Court School Desegregation Cases, 1969–1986

Case	Vote	Outcome
Alexander v. Holmes County Board of Education (1969)	8–0	Held that the "all deliberate speed" standard was no longer constitutionally permissible (L)
Dowell v. Board of Education of Oklahoma City Public Schools (1969)	8–0	Held that the school board must issue a desegregation plan at once on the authority of *Alexander* (L)
Carter v. West Feliciana Parish School Board (1970)	6–2	Held that the school board must take the necessary steps to desegregate schools on the authority of *Alexander* (L)
Swann v. Charlotte-Mecklenburg Board of Education (1971)	9–0	Held that the nature of the constitutional violation determined the scope of the remedy to achieve a desegregated school system (L)
Davis v. Board of School Commissioners of Mobile County (1971)	9–0	Held that the use of busing and split zoning to desegregate schools was permissible (L)
McDaniel v. Barresi (1971)	9–0	Held that a school board could take race into account to convert to a unitary school district without violating Title IV of the CRA of 1964 (L)
North Carolina Board of Education v. Swann (1971)	9–0	Struck down the state's antibusing law (L)
Wright v. Council of Emporia (1972)	5–4	Struck down the creation of a new school district from an existing one because it impeded the dismantling of its dual school system (L)
United States v. Scotland Neck City Board of Education (1972)	9–0	Struck down an attempt to carve out a new school district from an existing one on the authority of *Wright* (L)
Keyes v. School District No. 1 (1973)	7–1	Held that a finding of segregative intent in one part of a school system was adequate for an inferential finding that de jure segregation was systemwide (L)
Milliken v. Bradley (1974)	5–4	Struck down the use of a systemwide remedy that included busing to desegregate Detroit's public schools (C)

continued on next page

Table 6.2. Continued.

Case	Vote	Outcome
Pasadena City Board of Education v. Spangler (1976)	6–2	Held that a district court had exceeded its authority to enforce a no majority of any minority requirement once segregation practices were eliminated (C)
Milliken v. Bradley (1977)	9–0	Upheld the use of remedial programs as part of a school desegregation decree (L)
Dayton Board of Education v. Brinkman (1977)	8–0	Set aside a systemwide remedy due to lack of evidence that the school board's actions intentionally segregated the schools (C)
Columbus Board of Education v. Penick (1979)	7–2	held that the school board actions had an unconstitutional segregative purpose and impact to warrant a systemwide remedy (L)
Dayton Board of Education v. Brinkman (1979)	5–4	Upheld the use of a systemwide remedy because the school board intentionally operated a dual school system (L)
Washington v. Seattle School District No. 1 (1982)	5–4	Struck down a state initiative that prohibited the use of busing as a remedy to desegregate schools on Fourteenth Amendment grounds (L)
Crawford v. Board of Education of the City of Los Angeles (1982)	8–1	Upheld a state proposition that prohibited state court ordered busing as a remedy to desegregate schools unless a federal court would be permitted to do so (C)

Source: Created by the author.

Note: C for conservative outcomes, and L for liberal outcomes.

Discriminatory Private School Admissions

Brown's mandate to desegregate public schools contributed to the rise of private segregated schools in the South. Title VI of the CRA of 1964 prohibited public and private education institutions that received federal funding from discriminating against students on the basis of race, color, or national origin. It was an open question whether nonsectarian private schools that maintained racially discriminatory admissions policies could be sued under § 1981 (formerly § 1 of the Civil Rights Act of 1866). The court resolved that question in *Runyon v. McCrary* (1976) after parents sued two private schools when they refused to admit their children on account of race. Citing *Jones v. Alfred H. Mayer Company* (1968), the court ruled that

§ 1981 reached acts of racial discrimination in the making and enforcement of private contracts. Justice Stewart acknowledged that white parents may have "a First Amendment right to send their children to educational institutions that promote the belief that racial segregation is desirable" and they "have an equal right to attend such institutions," but it does not follow that the "*practice* of excluding racial minorities from such institutions is also protected by the same principle." Justice White, joined by Rehnquist in dissent, asserted that the right to make contracts "was therefore a right to enter into binding agreements only with willing second parties."

In 1970, the Internal Revenue Service (IRS) revoked the tax exemption and deduction privileges from two private Christian institutions, Bob Jones University and the Goldsboro Christian Schools, because of their racially discriminatory admissions policies. In response to pressure from the religious right, the Reagan administration reversed its policy to deny tax exempt status to segregated private schools and it petitioned the court to dismiss the IRS case against the schools on mootness grounds. In *Bob Jones University v. United States* (1983), the court found that the IRS policy

Table 6.3. Burger Court Private School Discrimination Cases, 1969–1986

Case	Vote	Outcome
Norwood v. Harrison (1973)	9–0	Held that Mississippi's textbook lending program to racially segregated private schools was unconstitutional (L)
Gilmore v. Montgomery, Alabama (1974)	9–0	Held that the lower court properly prohibited the City of Montgomery from permitting racially segregated private schools' exclusive access to its recreational facilities (L)
Runyon v. McCrary (1976)	7–2	Held that § 1981 applied to the making and enforcement of contracts in private school admissions (L)
Bob Jones University v. United States (1983)	8–1	Upheld the denial of federal tax benefits to religious schools that maintained racially discriminatory admissions policies (L)
Allen v. Wright (1984)	5–3	Held that black parents lacked standing to sue the IRS in a nationwide class action lawsuit to deny tax exempt status to racially segregated private schools (C)

Source: Created by the author.

Note: C for conservative outcomes, and L for liberal outcomes.

was consistent with Titles IV and VI of the Civil Rights Act of 1964 that "racial discrimination in education violates a fundamental public policy." Chief Justice Burger explained that Congress vested the interpretation of federal tax laws in the IRS and it could exercise its authority to "meet changing conditions and new problems." He went on to say that as part of the oversight process, Congress had the authority to overturn the IRS's interpretations of the tax laws but failed to do so. Justice Rehnquist asserted in his dissent that Congress's failure to statutorily reverse the IRS's position should not constitutionally empower the court to act for it. In *Allen v. Wright* (1984), the court made it more difficult for black parents to challenge the tax-exempt status of segregated private schools on standing to sue grounds.

ADDITIONAL BARRIERS TO EQUAL EDUCATIONAL OPPORTUNITY

The landmark case *San Antonio Independent School District v. Rodriguez* (1973) was the most important public education case affecting students of color since *Brown*. Latino parents filed a class action lawsuit that challenged the constitutionality of the property tax system used to finance public education in Texas. Public school financing was shared between the state, which supplied eighty percent of the funding, and school districts, which were responsible for the remaining twenty percent. School districts imposed a property tax to pay their share of funding, but the dual funding system resulted in wide disparities between wealthy school districts and poorer districts, because wealthier school districts could generate more revenue at a lower tax rate than poorer districts that taxed at a much higher rate. A three-judge district court applied the strict scrutiny standard to the case and found that discrimination based on wealth was suspect and education was a fundamental right that required the state to demonstrate a compelling interest to justify its method of financing public schools.

In *Rodriguez*, the court upheld the school financing scheme under the equal protection clause's rational basis test. Justice Lewis Powell found that the poorest families were not necessarily clustered in the poorest property districts. He asserted that the equal protection clause did not guarantee absolute equality or precisely equal advantages, at least where wealth was concerned. Powell explained that the school financing scheme did not operate to the disadvantage of any suspect class, because wealth lacked the traditional indicia of suspectness for equal protection analysis—"the class is not saddled with such disabilities, or subjected to such a history of purposeful unequal treatment, or relegated to such a position of political powerlessness as to command extraordinary protection from the majoritarian political process." Although *Brown* recognized that education was perhaps the most important function of state and local governments, Powell asserted that education as a fundamental right was not explicitly or implicitly protected under the Constitution. Powell concluded that it was best left up to lawmakers at the state and local levels to determine the best fiscal plan for financing public schools; otherwise, all local fiscal schemes would be subjected to equal protection challenges.

Justice Thurgood Marshall understood the implications of the majority's decision—that it would shut off an important avenue to address educational inequality based on claims of racial discrimination and economic status. In his dissent, Marshall criticized the majority's application of the rigid two-tiered approach to equal protection cases, and he believed that "careful judicial scrutiny" should have been applied to the case, because poverty was not a permanent disability. Three years later, the court reached a consensus to add a third level of scrutiny to analyze equal protection claims in the landmark gender discrimination case *Craig v. Boren* (1976). Under the less demanding intermediate level of review, statutory classifications must serve important governmental objectives, and they must be substantially related to the achievement of those objectives.

The revised equal protection framework was applied to a class action lawsuit that challenged the constitutionality of a Texas law that required the withholding of state funds from local school districts that enrolled undocumented children. In *Plyler v. Doe* (1982), the state argued that congressional immigration policy permitted the state to deny benefits to undocumented children, that it needed to protect itself from an influx of undocumented immigrants and that undocumented children placed economic burdens on the state. Justice Brennan acknowledged that undocumented immigrants cannot be treated as a suspect class and education was not a fundamental right. However, Brennan asserted that the Texas law imposed a lifetime of hardship on undocumented children who had no control over their parents' conduct or their own disabling status. To penalize them would "not comport with fundamental conceptions of justice," and to withhold education from undocumented children would mark them with the stigma of illiteracy and deny them the ability "to live within the structure of our civic institutions." Writing for the dissenters, Chief Justice Burger argued that it was not irrational for the state to conclude that it did not have the same responsibility to provide benefits to undocumented immigrants at the expense of persons lawfully present in the United States.

Although Title VI of the Civil Rights Act of 1964 prohibited discrimination on the basis of race, religion, or national origin by any educational institution receiving federal funds, it did not specifically address language discrimination. In the late 1960s, Chinese parents filed a class action lawsuit against the San Francisco public school system for its failure to provide non-English speaking Chinese children English language instruction on Title VI and equal protection grounds. In *Lau v. Nichols* (1974), the court did not reach the constitutional question, but it ordered the end to denying children of language minority groups equal access to English language learning in public schools under Title VI. Writing for the unanimous court, Justice William Douglas found that "there is no equality of treatment merely by providing students with the same facilities, textbooks, teachers, and curriculum; for students who do not understand English are effectively foreclosed from any meaningful education."

Affirmative Action in Higher Education

Prior to the civil rights movement, black students had limited access to higher education outside of historically black colleges and universities. In response to student protests and the demands of the civil rights movement, administrators at selective public and private colleges and universities developed affirmative action programs in the late 1960s and 1970s to enroll more minority students at the undergraduate and graduate levels (Bowen and Bok 1998; Urofsky 2020). Reverse discrimination lawsuits were filed by white males who claimed that they were denied entry into selective professional universities because lesser qualified minority applicants were given preferential admission. When Marco DeFunis was denied admission to the University of Washington's law school, he sued the university on the ground that its preferential admissions policy discriminated against him in violation of the equal protection clause. The trial court ordered his admission for the fall 1971 class, and by the time the case reached the court, DeFunis was in his final year of law school. In *DeFunis v. Odegaard* (1974), the court dismissed the case on mootness grounds in a 5–4 per curiam decision.

Alan Bakke was a thirty-one-year-old white male who decided to change careers from engineering to medicine. He applied to two medical schools for fall 1973 admission, but he was rejected by both. The following year, Bakke applied to eleven medical schools, and his applications were rejected by all of them. Bakke and his attorney devised a litigation plan to challenge the legality of the medical school's special admissions program at the University of California, Davis, with the real objective to get him admitted in time to join the 1974 fall class (Dreyfuss and Lawrence 1979, 35–36). The medical school's special admissions program reserved sixteen seats out of one hundred for disadvantaged applicants who were black, Latino, and Asian American. In his lawsuit, Bakke claimed that he would have been admitted but for the admission of minority students with significantly lower GPA, MCAT, and benchmark scores. The California Supreme Court found that the admissions program violated the equal protection clause, race could not be taken into account in the admissions process, and it ordered Bakke's admission, which was stayed pending review by the Supreme Court.

In *Regents of the University of California v. Bakke* (1978), the court upheld the constitutionality of affirmative action admissions programs in a narrow 5–4 plurality opinion written by Justice Powell. Justice Stevens's opinion, joined by Chief Justice Burger, Stewart, and Rehnquist, asserted that there was no need to reach the constitutional issues because the admissions program violated Title VI of the Civil Rights Act of 1964 and Bakke should be admitted to the university. Justice Brennan's opinion, joined by White, Marshall, and Blackmun, asserted that the intermediate level of scrutiny should be applied to the case because the university's goal to remedy the effects of past societal discrimination was sufficiently important to justify the use of the race-conscious admissions program.

Justice Powell assumed that Bakke had a statutory right to sue the university under Title VI, and he found that racial classifications that violated Title VI also violated the equal protection clause. Turning to the constitutional question, Powell established that racial classifications were always suspect, and therefore the special admissions program must be tested under the strict scrutiny standard. Powell found that the university's interest in the attainment of a diverse student body was compelling to satisfy the first part of the strict scrutiny test, but he rejected the means used by the university to achieve diversity. Because the two-track, sixteen seat set-aside program operated as a quota, Powell asserted that there were other permissible ways to take race into account in the admissions process. He concluded that the medical school's admissions program violated Bakke's equal protection rights under strict scrutiny, and he should be admitted, but race could be used as a factor in the admissions process.

Justice Marshall wrote a lengthy separate opinion that justified the use of affirmative action programs based on the two-hundred-year legacy of societal discrimination experienced by blacks in America. After chronicling the extensive history, Marshall concluded that "it is more than a little ironic that, after several hundred years of class-based discrimination against Negroes, the Court is unwilling to hold that a class-based remedy for that discrimination is permissible." He explained that blacks were discriminated against not as individuals but solely because of the color of their skins. "Because of a legacy of unequal treatment," Marshall concluded that "we now must permit the institutions of this society to give consideration to race in making decisions about who will hold the positions of influence, affluence, and prestige in America."

In the landmark *Bakke* case, the court upheld the use of a race-conscious remedy to promote the goal of diversity in higher education under the demanding strict scrutiny test. However, the precedent was on shaky constitutional ground because the justices failed to reach a consensus about how to approach the issue under the equal protection clause. Messer-Davidow (2021) found that the most important consequence of the *DeFunis* and *Bakke* decisions for the development of the law was that they galvanized the conservative legal movement to frame the affirmative action debate as reverse discrimination to dismantle affirmative action programs by litigation.

Voting Rights

The Voting Rights Act of 1965 expanded the electorate in the South by removing race-based obstacles to voting. Because the transformative law threatened the political power base of white elected officials, Southern state and local governments responded by instituting race neutral voting schemes to prevent blacks and Latinos from winning or deciding elections (Derfner 1973, 552–57). The schemes consisted of vote dilution practices (racial gerrymandering, annexations, run-off elections, at-large elections, and multimember districts), barriers to obtaining public office (abolishing offices, making elective offices appointive, limiting the responsibilities of offices likely to be won by blacks, imposing stiff requirements for qualifying to run in primaries), and hindrances to black voting (withholding information about registration, voting procedures, or party activities from black voters, conducting reregistrations or purging the voter rolls, moving polling places or failing to provide adequate voting facilities in areas of increased black registration). Minority voters filed second generation voting rights lawsuits to prevent the dilution of their votes in local, state, and national elections under the Voting Rights Act and the Fourteenth and Fifteenth Amendments.

Section 2 of the Voting Rights Act

Political equality encompasses the right to be protected from electoral arrangements that pose serious threats to the maximization of minority groups' political influence. Davidson (1992, 24) defined minority vote dilution as the "process whereby election laws or practices, either singly or in concert, combine with systematic bloc voting among an identifiable group to dominate or cancel the voting strength of at least one minority group." In *Whitcomb v. Chavis* (1971), the Burger Court rejected a challenge brought by black voters that claimed that the use of multimember districts for electing members of the Indiana state legislature diluted their votes under the equal protection clause. The court found that they failed to prove that the multimember districts were conceived or operated as purposeful devices to further racial discrimination. Two years later, the court reconsidered the dilutive effect of multimember districts in *White v. Regester* (1973) after Latino and black voters challenged a Texas state house reapportionment plan that drew super-sized multimember districts for Bexar and Dallas counties. Justice White found that in light of the past and present documented history of racial discrimination against minority voters, which affected their ability to participate in the political process, the plaintiffs met *Whitcomb*'s burden of proof standard that the multimember districts diluted their votes.

In 1975, black voters sued the city of Mobile, Alabama on the ground that the city's use of at-large elections to select its commissioners diluted their voting strength in violation of the Fourteenth and Fifteenth Amendments and § 2 of the Voting Rights Act. In *Mobile v. Bolden* (1980), the court reversed the lower court's finding that the at-large electoral arrangement was unconstitutional. Writing for the 6–3 plurality, Justice Potter Stewart applied the discriminatory intent standard to the case that required black voters to prove racially discriminatory motivation under the Fifteenth Amendment. When Stewart examined the evidence presented in the case, he found that it fell far short of proving that white officials conceived or operated a purposeful electoral arrangement to further racial discrimination. The dissenters, Justices White, Brennan, and Marshall, pointed out that prior vote dilution cases required only a showing of discriminatory impact to justify invalidating a multimember electoral arrangement and the intent requirement was inconsistent with the protection against denial or abridgment of the vote on account of race under § 2 and the Fifteenth Amendment.

The *Bolden* decision was controversial, because it required minority plaintiffs to find smoking gun evidence based on the motives of legislators to successfully challenge electoral arrangements that minimized or canceled out the effects of their votes. Civil rights groups and voting rights attorneys responded to the court's restrictive approach to vote dilution cases by pressuring Congress to statutorily reverse the decision based on Stewart's declaration that the language of § 2 was simply a restatement of the Fifteenth Amendment. The Voting Rights Act Amendments of 1982 changed the language of § 2 to require a totality of the circumstances approach for proving minority vote dilution—a violation of § 2 is established if, based on the totality of the circumstances, it is shown that any voting law or practice results in members of a protected class to have less opportunity than other members to elect representatives of their choice.

Thornburg v. Gingles (1986) was the first vote dilution case to interpret the amended § 2 of the Voting Rights Act. Black voters challenged a North Carolina state redistricting plan that consisted of one single-member and six multimember districts on the ground that it impaired their ability to elect representatives of their choice. In a fractured plurality opinion, the court agreed that the discriminatory effect of the redistricting plan diluted the minority vote in violation of § 2. Justice Brennan devised a new test for proving vote dilution under § 2 that required a determination whether the minority group in a district is sufficiently large and geographically compact, whether the minority group is politically cohesive, whether the minority group can demonstrate that a white majority voting bloc usually defeats their preferred candidate, and based on the totality of the circumstances, whether the minority group has less opportunity than other voters to elect their preferred candidate. Because Congress exercised its power to statutorily override the *Bolden* decision, the court was given the opportunity to break new ground in *Gingles* by devising a results test that made it easier for minority voters to challenge vote dilution schemes that weakened their political influence. The policy impact of the landmark *Thornburg v. Gingles* decision was significant because § 2 of the Voting Rights Act applies nationwide and the results test would be applied to vote dilution challenges that were subject to § 5's preclearance provision.

Table 6.4. Burger Court Vote Dilution Cases, 1969–1986

Case	Vote	Outcome
Whitcomb v. Chavis (1971)	6–3	Held that minority plaintiffs must prove that multimember districts were conceived as purposeful devices to dilute their votes under the equal protection clause (C)
White v. Regester (1973)	6–3	Held that the use of multimember districts in a state redistricting plan violated the equal protection clause based on past and present findings of voting discrimination against blacks and Latinos (L)
Connor v. Finch (1977)	7–1	Held that the lower court's reapportionment plan failed to draw legislative districts that were reasonably contiguous and compact to avoid diluting black voting strength (L)
Mobile v. Bolden (1980)	6–3	Held that minority plaintiffs must prove discriminatory intent when challenging the constitutionality of at-large electoral arrangements under the equal protection clause and the Fifteenth Amendment (C)
Rogers v. Lodge (1982)	6–3	Held that the at-large election of members to the board of commissioners unconstitutionally diluted the votes of black citizens under the Fourteenth and Fifteenth Amendments (L)
Thornburg v. Gingles (1986)	9–0	Established a results test that made it easier to prove minority vote dilution under amended § 2 of the Voting Rights Act (L)

Source: Created by the author.

Note: C for conservative outcomes, and L for liberal outcomes.

SECTION 5 OF THE VOTING RIGHTS ACT

The preclearance provision of the Voting Rights Act prohibited any state or political subdivision from implementing any voting changes unless they had been approved by the attorney general or by a declaratory judgment issued by a three-judge district court in the District of Columbia. Section

5 fully covered nine states: Alabama, Alaska, Arizona, Georgia, Louisiana, Mississippi, South Carolina, Texas, and Virginia. Six states were partially covered by the law: California, Florida, New York, North Carolina, South Dakota, and Michigan. Section 5 worked in tandem with § 4(a), the coverage provision, which established a formula to identify areas of the country where racial discrimination in voting was more prevalent. Section 4(b), the bailout provision, allowed state and local jurisdictions to be released from coverage by judicial preclearance if they had met the rigorous criteria required in the law.

As shown in table 6.5, the Burger Court applied the principle established in *Allen v. State Board of Elections* (1969) that § 5 reached any state

Table 6.5. Burger Court Preclearance Cases, 1969–1986

Case	Vote	Outcome
Perkins v. Matthews (1971)	8–1	Held that polling place, annexation, and changes from ward to at-large elections were subject to preclearance (L)
Georgia v. United States (1973)	6–3	Held that Georgia's 1972 house reapportionment plan had the potential of diluting black voting strength under § 5 (L)
Richmond v. United States (1975)	5–3	Held that annexation did not violate § 5 because the post-annexation system fairly recognized minority voters' political potential (C)
Beer v. United States (1976)	5–3	Held that § 5 prohibited voting changes that would lead to retrogressive effects (C)
United Jewish Organizations v. Carey (1977)	7–1	Held that a state reapportionment plan that created majority-minority districts did not violate the rights of the Hasidic Jewish community as white voters (L)
United States v. Sheffield Board of Commissioners (1978)	6–3	Held that a city is a subdivision as defined by § 5, and voting changes must be precleared (L)
Doughtery County Board of Education v. White (1978)	5–4	Held that a requirement that candidates take an unpaid leave of absence while seeking elective office was subject to preclearance (L)
Rome v. United States (1980)	6–3	Held that a city may not use the bailout procedure to escape § 5's preclearance requirements (L)
McDaniel v. Sanchez (1981)	7–2	Held that a court-approved reapportionment plan to elect county commissioners must be precleared under § 5 (L)

Case	Vote	Outcome
Port Arthur v. United States (1982)	6–3	Held that a district court did not exceed its authority by conditioning preclearance of an electoral plan that favored a plurality vote requirement for city council at-large elections (L)
Lockhart v. United States (1983)	6–3	Held that the use of a numbered post system and staggered terms for electing members of a city council did not have a retrogressive effect on Latino voting strength (C)
McCain v. Lybrand (1984)	9–0	Held that a jurisdiction with a history of discrimination must specifically identify proposed changes in their voting practices or procedures for a preclearance request (L)

Source: Created by the author.

Note: C for conservative outcomes, and L for liberal outcomes.

enactment that altered the election law of a covered jurisdiction in even a minor way in most cases. In an important preclearance case that involved competing group demands for representation, the court in *United Jewish Organizations v. Carey* (1977) rejected an attack on the use of race-conscious remedies in redistricting. The Hasidic Jewish community argued that a 1974 New York redistricting plan that split the community into two districts diluted their voting strength for the purposes of achieving a racial quota under the Fourteenth and Fifteenth Amendments. Justice White viewed their objections as claims of discrimination against white voters. He explained that the use of racial criteria was not confined to eliminating the effects of past discriminatory redistricting, and it was left up to the states to decide how to draw black majority districts to comply with § 5. He concluded that as long as whites as a group have fair representation, no individual white voter has a constitutional right to live in a district in which his or her race is in the majority.

Economic Equality

The Civil Rights Act of 1964 contained a provision that advanced an important policy goal of the transformative egalitarian alliance—economic equality. Title VII of the Civil Rights Act made employment discrimination practices illegal against any person on account of race, color, religion, sex, or national origin—classes of individuals who were considered protected because of their history of unequal treatment in the workplace. Title VII recognized two types of illegal employment discrimination: disparate treatment and disparate impact. Disparate treatment occurs when an employer intentionally treats a member of a protected class differently. Disparate impact cases involve a neutral employment practice that negatively affects members of a protected class. Title VII applies to private employers with fifteen or more employees, public employers at the federal, state, and local levels, employment agencies, and labor unions. The law created the Equal Employment Opportunity Commission to enforce Title VII's provisions. Title VII would become the primary statutory weapon used by members of protected classes to challenge discriminatory employment practices.

Title VII Remedies

The first employment discrimination cases established the standards and tests to apply in Title VII lawsuits and the legal remedies available for victims of employment discrimination. The court interpreted Title VII for the first time in the landmark case *Griggs v. Duke Power Company* (1971). In *Griggs*, the LDF represented black employees who challenged the company's stringent education and promotion requirements for employment and transfer to nonlabor departments. Chief Justice Burger found that the objective of Title VII "was to achieve equality of employment opportunities and remove barriers that have operated in the past to favor an identifiable group of white employees over other employees." He explained that "practices, procedures, or tests neutral on their face, and even neutral in terms of intent, cannot be maintained if they operate to 'freeze' the status quo of prior discriminatory practices." Burger asserted that Title VII "proscribes not only overt discrimination but also practices that are fair in form, but discriminatory in operation. The touchstone is business necessity. If an employment practice, which operates to exclude Negroes cannot be shown to be related to job performance, the practice is prohibited." *Griggs* established the adverse impact standard of proof—Title VII was violated when employer practices had a discriminatory impact on protected groups regardless of the employer's intent unless business necessity justified such practices.

Title VII authorized a private right to file discrimination lawsuits, and the Equal Employment Opportunity Commission was granted the authority to file pattern or practice lawsuits in the public's interest to attack systemic discrimination by businesses that maintained racially discriminatory practices. In *Teamsters v. United States* (1976), the federal government brought a pattern or practice lawsuit against the Teamsters union and a trucking company because of their discriminatory hiring, assignment, and promotion policies. Blacks and Latinos were given lower paying, less desirable jobs as local city drivers, and the more desirable and better paying long haul line driver jobs were reserved for whites. Justice Stewart found that the government successfully presented statistical evidence that proved the existence of a pattern or practice of discrimination against minority workers, and the company's attempts to rebut that conclusion were unsuccessful. The court was less receptive to the federal government's argument that the minority employees should be granted retroactive seniority for injuries suffered because of the union's unlawful employment discrimination. Stewart found that the seniority system was bona fide and minority employees who suffered discrimination prior to the enactment of Title VII were not entitled to relief. Justices Marshall and Brennan argued in dissent that the union's seniority system should not be protected because it put minority workers in a position to surrender seniority accumulated in their old jobs to take advantage of the opportunity to advance to more desirable jobs. In subsequent decisions, the court shielded seniority systems from racial discrimination lawsuits.

In 1970, black police officers sued the District of Columbia's police department, city officials, and the Civil Service Commission for racially discriminatory promotion policies. The complaint alleged that a written personnel test that had no relationship to job performance excluded a disproportionately high number of black applicants for police officer positions in the department in violation of the due process clause of the Fifth Amendment. The appeals court applied the *Griggs* disparate impact standard and found that a far greater proportion of blacks failed the test than did whites. In *Washington v. Davis* (1976), the court addressed a question that the parties had not raised or briefed: whether the equal protection intent standard or Title VII's disproportionate impact standard should apply to a public sector employment discrimination lawsuit (Graetz and Greenhouse 2016, 287–91). Justice Byron White found that the disparate impact standard was "not the constitutional rule" and the court has "never held that the constitutional standard for adjudicating claims of invidious racial discrimination is identical to the standards applicable under Title VII." After an extensive analysis of prior precedents, White established that a law that is claimed to be racially discriminatory "must ultimately be traced to a racially discriminatory purpose." A lesser standard would invalidate "a whole range of tax, welfare, public service, regulatory, and licensing statutes that may be more burdensome to the poor and to the average black than to the more affluent white."

Justice Brennan, joined by Marshall, dissented on the statutory ground that the police department did not meet its burden of proof with regard to the personnel test, and when Congress amended Title VII to include public employees in 1972, the same substantive protections were given to the black police officers and applicants. The landmark case *Washington v. Davis* (1976) made it more difficult to prove racial discrimination in the workplace. The court held that proof of discriminatory intent, not proof of disparate impact, was necessary to establish a claim of racial discrimination under the equal protection clause. The intent to discriminate standard required a burden of proof that was difficult to satisfy, and it was extended to cases outside the employment discrimination context: school desegregation, voting rights, housing discrimination, and death penalty challenges.

Table 6.6. Burger Court Employment Discrimination Cases, 1969–1986

Case	Vote	Outcome
Griggs v. Duke Power Company (1971)	8–0	Held that Title VII is violated when employer practices have a disparate impact on minority employees unless business necessity justified the practices (L)
McDonnell Douglas Corporation v. Green (1973)	9–0	Established a burden-shifting framework to prove a prima facie case of racial discrimination under Title VII (L)
Alexander v. Gardner-Denver Company (1974)	9–0	Held that minority employees were not bound by a union arbitration decision and could pursue their rights independently under Title VII (L)
Albemarle Paper Company v. Moody (1975)	7–1	Held that backpay should be denied only for reasons that do not frustrate the purpose of Title VII (L)
Johnson v. Railway Express Agency (1975)	9–0	Held that § 1981 affords a federal remedy against racial discrimination in private employment separate, distinct, and independent from Title VII (L)
McDonald v. Santa Fe Trail Transportation Company (1976)	7–2	Held that the language and legislative history of Title VII apply to whites and nonwhites alike (L)
Franks v. Bowman Transportation Company (1976)	5–3	Held that a retroactive seniority award was appropriate to a protected class since they had been victims of discrimination by the company (L)

Case	Vote	Outcome
Washington v. Davis (1976)	7–2	Required a showing of discriminatory intent under the equal protection clause to prove public sector employment discrimination (C)
Teamsters v. United States (1977)	7–2	Held that the seniority system was bona fide under Title VII, and minority employees who suffered pre-act discrimination were not entitled to retroactive seniority (C)
Hazelwood School District v. United States (1977)	8–1	Upheld the use of statistical evidence to establish a prima facie case of workforce disparities under Title VII (L)
Furnco Construction Corporation v. Waters (1978)	7–2	Held that employers must be given latitude to introduce statistics to determine whether the workforce was racially balanced under Title VII (C)
American Tobacco Company v. Patterson (1982)	5–4	Held that Congress did not intend to distinguish between seniority systems adopted before and after the Civil Rights Act of 1964, and Title VII protects bona fide seniority systems created after the law's passage (C)
Pullman-Standard v. Swint (1982)	7–2	Held that a showing of discriminatory purpose was required to invalidate a seniority system under Title VII even though the seniority system had some discriminatory consequences (C)
Connecticut v. Teal (1982)	5–4	Held that an employer's fair treatment of a protected class was not a defense to an individual claim of discrimination with regard to the hiring or promotion process under Title VII (L)
United States Postal Service Board of Governors v. Aikens (1983)	9–0	Held that victims of discrimination can prove their case by direct or circumstantial evidence under Title VII (L)
Bazemore v. Friday (1986)	9–0	Held that an extension service was obligated to eradicate salary disparities between white and black employees that began prior to the date Title VII was made applicable to public employees (L)

Source: Created by the author.

Note: C for conservative outcomes, and L for liberal outcomes.

Affirmative Action in Employment

One year after the *Bakke* case was decided, the Burger Court considered whether private affirmative action employment plans were permissible under Title VII. In 1974, the steelworkers' union and the Kaiser Aluminum company agreed to eliminate racial imbalances at Kaiser's almost all-white craft plants. The voluntary affirmative action plan reserved fifty percent of the openings in in-plant craft-training programs for black employees until the percentage of black craftworkers in a plant was commensurate with the percentage of blacks in the local labor force. When Brian Weber's bid for admission as a craft trainee was rejected, he brought a reverse discrimination class action lawsuit against the company and the union. In *United Steelworkers of America v. Weber* (1979), the court held that a private, voluntary, race-conscious affirmative action plan did not violate Title VII. Justice Brennan found that the training program was consistent with the purpose and legislative history of Title VII to allow the private sector to take effective steps to accomplish the statute's objective. When Brennan examined the operation of the program, he found that it did not unnecessarily trammel the interest of white employees, it did not require the discharge of white workers, it was a temporary measure, and it was intended to eliminate a manifest racial imbalance. Justice Rehnquist, joined by Chief Justice Burger in dissent, reached the opposite conclusion that Title VII outlawed all racial discrimination, especially in the context of Kaiser's "racially discriminatory admissions quota."

By 1980, the color-blind approach to race had gained considerable support among legal conservatives and a minority of justices on the Burger Court. In *Fullilove v. Klutznick* (1980), the court addressed the constitutionality of a federal program that gave preferential treatment to minority business enterprises (MBEs) under the Public Works Employment Act of 1977. The law required at least ten percent of the federal public works funds be set aside for minority owned businesses at the state and local levels. White construction contractors challenged the MBE provision on the ground that it established an impermissible racial quota. Six justices voted to uphold the constitutionality of MBE provision on different constitutional grounds. The Burger, White, and Powell bloc asserted that the law was valid under Congress's spending power in Article I, § 8, Clause 1. At the outset, Burger rejected the "contention that in the remedial context the Congress must act in a wholly 'color-blind' fashion." Burger found that the MBE provision was carefully crafted and had a number of safeguards in place to prevent unjust participation by businesses that were not bona fide MBEs. He concluded that the MBE provision would survive judicial review under the *Bakke* precedent. The Marshall, Brennan, and Blackmun bloc took the position that the MBE program was constitutional under the intermediate level of scrutiny. Justice Stewart, joined by Rehnquist in dissent, asserted that the MBE provision violated the "our constitution is color-blind" principle and that the equal protection clause "has one clear and central meaning—it absolutely prohibits invidious discrimination by government."

In *Wygant v. Jackson Board of Education* (1986), the court singled out layoffs as a remedy that was too intrusive and burdensome on whites in a challenge to a collective bargaining agreement between the school board and the teachers' union that gave minority teachers preference during layoffs. Justice Powell rejected the school board's societal discrimination justification as being "insufficient and overexpansive" "for imposing discriminatory legal remedies that work against innocent people." When Powell applied the strict scrutiny test to the case, he found that the layoff plan was not narrowly tailored, and less intrusive means to achieve the desired objectives were available. Writing for the dissenters, Justice Marshall asserted that he also believed that layoffs were unfair, but "unfairness ought not be confused with constitutional injury." The dissenters agreed with the evidence presented by the union and school officials that the goal of integrating the faculty could not be achieved by eliminating those last hired when layoffs became necessary. As shown in table 6.7, the Burger Court's approval of affirmative action employment plans was mixed. The court was less likely to uphold plans involving layoffs of white employees and remedies that threatened existing seniority systems.

Fair Housing

The issue of fair housing was virtually absent from the national political agenda between the *Shelley v. Kraemer* (1948) decision and the Kennedy administration (Lamb 1981). In 1962, President Kennedy signed Executive Order 11063 to curtail racial discrimination in federally assisted housing, but the order was ineffective because it only reached a small proportion of housing. In 1968, the Johnson administration and Congress responded to the demand for federal legislation to remedy discriminatory housing practices and housing segregation in the Civil Rights Act of 1968. Title

Table 6.7. Burger Court Affirmative Action Employment Cases, 1969–1986

Case	Vote	Outcome
United Steelworkers of American v. Weber (1979)	5–2	Upheld a voluntary private sector affirmative action plan under Title VII (L)
Fullilove v. Klutznick (1980)	6–3	Upheld a federal 10% set-aside plan for minority businesses under the spending clause (L)
Firefighters v. Stotts (1984)	6–3	Invalidated a modified layoff plan to prevent black firefighters from layoffs (C)
Sheet Metal Workers v. EEOC (1986)	5–4	Held that fines and race-conscious relief were appropriate remedies when a union has engaged in persistent discrimination against blacks and Latinos under Title VII (L)
Firefighters v. Cleveland (1986)	6–3	Held that Title VII does not preclude the adoption of a voluntary consent decree to benefit individuals who were not identified victims of the city's discriminatory practices (L)
Wygant v. Jackson Board of Education (1986)	5–4	Struck down a provision in a collective bargaining agreement that required the layoffs of white teachers with more seniority and the retention of minority teachers with less seniority under the equal protection clause (C)

Source: Created by the author.

Note: C for conservative outcomes, and L for liberal outcomes.

VIII, also known as the Fair Housing Act, prohibited discrimination on the basis of race, color, national origin, sex, and religion in the sale, rental, or financing of housing. The law made the following practices illegal: refusal to sell or rent to people of color, advertising discriminatory preferences, using different prices and qualification criteria for people of color, racial steering, blockbusting, mortgage and insurance discrimination, redlining, predatory lending practices, exclusionary zoning, and racial harassment. Title VIII created the Department of Housing and Urban Development (HUD) to administer the law.

The court signaled in *James v. Valtierra* (1971) that it would not interfere with the state's use of democratic processes such as referenda to defeat low-cost housing proposals by voters. Justice Black distinguished the charter amendment in *Hunter v. Erickson* (1969) from the referendum requirement in *James* by pointing out that the former provision rested on race, but California's referendum rested on the state's long history of using the procedure to give citizens a voice on questions of public policy. The court was more responsive to a lawsuit brought against the agencies directly responsible for administering fair housing laws when they engaged in unconstitutional conduct in selecting sites for public housing. Black residents who lived in public housing sued the Chicago Housing Authority and HUD on the ground that both agencies deliberately worked together for fifteen years to avoid placing family public housing sites in white neighborhoods. In *Hills v. Gautreaux* (1976), a unanimous court found that HUD's site selection policy confined black residents to segregated public housing in the city even though the relevant geographic area was the Chicago housing market. *Gautreaux* authorized a metropolitan wide remedy that enabled several thousand low-income black families to move from the Chicago inner city to the middle-class suburbs (Rubinowitz and Rosenbaum 2000). Lamb (2005, 231) found that the decision "had relatively little effect on segregated public housing patterns in other major cities."

Title VIII authorized private lawsuits to enforce its antidiscrimination provisions. Section 810(a) provided that persons who claim to have been injured by a discriminatory housing practice or believe that they will be injured may file a lawsuit. The meaning of § 810(a) was addressed in the first Title VIII case to reach the court, *Trafficante v. Metropolitan Life Insurance Company* (1972). The court attached a broad interpretation to the words "person aggrieved" in the statute to give standing to sue to all in the same housing unit who were injured by racial discrimination, including persons who were not direct victims of housing discrimination but suffered from the loss of important benefits from interracial associations. *Gladstone, Realtors v. Village of Bellwood* (1979) and *Havens Realty Corporation v. Coleman* (1982) extended *Trafficante's* broad standing interpretation to testers of housing discrimination—residents who inquire about purchasing homes or renting apartments to determine whether real estate companies were engaged in the illegal practice of racial steering. The court applied a more restrictive interpretation to standing rules when black and Puerto Rican residents brought a class action lawsuit against the all-white suburb of Penfield, New York, for engaging in exclusionary zoning practices. In *Warth v. Seldin* (1975), the court required that "a plaintiff who seeks to challenge exclusionary zoning practices must allege specific, concrete facts demonstrating that the challenged practices harm *him*, and that he personally would benefit in a tangible way from the court's intervention."

In *Village of Arlington Heights v. Metropolitan Housing Corporation* (1977), the court applied the *Washington v. Davis* intent to discriminate standard to make it more difficult to challenge exclusionary zoning practices. A nonprofit developer and black plaintiffs sued the residentially segregated municipality of Arlington Heights, a suburb of Chicago, on Title VIII and equal protection grounds after the municipality denied their rezoning request to build federally subsidized townhouses. The black plaintiffs met the standing requirements, but they failed to carry their burden of proving that racially discriminatory intent was a motivating factor in the municipality's rezoning decision. Justice Powell found that the impact of the municipality's decision "does arguably bear more heavily on racial minorities," but the plaintiffs "simply failed to carry the burden of proving that discriminatory purpose was a motivating factor in the Village's decision. This conclusion ends the constitutional inquiry." Powell moderated the intent to discriminate standard to a certain degree to allow for the submission of "circumstantial and direct evidence of intent as may be available." The dissenters criticized the majority's failure to follow the court's usual practice of remand in the case because *Washington v Davis* was decided after the lower courts ruled on the case.

Architectural exclusion refers to the use of elements of the physical environment to separate people of color and the poor from affluent white communities. Schindler (2015, 1939) found that urban design features such as street grid design, one-way streets, the absence of sidewalks and crosswalks, and the location of highways and transit stops operated intentionally to shape the demographics of a city and to isolate minority neighborhoods. The Memphis city council decided to close off a street at the point where it adjoined a black neighborhood at the request of residents of an affluent, all-white neighborhood. Black residents and civic associations sued the city on the ground that the street closure violated § 1982 and the Thirteenth Amendment. In *City of Memphis v. Greene* (1981), the court ruled that the street closure did not impair the kind of property interest identified as being within the reach of § 1982. Justice Stevens explained that the record did not disclose any racially discriminatory motive on part of the city council and that its interests in safety and tranquility were sufficient to justify the adverse impact on black motorists who were merely inconvenienced by the street closing. Writing for the dissenters, Justice Marshall asserted that Stevens's analysis ignored the plain and powerful symbolic message of the "inconvenience" to black drivers. Marshall found that ample evidence existed in the record to indicate that the city council's actions were racially motivated.

As shown in table 6.8, the outcomes in the Burger Court's fair housing decisions were mixed. The court applied a broad interpretation to Title VIII

Table 6.8. Burger Court Fair Housing Cases, 1969–1986

Case	Vote	Outcome
Sullivan v. Little Hunting Park (1969)	5–3	Held that whites could sue under § 1982 to vindicate the rights of black renters in the leasing of property (L)
James v. Valtierra (1971)	5–3	Held that a mandatory public housing referendum was not an impermissible racial classification under the equal protection clause (C)
Trafficante v. Metropolitan Life Insurance Company (1972)	9–0	Held that Title VIII granted standing to sue to all persons in the same housing unit who are injured by racial discrimination (L)
Warth v. Seldin (1975)	5–4	Held that minority plaintiffs lacked standing to challenge a predominantly white suburb's exclusionary zoning ordinance (C)
Hills v. Gautreaux (1976)	8–0	Held that a metropolitan-wide remedy was appropriate to correct segregated housing site selection (L)
Village of Arlington Heights v. Metropolitan Housing Corporation (1977)	5–3	Held that proof of discriminatory intent was required to challenge the denial of a rezoning application to build federally subsidized low-income housing in an all-white suburb (C)
Moore v. City of East Cleveland (1977)	5–4	Held that a municipal zoning ordinance's definition of the family violated the due process clause of the Fourteenth Amendment (L)
Gladstone, Realtors v. Village of Bellwood (1979)	7–2	Held that indirect victims of housing discrimination had standing to sue under Title VIII to obtain information about real estate firms' racial steering practices (L)
City of Memphis v. Greene (1981)	6–3	Held that a street closing that adjoined a black neighborhood did not violate § 1982 or the Thirteenth Amendment (C)
Havens Realty Corporation v. Coleman (1982)	9–0	Held that testers and fair housing organizations had standing to sue violators of racial steering practices under Title VIII (L)

Source: Created by the author.

Note: C for conservative outcomes, and L for liberal outcomes.

to allow testers to legally pose as renters or purchasers to gather information to bring lawsuits against real estate firms and apartment complexes that did not comply with fair housing laws, but the court made it more difficult for minority plaintiffs to challenge exclusionary zoning laws that would integrate all-white suburbs.

Jury Discrimination

The Burger Court expanded the concept of a representative jury with regard to race and gender. In *Peters v. Kiff* (1972), the court ruled that a white defendant had standing to challenge the system used to select juries when the process arbitrarily excluded from service members of any race. In *Taylor v. Louisiana* (1975), the court found that Louisiana's systematic exclusion of women from jury service deprived the male defendant of his Sixth and Fourteenth Amendment rights to an impartial jury trial. The decision overturned *Hoyt v. Florida* (1961), which held that a jury selection system that excluded women did not violate the Fourteenth Amendment. The *Taylor* decision expanded the jury pool to include women of color.

During its final term, the Burger Court reconsidered *Swain v. Alabama* (1965), which made prosecutors' use of peremptory challenges largely immune from judicial scrutiny. In *Batson v. Kentucky* (1986), Justice Powell rejected *Swain*'s placement of the burden of proof on black defendants by shifting the burden to the state "to come forward with a neutral explanation for challenging black jurors. . . . The trial court then will have the duty to determine if the defendant has established purposeful discrimination." Acknowledging that peremptory challenges had been used to discriminate against black jurors, Powell required "trial courts to be sensitive to the racially discriminatory use of peremptory challenges" to enforce the mandate of equal protection and further the ends of justice. Chief Justice Burger dissented on the ground that the majority's decision would upset the historical role and settled practice of peremptory challenges in the American jury system. Justice Rehnquist found nothing unequal about the state's use of peremptory challenges as long as the state "does not single out blacks, or members of any other race for that matter, for discriminatory treatment." In the landmark *Batson v. Kentucky* decision, a majority of the justices finally confronted the reality that prosecutors used peremptory challenges in a racially discriminatory manner and their discretion needed to be curbed to protect the constitutional rights of defendants of color and the integrity of the jury selection process.

Table 6.9. Burger Court Jury Discrimination Cases, 1969–1986

Case	Vote	Outcome
Carter v. Jury Commission of Greene County (1970)	7–1	Upheld the state's jury selection statute because it could be applied in a nondiscriminatory way (C)
Turner v. Fouche (1970)	8–0	Held that comparing the percentage of minority jurors with the percentage of minority residents in the population made out a prima facie case of jury discrimination (L)
Peters v. Kiff (1972)	6–3	Held that a white defendant had standing to challenge the exclusion of blacks from jury service (L)
Alexander v. Louisiana (1972)	7–0	Held that a black defendant made out a prima facie case of racial discrimination by showing that the grand jury selection procedures were not racially neutral (L)
Ham v. South Carolina (1973)	7–2	Held that the trial judge's refusal to make any inquiry about jurors' racial bias violated a black defendant's due process rights (L)
Taylor v. Louisiana (1975)	8–1	Held that the systematic exclusion of women from jury panels violated the Sixth and Fourteenth Amendments (L)
Ristaino v. Ross (1976)	6–2	Held that a black defendant's due process rights were not violated when the trial court denied his request to ask the jury about racial prejudice during the voir dire (C)
Castaneda v. Partida (1977)	5–4	Held that a Latino criminal defendant established a prima facie case of jury discrimination by comparing the percentage of Latinos summoned for grand jury duty and the percentage of Latinos in the local population (L)
Rosales-Lopez v. United States (1981)	6–3	Held that the due process rights of a defendant of Mexican descent were not violated when the trial judge refused a request to ask questions about bias toward Mexicans during the voir dire (C)
Turner v. Murray (1986)	7–2	Held that a black man convicted of murdering a white store owner and sentenced to death was entitled to have prospective jurors questioned about their racial bias (L)

Table 6.9. Continued.

Case	Vote	Outcome
Batson v. Kentucky (1986)	7–2	Held that once a defendant makes a prima facie showing of peremptory challenge abuse, the burden shifts to the prosecutor to present a race neutral explanation for challenging black jurors (L)

Source: Created by the author.

Note: C for conservative outcomes, and L for liberal outcomes.

The Death Penalty

In the mid-1960s, the LDF and the ACLU instituted a coordinated litigation campaign to attack the constitutionality of capital punishment (Meltsner 1973). In 1971, the Burger Court accepted three LDF backed cases for review. William Furman was a poor, mentally ill, and intellectually disabled young black man who was sentenced to death for killing a white homeowner during a botched robbery. In two companion cases, black men were sentenced to death for the rape of white women. In the landmark case *Furman v. Georgia* (1972), the court ruled in a 5–4 per curiam decision that the imposition and carrying out of the death penalty constituted cruel and unusual punishment in violation of the Eighth and Fourteenth Amendments.

All nine justices expressed their concurring or dissenting views separately in a 233-page decision. Justices Douglas, Brennan, Stewart, White, and Marshall took the position that the death penalty violated the cruel and unusual punishments provision. Douglas argued that the death penalty was applied discriminatorily against minorities and the poor under the equal protection clause. Brennan argued that the death penalty was no more effective than imprisonment, and it did not comport with human dignity under the Eighth Amendment. Stewart explained that the sentence was cruel and unusual in the same way that being struck by lightning was cruel and usual—it was wantonly and freakishly imposed. White found that the death penalty did not justify the social ends of deterrence and retribution due to its infrequent imposition. Marshall believed that the death penalty served no valid legislative purpose, it was morally unacceptable, it was cruel and unusual due to its infliction of physical pain, excessiveness, and arbitrariness, and it was discriminatorily applied.

Chief Justice Burger, Blackmun, Powell, and Rehnquist expressed opposing views in their dissents. Burger asserted that the Framers never intended to eliminate capital punishment, and it was not cruel by contemporary standards. Blackmun expressed his personal opposition to the death penalty, but he believed the majority overstepped as a matter of history and law by striking down the capital punishment laws of thirty-nine states. Powell explained that declaring the death penalty unconstitutional subordinated national and local democratic processes, and that racial bias in the trial and sentencing process had diminished in recent years. Rehnquist asserted that the court failed to follow the principle of judicial self-restraint, and he argued in favor of deference to legislative judgments in death penalty cases.

An immediate moratorium on executions was put in place until states revised their death penalty statutes to conform with the concerns expressed in *Furman*. The abolition of the death penalty in the United States lasted four years. In *Gregg v. Georgia* (1976), the court upheld Georgia's revised death penalty law in a 7–2 plurality decision. Justice Stewart, joined by Powell and Stevens, asserted that the imposition of the death penalty does not, under all circumstances, violate the Eighth Amendment. Stewart explained that the Eighth Amendment must be interpreted according to evolving standards of decency—it forbids punishment that is excessive because it involves the unnecessary and wanton infliction of pain or because it is grossly disproportionate to the severity of the crime. Stewart added that the legislature was not required to select the least severe penalty possible, and a heavy burden was placed upon those attacking its judgment.

The issue of race was prevalent throughout the *Furman* opinions, but it was missing in *Gregg*. Oshinsky (2010, 61) suggested that the court carefully selected *Gregg* and two companion cases that involved only white defendants sentenced to death from the deep South to temporarily take race off the table. Steiker and Steiker (2016, 98–99) suggested that some of the justices were trying to take a race neutral approach to the racially charged issue of capital punishment. The justices avoided the issue of race again in a challenge to a revised death penalty statute that required the death sentence in rape cases. Erlich Coker, a white convicted felon who was already serving multiple life sentences, escaped from a Georgia prison and entered the home of a young married couple, robbed them, and raped the sixteen-year-old wife. In *Coker v. Georgia* (1977), the court ruled in a 7–2 decision that the death penalty was grossly disproportionate and excessive for the crime of rape. The court's decision made no reference to the historical connection between race, rape, and the death penalty even though the LDF directly addressed the connection on behalf of Coker's defense.

Pulley v. Harris (1984) involved the brutal murder of two white teenagers during the course of a bank robbery by Robert Alton Harris, a previously convicted white felon. Harris sought to halt his execution on the ground that the Eighth Amendment's prohibition on cruel and unusual punishments required proportionality in sentencing. Writing for the 7–2 majority, Justice White found that *Gregg* did not establish a constitutional requirement of proportionality review nor was it constitutionally required under the Eighth Amendment. Justice Brennan's dissent, joined by Marshall, brought race back into the death penalty debate. Brennan challenged the majority's assumption that the death penalty was imposed in a rational and nondiscriminatory way. He cited several scholarly studies that reached the conclusion that the race of the defendant and the race of the victim were factors that determined whether the death penalty was impermissibly applied. He concluded that comparative proportionality review was mandated by the Constitution.

Conclusion

During an interview with a *New York Times* reporter that took place shortly before his death on July 9, 1974, retired Chief Justice Earl Warren declared, "If I had ever known what was going to happen to the country and this Court, I *never* would have resigned. They would have had to carry me out of here on a plank!" (Schwartz 1983, 771). Warren was referring to the election of Richard Nixon and his role in the Watergate scandal. He thought "Tricky" was the "most despicable President this nation has ever had," who "had abused both the office and the people" (Schwartz 1983, 771). Warren (1969, ix–x) expressed his concerns about the incoming Burger Court in the speech he delivered on his last day as chief justice in the presence of Nixon and Warren Burger. Nixon's remarks emphasized "continuity with change," which was essential to the nation's progress, but Warren responded by stressing the theme of continuity when he stated, "I might point out to you . . . that [the court] is a continuing body . . . and how it is that the Court develops consistently the eternal principles of our Constitution in solving the problems of the day."

Warren's concern that the Nixon appointees would resist the path of continuity with regard to race and rights was justified. The Nixon and Reagan administrations exercised their executive powers to shift the policy direction of the court to the right. Over time, Burger Court policymaking began to reflect the New Right alliance's negative civil rights agenda. As shown in this chapter, the Burger Court's exercise of power to advance the policy goal of equal rights under law was significantly weaker compared to the Warren Court's record. Of the ninety-nine race cases examined in this chapter, 32 percent of the outcomes were decided in a conservative direction and 68 percent were decided in a liberal direction in favor of people of color or pro–civil rights claimants. My analysis of the decisions revealed that the court was willing to expand rights on behalf of people of color, but it was also willing to restrict them. A noticeable rightward shift in the court's policymaking began in the mid-1970s after the Nixon and Ford appointees took their seats on the court. The justices became more divided and increasingly conservative in their decision making in race cases. The moderate justices wielded considerable power on the Burger Court—Lewis Powell, Potter Stewart, and Byron White—along with the liberal William Brennan, who was able to form coalitions among the justices to advance egalitarian policy goals. President Jimmy Carter's loss to Ronald Reagan in the 1980 presidential election had serious consequences for the policy direction of the court. Nixon's most conservative appointment to the court, William Rehnquist, would become the sixteenth chief justice in 1986.

Chapter 7

The Rehnquist Court, 1986–2005

During the tenure of the Rehnquist Court, the clash between the policy goals of the rival racial orders played out at the national level as politics became increasingly partisan and polarized. The Reagan administration was coming to an end, and another Republican president won the White House for a single term, George H. W. Bush (1988–1992). The Gulf War became the defining issue of the Bush presidency, and he was defeated by the Democratic candidate, Bill Clinton, who served two terms in the White House (1992–2000). The Rehnquist Court intervened in the 2000 presidential election between George W. Bush and Al Gore after the November election results failed to declare a winner. In one of the most controversial decisions of the modern era, five of the seven Republican appointees on the court voted to reverse a decision by the Florida Supreme Court that called for a manual recount of votes. After the *Bush v. Gore* (2000) decision, Bush was declared the winner of the presidential election by a narrow 271 electoral college vote. Phrases used to describe judicial policymaking such as judicial activism and judicial restraint lost whatever substantive meaning they had when applied to a Republican dominated court that was willing to invalidate federal and state laws based on its conservative policy preferences.

Because the policy goals of the transformative egalitarian order were enshrined in authoritative precedents, civil rights laws, and federal agency rules, the rival New Right alliance sought to reinterpret egalitarian ideals in ways to maintain superior white status and political power. The Federalist Society became an important ally of the New Right alliance by countering liberal legal thinking in elite law schools and by influencing the selection of federal judges in Republican administrations. The racial policy dichotomy used to appraise Rehnquist Court policymaking in race cases is color-blindness versus race consciousness. As shown in this chapter, Rehnquist Court policymaking represents a significant departure from the liberal policymaking of the New Deal and the Warren and Burger Courts. The court exercised its power to advance the policy goals of the New Right alliance, but Congress and shifting coalitions on the court prevented it from instituting a backward-looking jurisprudence with regard to race and rights. Unlike his predecessor, William Rehnquist strategically used his position as chief justice to shape outcomes in race cases according to his sincerely held policy preferences and those of like-minded justices that were hostile to the constitutional and statutory rights of people of color.

The Composition of the Rehnquist Court

On May 27, 1986, Chief Justice Warren Burger informed President Reagan of his decision to retire at the end of the 1985 term to chair the Commission on the Bicentennial of the US Constitution. Reagan nominated the most conservative justice on the court, William Rehnquist, to become the sixteenth chief justice and DC Circuit judge Antonin Scalia was nominated to fill Rehnquist's seat. Rehnquist was sharply questioned by Democrats on the Senate Judiciary Committee about his views on civil rights, the memo he wrote as a law clerk for Justice Robert Jackson, and allegations that he harassed and challenged the rights of minorities to vote in Arizona during his prior political activities. The harsh questioning had no impact on the Republican-controlled Senate's decision to confirm Rehnquist by a 65–33 vote. Fifty-year-old Antonin Scalia was well-known for his conservative voting record on the DC Circuit. His confirmation hearing turned out to be a mere formality, and he was unanimously confirmed by the Senate. Scalia became the first Italian American to serve on the court.

When seventy-nine-year-old Lewis Powell announced his retirement decision in 1987, President Reagan initiated a fierce confirmation battle when he nominated DC Circuit judge Robert Bork as Powell's successor. Bork was a controversial nominee because of his very conservative legal views with regard to individual and civil rights, which he had expressed in extensive writings and speeches over two decades. Several factors contributed to Bork's 42–58 Senate vote defeat: unprecedented liberal interest group opposition, Democrats had regained control of the Senate, his policy views were ideologically distant from the views of the median senator, and Reagan's popularity had declined due to the administration's involvement in the Iran-Contra Affair. Reagan's second attempt to fill Powell's seat collapsed within nine days when his nominee, DC Circuit judge Douglas Ginsburg, withdrew his name from consideration due to allegations of illegal drug use. Reagan succeeded in his third attempt to fill Powell's seat with the nomination of fifty-one-year-old Ninth Circuit judge Anthony Kennedy. Kennedy, who was a conservative but not a rigid ideologue like Bork, was confirmed by a unanimous vote in February 1988.

In July 1990, the first of two remaining liberal icons on the court, William Brennan, announced his retirement at the age of eighty-four due to his advancing age and medical condition. President George H. W. Bush nominated First Circuit judge David Souter to succeed Brennan. Souter served as an associate justice on the New Hampshire Supreme Court for seven years prior to his brief service on the First Circuit. His paper trail was thin, and not much was known about his positions on culture war issues and civil rights. Despite efforts to derail his nomination by civil rights groups, fifty-one-year-old David Souter was confirmed by a 90–9 vote. One year later, eighty-three-year-old Thurgood Marshall announced his retirement from the court due to his advancing age and medical condition. On July 1, 1991, George H. W. Bush nominated forty-three-year-old DC Circuit judge Clarence Thomas to succeed Marshall. Prior to his judicial appointment in 1990, Thomas served as chair of the Equal Employment Opportunity Commission and assistant secretary for civil rights in the Education Department.

The Thomas nomination caused deep divisions in the civil rights community because of his conservative views on civil rights and criticisms of civil rights organizations. Prior to the full Senate confirmation vote, NPR reporter Nina Totenberg broke a story on October 6 that Thomas's FBI background check revealed that he had been accused of sexual harassment by University of Oklahoma Law School professor Anita Hill, who worked with Thomas at the Education Department and the Equal Employment Opportunity Commission. Hill testified during the second committee hearing that Thomas used the workplace to discuss sex and pornographic films in graphic detail, and he boasted of his sexual prowess (Senate Judiciary Committee 1991, 36–39). Thomas categorically denied Hill's accusations and accused the committee of engaging in a "high-tech lynching for uppity-blacks who in any way deign to think for themselves" (157–58). Hill's sexual harassment accusations failed to derail Thomas's confirmation by the Democratic-controlled Senate. He was confirmed by a 52–48 vote. Shortly after Thomas took his seat on the court, retired Third Circuit judge A. Leon Higginbotham, Jr. (1992, 1007), wrote an open letter to Thomas that criticized him for identifying as a black conservative, because conservatives at every turn tried to derail the struggle for equal rights. Higginbotham (1019) was especially harsh about Thomas's criticism of the *Brown* decision because it "was primarily the conservatives who attacked the Warren Court relentlessly because of *Brown v. Board of Education* and who stood in the way of almost every measure to ensure gender and racial advancement." Higginbotham pointed out that if it were not for those civil rights organizations and leaders criticized by Thomas, he would probably still be in Pin Point or Savannah, Georgia, working as a laborer and not on the court.

Bill Clinton's 1992 election ended the twenty-six-year lack of Democratic appointments to the court when Byron White announced his retirement in March 1993. Clinton nominated sixty-year-old DC Circuit judge Ruth Bader Ginsburg to succeed White. Prior to her appointment to the DC Circuit, Ginsburg taught law at Columbia University, and she directed the ACLU's Women's Rights Project. Ginsburg was confirmed by a 96–3 vote. The following year, Harry Blackmun announced his retirement at the age of eighty-five. Clinton nominated fifty-five-year-old First Circuit judge Stephen Breyer to succeed Blackmun. Breyer, who had previously served as the Senate Judiciary Committee's chief counsel, was confirmed by an 87–9 vote.

Education

School Desegregation Remedies

Public school systems were becoming resegregated and school districts returned to federal courts to obtain favorable rulings that would release them from federal court supervision. The Rehnquist Court pursued a federalism education agenda that successfully navigated the issue of school desegregation away from the authority of federal district courts to return the process to local control. The court's school desegregation decisions resulted in the termination of desegregation orders by federal courts and the substantial resegregation of public schools (Orfield and Jarvie 2020).

In *Board of Education of Oklahoma City Public Schools v. Dowell* (1991), black parents challenged the Oklahoma City school district's plan that adopted neighborhood schools for K–4 students and busing for students in grades 5–12 on the ground that the school district had not achieved unitary status and its neighborhood school policy was a return to segregation. Chief Justice Rehnquist asserted that desegregation decrees were intended to operate temporarily to remedy past discrimination; otherwise, a school district could be condemned "to judicial tutelage for the indefinite future." Rehnquist explained that after local authorities have complied with a decree for a reasonable time period and the evidence indicated that they were not likely to return to their former ways, dissolution of a decree was appropriate. In his last school desegregation opinion, Justice Marshall asserted that "a desegregation decree cannot be lifted so long as conditions likely to inflict the stigmatic injury condemned in *Brown I* persist and there remain feasible methods of eliminating such conditions."

The following year, the court provided greater clarity to school districts seeking to terminate federal judicial supervision. In the landmark case *Freeman v. Pitts* (1992), the court held that a district court may relinquish supervisory authority of a school district in incremental stages before achieving full compliance in every area of school operations. Writing for the unanimous court, Justice Anthony Kennedy identified three factors that must inform the district court's discretion to order partial withdrawal: whether there has been satisfactory compliance in those aspects of the system where supervision is to be withdrawn, whether retention of judicial control was necessary to achieve compliance in other facets of the school system, and whether the school district had demonstrated its good-faith commitment to the whole of the court's decree. Kennedy explained that if resegregation of a school district was not a product of state action but of private choices, then "it does not have constitutional implications" and cannot be addressed by judicial remedies. The *Freeman v. Pitts* decision signaled the court's retreat from *Brown*'s constitutional mandate to desegregate public schools.

The *Brown* decision applied to public colleges and universities that refused admission to black students. The desegregation of postsecondary institutions was ignored until the LDF sued the Nixon administration for its failure to enforce Title VI of the Civil Rights Act of 1964. In 1975, the federal government intervened in a lawsuit brought by black parents that alleged that Mississippi unlawfully maintained a dual university system in violation of the equal protection clause and Title VI. For twelve years, the parties attempted to resolve the dual university system voluntarily, but the university system's board of trustees failed to take meaningful actions to desegregate its public colleges and universities. In 1987, the case proceeded to trial, and the district court found that the race-neutral policies adopted and implemented by state officials conclusively demonstrated that they had fulfilled their affirmative duty to desegregate. In *United States v. Fordice* (1992), the court found that race-neutral policies and free choice were not enough to cure the constitutional violation. Writing for the 8–1 majority, Justice White asserted that if a state "perpetuates policies and practices traceable to its prior system that continue to have segregative effects—whether by influencing student enrollment decisions or by fostering segregation in other facets of the university system—and such policies are without sound educational justification and can be practicably eliminated, the State has not satisfied its burden of proving that it has dismantled its prior system." White found that the university system's policies contributed to the racial identifiability of the eight public universities in Mississippi. The *Fordice* decision is often depicted as the *Brown* of higher education. Like *Brown*, implementing *Fordice* would prove to be problematic, especially for the nation's historically black colleges and universities.

Affirmative Action in Higher Education

Conservative legal groups devised a strategy to overturn the *Bakke* decision by locating student plaintiffs to challenge the constitutionality of race-conscious admissions in higher education. The Center for Individual Rights represented Cheryl Hopwood, a white female, and three white males who were denied admission to the University of Texas's law school in 1992. In *Hopwood v. Texas* (1996), the Fifth Circuit ruled that racial diversity could never be a compelling governmental interest under the strict scrutiny test. The Rehnquist Court declined to review the decision and its impact was limited to the Fifth Circuit states. To locate additional plaintiffs, the Center for Individual Rights placed an advertisement in fourteen major college and university student newspapers with the caption—"Guilty by Admission: Nearly Every Elite College in America Violates the Law. Does Yours?"—to encourage students to sue (Cross 1999, 95). The law firm was successful in finding white plaintiffs who were willing to sue the University of Michigan in two lawsuits that challenged the use of race in admitting students to the law school and the undergraduate school.

In *Grutter v. Bollinger* (2003), the court upheld the law school's race conscious admissions process under *Bakke*'s strict scrutiny test. Writing for the 5–4 majority, Justice Sandra Day O'Connor accepted the law school's position that diversity was a compelling interest because it yielded various educational benefits and a critical mass of underrepresented minorities was needed to further the educational benefits of a diverse society. O'Connor cited amicus curiae briefs submitted by corporations and the military that took the position that student body diversity prepared students for an increasingly diverse workforce and it was essential to the military's ability to provide national security. O'Connor found that the means used by the law school to obtain a diverse student body was narrowly tailored because it did not operate as a quota, the program was flexible enough to rely on a wide range of factors besides race and ethnicity, and the law school accepted nonminority applicants with grades and test scores lower than underrepresented minority applicants.

In response to the dissenters' criticism that the law school's admissions policy lacked any reasonable precise time limit, O'Connor pointed out that twenty-five years had passed since *Bakke* approved the use of race to further student body diversity. Because the number of minority applicants with high grades and test scores had increased since that time, O'Connor speculated that "25 years from now, the use of racial preferences will no longer be necessary to further the interest approved today." Chief Justice Rehnquist, joined by Justices Scalia, Kennedy, and Thomas in dissent, criticized O'Connor's acceptance of the university's critical mass of underrepresented minorities argument to justify its affirmative action policy. Rehnquist called the law school's goal to obtain a critical mass of minority students "a sham." He believed it was "a carefully managed program designed to ensure proportionate representation of applicants from selected minority groups," which was forbidden by the Constitution.

Gratz v. Bollinger (2003) challenged the constitutionality of the race-conscious admissions process by the undergraduate school. The undergraduate admissions office used a numerical selection index system to process the 25,000 applications to obtain an entering class of 5,000 (Urofsky 2020, 367). Each applicant received points based on a variety of criteria, including points based on their membership in underrepresented groups (blacks, Latinos, and Native Americans). The *Gratz* decision produced a different outcome because Justices O'Connor and Breyer switched their votes. Writing for the 6–3 majority, Chief Justice Rehnquist found that the use of race by the undergraduate school violated the equal protection clause because the automatic distribution of twenty points to every single underrepresented minority applicant did not allow for individualized assessment. O'Connor explained in her concurrence that the undergraduate admissions program was different from the law school admissions program, because the law school considered the diversity qualifications of each applicant on a case-by-case basis, whereas the undergraduate program automatically gave twenty-points to each minority applicant. Justice Breyer wrote a four-sentence opinion concurring in the judgment that simply stated his vote without explanation.

Justice Souter, joined by Ginsburg in dissent, argued that the undergraduate admissions process "is closer to what *Grutter* approves than what *Bakke* condemns, and should not be held unconstitutional." He explained that the undergraduate school awarded value to diversity on a numbered scale, whereas the law school accomplished the same thing in its holistic review. Souter acknowledged that minority applicants received twenty points for their race or ethnicity, but nonminority students were assigned twenty points for their athletic ability, socioeconomic disadvantage, attendance at a socioeconomically disadvantaged high school or predominantly minority high school, and at the discretion of the provost.

Devins (2003) found that strong social and political forces provided the incentive for the court to uphold at least one of the plans. The *Grutter* and *Gratz* cases attracted an unprecedented number of amicus brief filings

Table 7.1. Rehnquist Court Education Cases, 1986–2005

Case	Vote	Outcome
Missouri v. Jenkins (1990)	9–0	Held that a district court had the authority to order a school district to levy property taxes to fund a desegregation remedy but the court could not impose a tax increase directly (L)
Board of Education of Oklahoma City Public Schools v. Dowell (1991)	5–3	Held that school districts may be released from desegregation decrees once they have complied in good faith and taken steps to eliminate vestiges of past discrimination (C)
Freeman v. Pitts (1992)	8–0	Held that under certain circumstances, partial withdrawal from a desegregation decree was permissible (C)
United States v. Fordice (1992)	8–1	Held that a state policy that could be traced to de jure segregation and continued to promote segregation in its colleges and universities violated the equal protection clause (L)
Missouri v. Jenkins (1995)	5–4	Held that an expensive court-ordered desegregation remedy that indirectly mandated the interdistrict transfer of students exceeded the remedial power of a district court (C)
Gratz v. Bollinger (2003)	6–3	Held that the University of Michigan's use of race in its undergraduate admissions program was not narrowly tailored under strict scrutiny (C)
Grutter v. Bollinger (2003)	5–4	Held that the University of Michigan's law school admissions program that used race to achieve a critical mass of underrepresented minority students was narrowly tailored under strict scrutiny (L)

Source: Created by the author.

Note: C for conservative outcomes, and L for liberal outcomes.

to influence the outcomes in the cases, including surprising amici that were not the usual advocates of liberal policies (Larsen and Devins 2016, 1954–55). Owens and Epstein (2005, 125) found that the Rehnquist Court was unusually attentive to arguments offered by amici. The mixed outcomes in *Grutter* and *Gratz* meant that conservative legal groups would continue to challenge the use of race-conscious admissions by elite private and public universities. The *Bakke* precedent survived constitutional scrutiny by a slim majority.

Voting Rights

Davidson and Grofman's (1994) empirical study of the impact of the Voting Rights Act of 1965 found that the law brought about a quiet revolution in the South with regard to increases in minority registration, voting, and representation at the national, state, and local levels. Congress continued to support the remedial goals of the Voting Rights Act by renewing and expanding the law. Advances in minority representation in the South were met with a variety of schemes designed to curtail the law's effectiveness and to dilute the political power of minority groups.

SECTION 5 PRECLEARANCE

The Rehnquist Court's approach to § 5's preclearance cases was mixed. The court expanded the meaning of political equality when it declared that §§ 2 and 5 of the Voting Rights Act applied to judicial elections. By contrast, the court refused to apply a broad interpretation to § 5's coverage of election changes as established in *Allen v. State Board of Elections* (1969). When three black commissioners were elected to the Etowah and Russell County commissions in Alabama for the first time, the county commissions adopted three resolutions that took budgetary powers away from their offices. In *Presley v. Etowah County Commission* (1992), the court ruled that the adoption of the county resolutions did not require preclearance because they did not involve changes covered by § 5. Justice Kennedy restricted the reach of the preclearance provision to changes that had a direct relation to voting, the election process, and the allocation of power among governmental officials. The court's restrictive preclearance decisions were criticized by voting rights experts who speculated that they signaled the end of § 5 as an enforcement tool (McCrary, Seaman, and Valelly 2006).

Table 7.2. Rehnquist Court Preclearance Cases, 1986–2005

Case	Vote	Outcome
City of Pleasant Grove v. United States (1987)	6–3	Held that a city's failure to annex a black area while annexing white areas was racially motivated and was subject to preclearance (L)
Clark v. Roemer (1991)	9–0	Held that § 5 applied to judicial elections (L)
Presley v. Etowah County Commission (1992)	6–3	Held that only procedural changes that have a direct relation to voting and the electoral process require preclearance (C)
Young v. Fordice (1997)	9–0	Held that changes made to Mississippi's voter registration procedures to comply with the National Voter Registration Act of 1993 required § 5 preclearance (L)
Reno v. Bossier Parish School Board (1997)	7–2	Held that a purpose inquiry is restricted to the question of retrogressive intent under § 5 (C)
Lopez v. Monterey County, California (1999)	8–1	Held that voting changes to select judges from a covered county must be precleared before taking effect (L)
Reno v. Bossier Parish School Board (2000)	5–4	Held that § 5 does not prohibit preclearance of a redistricting plan enacted with a discriminatory but nonretrogressive purpose (C)
Georgia v. Ashcroft (2003)	5–4	Applied a more burdensome retrogression standard under § 5 (C)

Source: Created by the author.

Note: C for conservative outcomes, and L for liberal outcomes.

RACE-CONSCIOUS REDISTRICTING

Conservatives attacked the successes of the Voting Rights Act in public discourse and academic publications by arguing that the law was transformed into a powerful affirmative action tool to promote black and Latino officeholders (Thernstrom 1987; but see Karlan and McCrary 1988). A bloc of justices on the Rehnquist Court was receptive to the revisionist color-blind interpretations of the Voting Rights Act and the Fourteenth and Fifteenth Amendments. After the 1990 census, the Justice Department objected to a

North Carolina congressional redistricting plan that included one majority-black congressional district on the ground that the legislature could have created a second majority-black congressional district to strengthen the votes of black citizens. The legislature submitted a revised plan that included a second majority-black district, District 12. The new district's boundary lines were described as having an irregular, snake-like shape because they were drawn along the 160 mile north central corridor of Interstate 85 to obtain enough black voters. Five white voters challenged the constitutionality of the plan on the ground that the use of race in the creation of congressional districts gave governmental approval to racial stereotypes and racial quotas (Everett 2001). A three-judge district court dismissed the lawsuit because the white plaintiffs failed to state a claim under the equal protection clause. On appeal, the white plaintiffs claimed that "the deliberate segregation of voters into separate districts on the basis of race violated their constitutional right to participate in a 'color-blind' electoral process." After the plan took effect, North Carolina elected its first black representatives to Congress since 1901—Eva Clayton and Mel Watt.

In the landmark case *Shaw v. Reno* (1993), the court found that the white plaintiffs' claim was cognizable under the equal protection clause. Writing for the 5–4 majority, Justice O'Connor applied the reasoning in *Gomillion v. Lightfoot* (1960) to District 12, and concluded that "reapportionment is one area in which appearances do matter." She asserted that a "reapportionment plan that includes in one district individuals who belong to the same race, but who are otherwise widely separated by geographical and political boundaries, and who may have little in common with one another but for the color of their skin, bears an uncomfortable resemblance to political apartheid." O'Connor explained that racial gerrymandering "may balkanize us into competing racial factions; it threatens to carry us further from the goal of a political system in which race no longer matters—a goal that the Fourteenth and Fifteenth Amendments embody, and to which the Nation continues to aspire." O'Connor concluded that race-based districting required the application of the strict scrutiny test and left it up to the district court on remand to determine whether the redistricting plan was narrowly tailored to further a compelling governmental interest.

On the day of his retirement, Justice Byron White argued in his dissent that the facts in *Shaw* mirrored those presented in *United Jewish Organizations v. Carey* (1977). White explained that he could not understand how the white plaintiffs presented a cognizable claim, especially since "whites constituted roughly 76 percent of the total population and 79 percent of the voting age population in North Carolina. Yet, under the State's plan, they still constitute a voting majority in 10 (or 83 percent) of the 12 Congressional districts." White criticized the majority for being fascinated with irregularly shaped districts as an indicator of some form of gerrymandering. He asserted that a "regularly shaped district can just as effectively effectuate racially discriminatory gerrymandering as an odd-shaped one." White concluded that "state efforts to remedy minority vote dilution are wholly unlike what typically has been labeled 'affirmative action,' " and, instead, it involved "an attempt to *equalize* treatment, and to provide minority voters with an effective voice in the political process."

The *Shaw* decision was harshly criticized on a number of grounds: it gave white voters standing to challenge race-conscious redistricting under the equal protection clause, O'Connor's reasoning was based on value judgments rather than empirical assessments, and the decision created a legal theory based on the appearance of a district even though naturally shaped legislative districts do not exist. In response to the criticism, the court clarified the *Shaw* decision in a similar Georgia redistricting case. In *Miller v. Johnson* (1995), Justice Kennedy asserted that *Shaw* never intended that the appearance of a district was a threshold requirement to challenge a racial gerrymander. He explained that the shape of a district may serve as persuasive circumstantial evidence, and the burden was on the plaintiff to show that "race was the predominant factor motivating the legislature's decision to place a significant number of voters within or without a particular district." The revised standard required plaintiffs to prove that the legislature subordinated traditional race neutral districting principles, including compactness, contiguity, and respect for communities defined by shared interests to racial considerations.

In *Bush v. Vera* (1996), Justice Souter argued in his dissent that the conceptual weaknesses in *Shaw v. Reno* were so great that the court should either overrule it or create a manageable constitutional standard "to allow some faith in the political process." The court's radical attempt to restrict the use of race-conscious redistricting in *Shaw* threatened to reverse hard won minority electoral gains in the South (Kousser 1999). As the outcomes in table 7.3 show, the Rehnquist Court took an aggressive approach to race-conscious redistricting and vote dilution claims to advance the New Right alliance's policy goals.

Table 7.3. Rehnquist Court Race-Conscious Redistricting Cases, 1986–2005

Case	Vote	Outcome
Chisom v. Roemer (1991)	6–3	Held that § 2 applied to the election of state supreme court judges (L)
Houston Lawyers' Association v. Attorney General of Texas (1991)	6–3	Held that § 2 applied to the election of state trial judges (L)
Voinovich v. Quilter (1993)	9–0	Held that a state's redistricting map complied with the court's vote dilution decisions (C)
Shaw v. Reno (1993)	5–4	Held that white plaintiffs who alleged that the deliberate segregation of voters into separate bizarre-shaped districts on the basis of race stated a cognizable claim under the equal protection clause (C)
Holder v. Hall (1994)	5–4	Held that the size of a governing body was not subject to a vote dilution challenge (C)
Johnson v. De Grandy (1994)	7–2	Upheld a state's legislative redistricting plan because it provided minority groups with a proportional number of majority-minority districts (L)
Miller v. Johnson (1995)	5–4	Clarified *Shaw*'s appearance standard of proof in race-based redistricting challenges (C)
Shaw v. Hunt (1996)	5–4	Held that North Carolina failed to present compelling interests to justify the creation of a second majority-minority district to comply with the Voting Rights Act (C)
Bush v. Vera (1996)	5–4	Held that race was used as a proxy for political gerrymandering in the creation of three majority-minority districts in violation of the equal protection clause (C)
Hunt v. Cromartie (1999)	5–4	Held that the lower court should not have granted summary judgment in favor of white challengers to the redrawn District 12 (L)
Easley v. Cromartie (2001)	5–4	Held that North Carolina's District 12 did not violate the equal protection clause under the *Shaw* framework because the redistricting was predominantly political and not racial (L)

Source: Created by the author.

Note: C for conservative outcomes, and L for liberal outcomes.

Economic Equality

Title VII of the Civil Rights Act of 1964 was enacted to remedy employment discrimination and to ameliorate the economic status of protected groups. The Rehnquist Court exercised its power to restructure the Burger Court's Title VII and § 1981 doctrines to defeat the purposes of the statutes. The court's 1988 term produced a series of conservative employment discrimination decisions that benefitted employers and businesses at the expense of victims of employment discrimination.

TITLE VII AND SECTION 1981

In *Watson v. Fort Worth Bank & Trust* (1988), a plurality of justices agreed to a new burden-shifting framework for disparate impact cases—"the ultimate burden of proving that discrimination against a protected group has been caused by a specific employment practice remains with the plaintiffs at all times." *Watson*'s burden shifting framework became law in *Wards Cove Packing Company v. Antonio* (1989). In 1974, a class of Filipino and Alaska Native workers sued two salmon cannery companies on the ground that they engaged in a variety of discriminatory hiring and promotion practices and operated segregated housing and dining facilities in violation of Title VII. In *Wards Cove*, the court required minority workers to "demonstrate that it is the application of a specific or particular employment practice that has created the disparate impact under attack." Justice White explained that to rule otherwise would burden employers, who would be forced into court to engage in the expensive and time-consuming task of defending business necessity methods and force them to adopt racial quotas. Justice Stevens found that the overt and institutionalized discrimination in the salmon industry was so bad that it resembled a plantation economy. In his dissent, Stevens criticized White's opinion for abandoning the *Griggs* disparate impact standard that had been in place for eighteen years and for turning a blind eye to the meaning and purpose of Title VII.

Section 1981 is the recodified version of § 1 of the Civil Rights Act of 1866 that protects against racial discrimination in the making and enforcement of contracts. In *Runyon v. McCrary* (1976), the Burger Court ruled that § 1981 reached private acts of racial discrimination in the making of contracts. Brenda Patterson filed a § 1981 lawsuit that alleged that her employer, the manager of a credit union, subjected her to racially motivated harassment. The lower courts ruled that racially motivated harassment on the job was not actionable under § 1981. After the Rehnquist Court heard oral arguments in the case, a majority of the justices asked the parties to rebrief and reargue the question—whether the *Runyon* decision should be reconsidered. The court's action was controversial because neither the parties to the case nor the solicitor general requested the court to overrule *Runyon*. Civil rights groups feared that the court was about to overturn the Civil Rights Act of 1866. In *Patterson v. McLean Credit Union* (1989), the court did not overrule *Runyon*, but it refused to expand § 1981's protection to racial harassment in the workplace. Writing for the 5–4 majority, Justice Kennedy found that none of the racially motivated conduct experienced by the black plaintiff involved either a refusal to make a contract or the ability to enforce an established contract right. Justice Brennan criticized Kennedy in his dissent for adopting "a formalistic method of interpretation antithetical to Congress' vision of a society in which contractual opportunities are equal." Schwartz (2013, 252) found that the prime mover behind the attempt to secure the reconsideration and overruling of *Runyon* was Chief Justice Rehnquist, who dissented in *Runyon*.

A broad coalition of civil rights groups condemned the Rehnquist Court's restrictive employment discrimination decisions, and they successfully mobilized to obtain a legislative solution to reverse them (Baum and Hausegger 2004). The Civil Rights Act of 1991 modified or reversed all or parts of eight decisions that made it harder for protected workers to bring and win employment discrimination lawsuits (Selmi 2011, 281). The legislation also added new remedial provisions to strengthen Title VII's enforcement. Despite the 1991 law, the Rehnquist Court continued its mission to restrict Title VII's protections. In *St. Mary's Honor Center v. Hicks* (1993), the court revised the framework used to decide disparate treatment cases. In *McDonnell Douglas v. Green* (1973), the Burger Court required the minority employee to show that the reason the employer gave for his dismissal was not credible and was a pretext for discrimination. In *Hicks*, Justice Antonin Scalia required the minority plaintiff to prove that his employer intentionally discriminated against him because of race. Justice Souter criticized Scalia's opinion for abandoning "settled law that sets out this structure for trying disparate-treatment Title VII cases, only to adopt a scheme that will be unfair to the plaintiff, unworkable in practice, and inexplicable in forgiving employers who present false evidence in court."

As shown in table 7.4, the Rehnquist Court exercised its power to transform Title VII and § 1981 evidentiary doctrines in ways that made it

Table 7.4. Rehnquist Court Employment Discrimination Cases, 1986–2005

Case	Vote	Outcome
Saint Francis College v. Al-Khazraji (1987)	9–0	Held that an American citizen professor of Iraqi descent could sue for denial of tenure under § 1981 (L)
Watson v. Fort Worth Bank & Trust (1988)	8–0	Held that the disparate impact standard applied to subjective and objective employment practices (L)
Wards Cove Packing Company v. Atonio (1989)	5–4	Held that employees were required to isolate and identify specific employment practices that were responsible for statistical disparities in disparate impact cases (C)
Martin v. Wilks (1989)	5–4	Held that white firefighters who failed to intervene in a Title VII lawsuit could challenge the decree even though they had not been parties to the proceedings when the decrees were entered (C)
Patterson v. McLean Credit Union (1989)	5–4	Held that racial harassment in the workplace was not actionable under §1981 (C)
University of Pennsylvania v. EEOC (1990)	9–0	Held that a state's compelling interest in eradicating sexual and racial discrimination in universities outweighs the need for confidentiality in peer review in a Title VII lawsuit (L)
EEOC v. Arabian American Oil Company (1991)	6–3	Held that Title VII did not apply to American citizens employed by an American company in a foreign country (C)
St. Mary's Honor Center v. Hicks (1993)	5–4	Held that plaintiffs must prove intentional discrimination beyond showing that the employer's explanation was pretextual in disparate treatment cases (C)

Source: Created by the author.

Note: C for conservative outcomes, and L for liberal outcomes.

more difficult to remedy racial discrimination in the workplace. Congress exercised its power to check the court's hostile approach to employment discrimination cases by passing the Civil Rights Act of 1991.

Affirmative Action in Employment

The liberal William Brennan and conservative Sandra Day O'Connor clashed over which equal protection standard to apply to affirmative action employment cases. The doctrinal stakes were high because an application of strict scrutiny would almost always result in a finding that race-conscious remedies were unconstitutional. The contest began in *United States v. Paradise* (1987) which involved a challenge to a court-ordered remedy that required the Alabama Department of Public Safety to promote one black trooper for each white trooper promoted as long as qualified black candidates were available to ameliorate the department's 37-year history of discriminatory hiring and promotion practices. Writing for the 5–4 plurality, Brennan found that the court ordered remedy was narrowly tailored to serve a compelling governmental interest to remedy past and present discrimination in the hiring and promotion of state troopers by state officials. O'Connor argued that *Wygant v. Jackson Board of Education* (1986) controlled the case, and she believed that the district court failed to consider whether other alternatives would have successfully compelled the department to comply with the consent decrees.

After the Burger Court upheld a federal set-aside program for minority businesses in *Fullilove v. Klutznick* (1980), state and local governments devised their own programs that set aside a portion of their contracts for minority businesses. In 1983, the Richmond, Virginia, city council adopted an affirmative action program that required prime contractors that held construction contracts awarded by the city to subcontract at least 30 percent of the dollar amount of the contract to one or more minority business enterprise to compensate for past discrimination in the industry and to promote wide participation by minority businesses. In *City of Richmond v. Croson* (1989), the court held that the affirmative action program violated the equal protection clause. Writing for the 6–3 majority, Justice O'Connor found that the program failed the first part of the strict scrutiny test because the city did not establish identified past discrimination in the construction industry to authorize race-based relief. The program failed the second part of the strict scrutiny test because it was not narrowly tailored—it was over-inclusive and race neutral means were not used to increase minority business participation in city contracting. Justice Marshall sharply criticized O'Connor's opinion for taking a step backward in the court's affirmative action jurisprudence, and he believed that the program was plainly constitutional under the intermediate level of scrutiny. Marshall described O'Connor's position as "constitutionalizing wishful thinking" by sending a signal that it regards racial discrimination as a phenomenon of the past and that government bodies need no longer preoccupy themselves with rectifying racial injustice.

The following term, the court addressed the constitutionality of two minority preference policies adopted by the Federal Communications Commission to promote program diversity: an enhancement for minority ownership in comparative proceedings for new licenses and a federal minority distress sale policy that permitted a limited category of existing television and radio broadcast stations in danger of losing their licenses to be sold to minority-controlled firms. In *Metro Broadcasting v. FCC* (1990), Justice Brennan persuaded Justices White and Stevens to uphold the minority preference policies under the intermediate standard of review. Brennan explained that the policies served the important governmental objective of broadcast diversity as expressed in extensive congressional hearings, testimony, and written materials. He also found that the policies were substantially related to the achievement of the federal government's interest in broadcast diversity for several reasons: they expanded minority ownership, broadcast diversity did not rest on impermissible stereotyping, the distress sale policy did not constitute a quota, and the policies did not impose an undue burden on whites, due to the small number of broadcast licenses. Brennan concluded that a congressionally mandated, benign race-conscious program was consistent with equal protection principles. Justice O'Connor argued in her dissent that *Croson* controlled the case and the strict scrutiny standard should have been applied to the commission's policies.

By 1995, Brennan, Marshall, and White were no longer on the Rehnquist Court. The court's ideological balance had shifted enough to make O'Connor's dissenting position in *Metro Broadcasting* the majority position in *Adarand Constructors v. Peña* (1995). In *Adarand*, the 5–4 majority overruled *Metro Broadcasting* and required the application of the strict scrutiny test to "all racial classifications, imposed by whatever federal, state, or local governmental actor." The conservative majority on the court—Chief Justice Rehnquist, O'Connor, Scalia, Thomas, and Kennedy—achieved their desired policy goal to compel the use of the strict scrutiny test to all cases challenging the constitutionality of racial classifications under the Fifth and Fourteenth Amendments. The jurisprudential regime change precedent was a significant victory for the New Right alliance that sought to have all race-based affirmative action programs declared unconstitutional.

Table 7.5. Rehnquist Court Affirmative Action Employment Cases, 1986–2005

Case	Vote	Outcome
United States v. Paradise (1987)	5–4	Held that the one-black-for-one-white promotion requirement for state troopers was permissible under strict scrutiny (L)
Johnson v. Transportation Agency (1987)	6–3	Held that a voluntary affirmative action plan for promoting women was valid under Title VII (L)
City of Richmond v. Croson (1989)	6–3	Held that a city's 30% minority business enterprise set-aside program was unconstitutional under strict scrutiny (C)
Metro Broadcasting v. FCC (1990)	5–4	Held that the FCC's minority preference policies were constitutional under the intermediate standard of review (L)
Adarand Constructors v. Peña (1995)	5–4	Held that all racial classifications imposed by all levels of government must be analyzed under strict scrutiny (C)

Source: Created by the author.

Note: C for conservative outcomes, and L for liberal outcomes.

Hate Crimes and Hate Speech

Congress responded to the proliferation of heinous crimes perpetrated against people of color and the LGBTQ community when it passed the Hate Crimes Statistics Act of 1990. The law required the Justice Department to track and report statistics about crimes that manifest evidence of prejudice based on race, religion, sexual orientation, or ethnicity. In response to the increased arsons directed at black churches, Congress passed the Church Arson Prevention Act of 1996, which prohibited the intentional defacement, damage, or destruction of religious property because of the race, color, or ethnic characteristics of the people associated with the churches. The Matthew Shepard and James Byrd, Jr., Hate Crimes Prevention Act of 2009 expanded the federal definition of hate crimes and the law criminalized willful violent conduct causing bodily harm through the use of fire, firearms, explosives, or other dangerous weapons because of the victim's actual or perceived race, color, religion, national origin, gender, sexual orientation, gender identity, or disability. For the first time in American history, Congress enacted an antilynching law—the Emmett Till Antilynching Act of 2022. The law made lynching a federal hate crime by imposing criminal penalties and fines on any person who conspired to commit a hate crime that resulted in death or serious bodily injury.

States and local governments responded to the rise in hate crimes by enacting laws designed to curtail violence against racial groups, Jews, and the LGBTQ community. The court considered the constitutionality of a hate crime law for the first time in *R. A. V. v. St. Paul* (1992). In 1990, the City of St. Paul enacted an ordinance that made it a misdemeanor for anyone to place on public or private property a symbol that aroused anger, alarm, or resentment in others on the basis of race, color, creed, religion, or gender. Seventeen-year-old high school dropout Robert Viktora, an avowed white separatist, and his accomplices burned a cross on a black family's yard. The police report indicated that Viktora instigated the cross burning when he asked his friends "if they wanted to cause some skinhead trouble." Viktora's hate crime charge was dismissed by a juvenile judge who ruled that the ordinance was unconstitutional. The Minnesota Supreme Court found that the ordinance prohibited fighting words, which were not protected by the First Amendment. In *R. A. V.*, all nine justices agreed that the St. Paul ordinance violated the First Amendment, but they were sharply divided on the rationale. Writing for the court, Justice Scalia found that the government could not regulate fighting words based on their content or viewpoint. He asserted that the government must remain neutral by not showing favoritism or hostility toward the underlying message. Justice White's concurrence, which resembled a dissent, criticized Scalia's opinion for failing to apply established First Amendment doctrine to the case. White believed that the law was too broad, because it risked making constitutionally protected speech unconstitutional and Scalia's approach appeared to legitimate hate speech as a form of public discussion.

After *R. A. V.* was decided, a federal prosecutor brought charges against Viktora and his accomplices for conspiring to violate the civil rights of the black family under § 241. The district court found the defendants guilty on all charges. The court revisited the question whether cross burning was protected speech in *Virginia v. Black* (2003). Three white men were convicted of violating a Virginia law that made it illegal to burn a cross on the property of another, a highway, or another public place with the intent to intimidate a person or group of persons. Writing for the 6–3 plurality, Justice O'Connor explained that cross burning was a form of protected symbolic speech, but unlike the ordinance in *R. A. V.*, the Virginia statute regulated a subset of intimidating messages in light of the long and pernicious history of cross burnings in the United States. O'Connor found that it was permissible for the state to ban cross burning with an intent to intimidate, but the part of the Virginia statute that treated any cross burning as prima facie evidence of intent to intimidate violated the First Amendment.

Some states enacted penalty enhancement legislation that required increased sentences if a crime was motivated by bias. Wisconsin's penalty enhancement law imposed a harsher sentence for an offense whenever the defendant intentionally selected the victim on account of race, religion, color, disability, sexual orientation, national origin, or ancestry. In 1989, nineteen-year-old Todd Mitchell and a group of his friends were watching the movie *Mississippi Burning*. After they left the apartment and while still discussing the movie, a fourteen-year-old white youth approached the complex on the opposite side of the street. Mitchell then stated, "There goes a white boy, go get him." The white youth was severely beaten by the group, and they were arrested, charged, and found guilty of the attack. Mitchell received a two-year prison sentence and two additional years under Wisconsin's penalty enhancement law. In *Wisconsin v. Mitchell* (1993), Chief Justice Rehnquist wrote the unanimous decision, which upheld the penalty enhancement legislation. Rehnquist explained that the main difference between the St. Paul ordinance and the penalty enhancement statute was that the ordinance violated the rule against content-based discrimination, whereas the penalty enhancement statute was aimed at conduct not protected by the First Amendment.

The hate crimes and hate speech cases revealed a tension between the important constitutional values of freedom of speech and racial equality. The Rehnquist Court was willing to protect racist speech but not racist conduct.

Jury Discrimination

The Rehnquist Court's jury discrimination decisions clarified and extended the *Batson* framework that required prosecutors to state a race neutral reason for striking jurors of color from venires. In *Powers v. Ohio* (1991), the court declared that a criminal defendant may object to the race-based exclusion of potential jurors by peremptory challenges notwithstanding the race of the defendant and the excluded jurors. In *Edmonson v. Leesville Concrete Company* (1991), the court extended *Batson* to the selection of juries in civil cases on state action grounds because a private litigant was deemed a government actor in the use of peremptories. In *Georgia v. McCollum* (1992), the court extended *Batson* to the discriminatory use of peremptories by defense counsel in criminal cases.

In *Hernandez v. New York* (1991), the court addressed the relationship between race, ethnicity, and language to decide whether a prosecutor's exclusion of prospective bilingual jurors should have been permitted in a murder case brought against a Latino defendant. During the voir dire, defense counsel objected to the prosecutor's use of four peremptory challenges to exclude potential Latino jurors because he felt uncertain that they would be able to listen and follow the interpreter. Justice Kennedy found no discriminatory intent inherent in the prosecutor's explanation for striking Latino jurors in a manner inconsistent with *Batson*. Kennedy explained that the prosecutor divided the prospective jurors into two classes—those who might have difficulty in accepting the translator's Spanish language testimony and those potential jurors who gave no such reason for doubt. Each category would include both Latinos and non-Latinos. Kennedy added that it "may well be, for certain ethnic groups and in some communities, that proficiency in a particular language, like skin color, should be treated as a surrogate for race under an equal protection analysis." As shown in table 7.6, the outcomes in

Table 7.6. Rehnquist Court Jury Discrimination Cases, 1986–2005

Case	Vote	Outcome
Holland v. Illinois (1990)	5–4	Held that *Batson* did not extend to peremptory challenges under the Sixth Amendment (C)
Ford v. Georgia (1991)	9–0	Held that a black defendant's pretrial motion preserved the *Batson* challenge (L)
Powers v. Ohio (1991)	7–2	Held that *Batson* applied regardless of the race of the defendant (L)
Edmonson v. Leesville Concrete Company (1991)	6–3	Held that *Batson* applied to civil cases (L)
Hernandez v. New York (1991)	6–3	Held that the use of peremptories to strike Spanish-speaking jurors was permissible (C)
Georgia v. McCollum (1992)	7–2	Held that *Batson* extended to defense counsel's use of peremptories in criminal cases (L)
J. E. B. v. Alabama ex rel. T. B. (1994)	6–3	Held that gender-based peremptory challenges violated the equal protection clause (L)
Purkett v. Elem (1995)	7–2	Upheld the use of peremptories based on the appearance of prospective black jurors (C)
Campbell v. Louisiana (1998)	7–2	Held that a white criminal defendant had standing to object to discrimination against blacks in the selection of grand jurors (L)

Source: Created by the author.

Note: C for conservative outcomes, and L for liberal outcomes.

the jury discrimination cases indicate that the Rehnquist Court exercised its power to ensure a fair trial and to obtain a representative jury.

The Death Penalty

During its first term, the Rehnquist Court decided the controversial case *McCleskey v. Kemp* (1987), which addressed the question of whether the imposition of the death penalty was racially discriminatory under the equal protection clause and the Eighth Amendment. In 1978, Warren McCleskey and three accomplices carried out a robbery of a furniture store in Atlanta, Georgia. The police officer who answered the silent alarm was shot and killed while walking through the store. McCleskey was arrested, convicted, and sentenced to death for armed robbery and murder. After exhausting post-conviction relief in state courts, McCleskey filed a petition for habeas relief in federal court that claimed that the Georgia death penalty statute was racially discriminatory under the Eighth and Fourteenth Amendments. During the trial, three expert witnesses presented statistical evidence to support McCleskey's contention that racial factors played a role in the application of the death sentence in Georgia. The experts examined more than two thousand murder cases that occurred in the state during the 1970s. The Baldus study found that blacks were more likely to receive the death penalty than any other defendant and black defendants who killed white victims were more likely to be sentenced to death.

Writing for the 5–4 majority, Justice Powell asserted that McCleskey failed to prove the existence of purposeful discrimination as required by the *Washington v. Davis* (1976) intent standard. Powell acknowledged that courts had relied on statistical data as proof of racial discrimination in Title VII cases, but in McCleskey's case, the state had no practical opportunity to rebut the Baldus study's findings. With regard to the operation of the criminal justice system, Powell explained that "we would demand exceptionally clear proof before we would infer that the discretion has been abused." Turning to the Eighth Amendment argument, Powell pointed out that the death penalty cases decided after *Gregg v. Georgia* (1976) imposed several requirements on the capital sentencing process to guarantee that decisions rested on individualized assessments. He found that McCleskey failed to successfully argue that his sentence was disproportionate to the crime in the traditional sense. Powell did not find any evidence that the Georgia capital punishment system was arbitrary and capricious based on the Baldus study statistics, because "they did not prove that race enters into any capital sentencing decision or that race was a factor in McCleskey's particular case."

Writing for the dissenters, Justice Brennan pointed out that since *Furman*, "the Court has been concerned with the risk of the imposition of an arbitrary sentence, rather than the proven fact of one." After an extensive examination of the Baldus study's findings, Brennan was persuaded that McCleskey's sentence was influenced by racial considerations, because "a majority of defendants in white-victim crimes would not have been sentenced to die if their victims had been black." When confronted with groundbreaking empirical evidence that the death penalty was racially discriminatory in its application, the court's response was that racial disparities in sentencing were an "inevitable part of our criminal justice system." The landmark *McCleskey v. Kemp* decision effectively closed the door to constitutional challenges alleging racial bias in death penalty cases based on statistical evidence.

Fair Housing

The Rehnquist Court decided three fair housing cases that did not break new ground, and two of the cases failed to advance fair housing protections. In *Town of Huntington v. Huntington Branch, NAACP* (1988), the court affirmed a Second Circuit decision that applied the disparate impact standard to a zoning classification that prohibited the construction of a multifamily housing project in the segregated New York suburb of Huntington. *Cuyahoga Falls v. Buckeye Community Hope Foundation* (2003) involved the repeal of an ordinance by voters that permitted the construction of low-income housing. The court unanimously found no intent to discriminate under the equal protection clause and subjecting the ordinance to the referendum process did not constitute arbitrary government conduct under the due process clause. In *Meyer v. Holley* (2003), an interracial couple sued the real estate sales agent and the president of the real estate company for racial discrimination when the agent prevented them from buying a home. The court unanimously held that the language of Title VIII of the Fair Housing Act of 1968 and its legislative history said nothing about extending vicarious liability and that corporate officers and shareholders were not automatically liable for the acts of the corporation's agents or employees. The court's limited policymaking in fair housing cases meant that it would be left up to the federal appellate courts to shape fair housing policies.

Conclusion

My examination of Rehnquist Court policymaking in race cases confirms that the court exercised its power to advance the negative civil rights agenda of the New Right alliance and to institute a color-blind jurisprudence to weaken liberal Warren and Burger Court precedents. The court's decisions undermined the intent of the Fourteenth and Fifteenth Amendments and federal civil rights statutes by restricting the rights of people of color in the issue areas of school desegregation, voting rights, employment discrimination, and capital punishment. The area of jury discrimination was the major exception to the court's adverse policymaking. During its nineteen-year operation, the Rehnquist Court decided fifty-five race cases. This low number can be explained in part by the passage of the Supreme Court Case Selection Act of 1988 that eliminated almost all of the court's mandatory jurisdiction (Owens and Simon 2012, 1279). The court exercised its new power by deciding significantly fewer cases than in the past. Compared to the Burger Court's 68 percent liberal policymaking record, the Rehnquist Court's record was significantly lower—51 percent of the race cases were decided in a conservative direction, and 49 percent were decided in a liberal direction in favor of people of color or pro–civil rights claimants.

Institutional constraints, both external and internal, prevented the Rehnquist Court from fully implementing its anti-egalitarian policy agenda. Congress responded to the court's attempt to radically alter the Burger Court's Title VII jurisprudence by overriding its adverse employment discrimination rulings. Congress and the executive remained committed to the democratic value of political equality by renewing and strengthening the Voting Rights Act. The strategic behavior of the justices affected the outcomes in race cases. During his thirty-three-year tenure on the court, Rehnquist played the long game, which empowered him to move the court in a conservative direction that was compatible with his sincerely held preferences on race and the views of like-minded justices: O'Connor, Thomas, Scalia, and Kennedy. Byron White, a Kennedy appointee, would vote as a swing justice in some race cases to give the conservative bloc the fifth vote to restrict the rights of people of color. The Democratic appointees, Ginsburg and Breyer, coalesced with the Republican appointees Blackmun, Stevens, and Souter, who drifted to the left on issues of race after the retirements of Brennan and Marshall. Despite these constraints, Rehnquist Court policymaking paved the jurisprudential path for the next court to advance an anti–civil rights policy agenda. Chief Justice Rehnquist lived long enough to see his former law clerk, John Roberts, Jr., nominated to the position of associate justice. Twenty-six days after Rehnquist's death, the Senate confirmed John Roberts to become the seventeenth chief justice.

Chapter 8

The Roberts Court, 2005–2025

A series of consequential domestic events occurred during the Roberts Court era. In 2007, the economy began to decline, and by 2008 the United States experienced a serious economic downturn. In the midst of this recession, a historic presidential election was taking place in 2008. The United States elected its first African American president, Barak Obama, and his running mate, Joe Biden, in a landslide election. The Obama administration policies successfully stabilized the economy, and his signature policy accomplishment, the Affordable Care Act, narrowly survived a constitutional challenge before the Roberts Court in 2012. During the two terms of the Obama presidency, hyperpartisanship and hyperpolarization at the national level and in the electorate became the status quo in the United States. New Right conservatism and conspiracy theories took center stage in American politics. The 2016 presidential election contest pitted a conventional Democratic nominee, Hillary Clinton, against an unconventional Republican nominee, Donald Trump. Trump's right-wing populist campaign pledge to "Make America Great Again" was sufficient for him to win the electoral college vote but not the popular vote in the November 2016 election. Another historic presidential election occurred in November 2020 when the Democratic nominee, Joe Biden, and his running mate, Kamala Harris, won the election, which had record levels of turnout despite the COVID-19 pandemic. Harris became the first woman and the first African American vice president in US history. Donald Trump attempted to remain in office by spreading the "Big Lie" that Biden stole the election. At the behest of Trump, MAGA supporters stormed the US Capitol on January 6, 2021, to prevent the peaceful transfer of power. In the 2024 presidential election, Trump defeated Harris and Republicans regained control of Congress.

For decades, the base of the Republican Party demanded that movement conservatives be appointed to the federal bench to carry out their social and political agenda. The Federalist Society, an influential legal organization backed by conservatives and big money donors, played an outsized role in federal judicial selection for the Republican Party. The 2016 presidential election was the watershed event that over time transformed the Roberts Court's conservative majority into a hard right supermajority. With regard to race, Roberts Court policymaking is not viewed as analytically distinct from Rehnquist Court policymaking. Both courts were fully committed partners of the New Right alliance, and they advanced the alliance's negative civil rights agenda. Both courts imposed a color-blind interpretation to the Fourteenth and Fifteenth Amendments, and they attempted to dismantle the protections of federal civil rights laws. Unlike the Rehnquist Court, Congress and the executive failed to check the Roberts Court's aggressive exercise of power to turn back the jurisprudential clock to an era of racial hierarchy and political powerlessness.

The Composition of the Roberts Court

When Sandra Day O'Connor informed President George Bush of her decision to retire on July 1, 2005, Bush nominated 50-year-old DC Circuit judge John G. Roberts, Jr., to succeed O'Connor. Roberts served in the Reagan and George H. W. Bush administrations prior to his appointment to the DC Circuit. Roberts's Senate confirmation was easy because he was considered to be exceptionally well-qualified for the position, he lacked a paper trail, and his views on conservative culture war issues were not publicly known. Three days prior to Roberts's confirmation hearing on September 7, Chief Justice William Rehnquist died from thyroid cancer at the age of 80. Bush promptly withdrew Roberts's associate justice nomination and renominated him for the position of chief justice. On September 29, 2005, the Senate confirmed Roberts to become the seventeenth chief justice by a 78–22 vote. Bush announced the nomination of Harriet Miers, his White House counsel and long-time friend, to fill O'Connor's seat. Right wing interest groups derailed the Miers nomination because of her apparent lack of commitment to movement conservatism and her underwhelming legal qualifications for a position on the court. Bush withdrew Miers's nomination and nominated fifty-five-year-old Third Circuit judge Samuel Alito, Jr., to fill O'Connor's seat. While serving on the Third Circuit, Alito was called "Scalito" because of the similarities between his conservative judicial philosophy and Justice Antonin Scalia's views. In January 2006, Alito was confirmed by a 58–42 vote.

Justice David Souter informed President Obama of his decision to retire at the end of the 2008 term. Obama nominated fifty-four-year-old Second Circuit judge Sonya Sotomayor to succeed Souter. Despite attempts by Republicans to galvanize opposition against her, Sotomayor was easily confirmed by the Democratic controlled Senate in August 2009 by a 68–31 vote. Born to Puerto Rican parents, Sotomayor became the first Latina Supreme Court justice. When ninety-year-old John Paul Stevens announced his retirement in 2010, Obama nominated fifty-year-old Elena Kagan to succeed Stevens. Kagan taught law at the University of Chicago and served as Dean of Harvard's law school prior to becoming US solicitor general—the first woman to hold that position. In August 2010, Kagan was easily confirmed by a 61–31 vote.

On February 13, 2016, the seventy-nine-year-old conservative judicial icon, Antonin Scalia, died of natural causes while he was vacationing at a hunting resort in Texas. About an hour after Scalia's death was confirmed, Senate majority leader Mitch McConnell announced that the vacancy should not be filled until after the upcoming presidential election. Obama nominated sixty-three-year-old DC Circuit judge Merrick Garland to fill Scalia's seat, but McConnell successfully blocked Obama's third nomination by refusing to hold confirmation hearings. McConnell's obstructionism paid off when Trump won the 2016 election. In January 2017, Trump nominated forty-nine-year-old old Tenth Circuit judge Neil Gorsuch to fill the eleven-month-old vacancy. The Republican controlled Senate confirmed Gorsuch by a 54–45 vote.

In 2018, eighty-one-year-old Anthony Kennedy informed Trump of his intention to retire at the end of the term. Trump nominated fifty-three-year-old DC Circuit judge Brett Kavanaugh to succeed Kennedy. It appeared that Kavanaugh would be easily confirmed by the Republican controlled Senate until allegations of sexual assault surfaced that dated back to his high school and college years. Psychology professor Christine Blasey Ford testified before the Senate Judiciary Committee that when she was fifteen, she attended a party at a private home in Bethesda, Maryland, where seventeen-year-old Kavanaugh, who was drunk, sexually assaulted her in the presence of his friend, Mark Judge. Kavanaugh's three-hour testimony rebutting Ford's allegations was filled with strong emotion, rage, and combativeness with Democratic Senators. He characterized Ford's allegations as "a calculated and orchestrated political hit fueled with apparent pent-up anger about

President Trump and the 2016 election, fear that has been unfairly stoked about my judicial record, revenge on behalf of the Clintons, and millions of dollars in money from outside left-wing opposition groups" (Senate Judiciary Committee 2018, 683). After the confirmation hearing spectacle, the Republican controlled Senate confirmed Kavanaugh by a 50–48 vote.

On September 18, 2020, eighty-seven-year-old Ruth Bader Ginsburg died from cancer. Democrats had pressured Ginsburg to retire during the Obama administration given her health challenges, but the window to retire during a Democratic administration closed after Trump won the 2016 election. Unlike the Scalia vacancy, McConnell announced that the Senate would quickly fill Ginsburg's seat despite the pending presidential election. On September 26, Trump nominated forty-eight-year-old Seventh Circuit judge Amy Coney Barrett to succeed Ginsburg. Barrett lacked the conventional Ivy League education credentials for a seat on the Supreme Court. Prior to her Seventh Circuit appointment, Barrett taught law at Notre Dame for fifteen years. Barrett's confirmation was extraordinarily fast. Hearings were held on October 12, and she was confirmed on October 26 by a 52–48 vote—eight days prior to the November election.

In January 2022, eighty-three-year-old Stephen Breyer heeded the call of Democrats to retire from the court. President Biden fulfilled his campaign promise to appoint an African American woman to the court when he nominated DC Circuit judge Ketanji Brown Jackson to succeed Breyer. Prior to her DC District Court appointment, Jackson served as an assistant federal public defender and a commissioner on the US Sentencing Commission. Jackson's confirmation hearing deteriorated into a contentious and disrespectful spectacle by Republicans on the Senate Judiciary Committee who sought to derail her nomination. During their questioning, Senators Josh Hawley and Lindsey Graham smeared Brown for being soft on pedophiles and pornographers to appease their QAnon and MAGA constituents. Senator Ted Cruz's demeaning antics included repeated questioning, which asked Jackson to define "what is a woman." Cruz interjected race into his questioning by asking Jackson if she thought babies were racist while holding up a children's picture book and whether critical race theory should be taught in the public schools. When Jackson attempted to answer their questions, the Republican senators frequently interrupted her in what became the most vile and racist Senate Judiciary Committee confirmation hearing for a court nominee ever held. Jackson was confirmed by the Democratic controlled Senate on April 7, 2022, by a 53–47 vote. The MAGA Senators' treatment of Jackson confirmed the findings of Boyd, Ringhand, and Collins

(2018) that minority female nominees are more likely to experience bias and disrespectful behavior during Supreme Court confirmation hearings than male nominees.

Education

Two issues appeared on the Roberts Court's education agenda: school resegregation and the use of race-conscious admissions in higher education. The court was asked to address the nationwide problem of an increasingly diverse but residentially segregated society and its impact on school desegregation. The attack on the use of race-conscious admissions by elite colleges and universities gained considerable momentum. Movement conservatives turned to the electorate via the initiative process and coordinated litigation strategies to prohibit the use of affirmative action programs in university admissions on a permanent basis. The Roberts Court applied principles of race neutrality, color-blindness, and revisionist interpretations to the Fourteenth Amendment and the *Brown* decision to advance the policy goals of movement conservativism.

SCHOOL DESEGREGATION

The Seattle and Louisville school districts voluntarily adopted school choice plans that considered the race of the student among other school assignment factors to desegregate schools. White parents challenged the constitutionality of the plans when their children were denied admission to their first-choice schools. The Ninth and Sixth Circuits found that the school choice plans were constitutional under the equal protection clause. In the lead case, *Parents Involved in Community Schools v. Seattle School District No. 1* (2007), Chief Justice Roberts wrote the 5–4 plurality decision that struck down the school districts' use of race in the assignment of students to public schools. Roberts applied the strict scrutiny test to the school choice plans, which required the school districts to demonstrate that the racial classification used to assign students was narrowly tailored to achieve a compelling governmental interest. The school districts argued that the use of race was necessary to achieve diversity because education and broader socialization benefits flow from a racially diverse learning environment. Roberts rejected the school districts' reliance on the *Grutter v. Bollinger* (2003) rationale to justify their plans because the broad-based interest in diversity was unique to higher education. He asserted that racial demographics were the driving force behind the diversity numbers in both plans and enrolling students without regard to their race would yield a substantially diverse student body under any definition of diversity. Roberts criticized the school districts for their failure to show that other methods besides race were considered to achieve diversity. Roberts concluded that both plans in design and operation were "directed only to racial balance, pure and simple, an objective this Court has repeatedly condemned as illegitimate."

Roberts applied a race-neutral interpretation to the *Brown* precedent to support his argument that racial classifications should not be used to assign children to schools. He asserted that "it was not the inequality of the facilities but the fact of legally separating children on the basis of race on which the Court relied to find a constitutional violation in 1954." He concluded that the school districts "have not carried the heavy burden of demonstrating that we should not allow this once again—even for very different reasons." Roberts insisted that "the way to stop discrimination on the basis of race is to stop discriminating on the basis of race." Justice Kennedy, who concurred in part and concurred in the judgment, criticized Roberts's opinion for implying "an all-too unyielding insistence that race cannot be a factor in instances when, in my view, it may be taken into account." Kennedy did not believe that the postulate, "the only way to stop discriminating on the basis of race is to stop discriminating on the basis of race," was sufficient to decide the cases. Not only was Kennedy skeptical of the view that the Constitution required school districts to ignore the problem of de facto resegregation, he criticized Roberts's embrace of a color-blind Constitution: "The statement by Justice Harlan that '[o]ur Constitution is color-blind' was most certainly justified in the context of his dissent in *Plessy v. Ferguson* (1896). . . . And, as an aspiration, Justice Harlan's axiom must command our assent. In the real world, it is regrettable to say, it cannot be a universal constitutional principle."

Justice Breyer wrote a seventy-seven-page dissent joined by Justices Stevens, Souter, and Ginsburg that strongly criticized Roberts's opinion on multiple grounds: "it distorts precedent, it misapplies the relevant constitutional principles, it announces legal rules that will obstruct efforts by state and local governments to deal effectively with the growing resegregation of public schools, it threatens to substitute for present calm a disruptive round of race-related litigation, and it undermines *Brown*'s promise of integrated primary and secondary education that local communities have sought to make this a reality. This cannot be justified in the name of the Equal Protection

Clause." Breyer pointed out that the Seattle and Louisville plans resembled many other plans adopted by school boards in the last fifty years that "represent local efforts to bring about the kind of racially integrated education that *Brown v. Board of Education* (1954) long ago promised—efforts that this Court has repeatedly required, permitted, and encouraged local authorities to undertake." The outcomes in the school desegregation decisions since the 1980s indicate that the court has played its part in the resegregation of public schools in the United States (Frankenberg and Orfield 2012, 5–8; Orfield and Jarvie 2020).

AFFIRMATIVE ACTION IN HIGHER EDUCATION

Universities responded to the *Grutter* decision by revising their admissions policies to use race in a holistic way. After Texas passed the Top Ten Percent law, which guaranteed admission to students who graduated from a Texas high school in the top ten percent of their class, a white high school student who was not in the ten percent of her class challenged the way the University of Texas used race under its holistic review process. In *Fisher v. University of Texas* (2013), the court ruled that the Fifth Circuit applied an incorrect standard to assess the constitutionality of the university's admission policy. When the case reached the court two years later, the constitutionality of the University of Texas's admission policy was upheld under strict scrutiny in *Fisher v. University of Texas* (2016). Justice Kennedy emphasized the uniqueness of the university's admissions policy, because it combined both holistic review and a percentage plan. Kennedy accepted the university's compelling interest in the educational benefits that flowed from student body diversity, and the university articulated concrete and precise goals to achieve that interest. The fact that Justice Kennedy wrote the majority opinion was surprising because he had previously voted against affirmative action policies. In his dissent, Justice Alito pointed out Kennedy's defection by using his own positions in prior cases against him.

In 2014, the Students for Fair Admissions group filed separate lawsuits against Harvard College and the University of North Carolina, alleging that their use of race-conscious admissions violated the equal protection. The affirmative action policies attacked in the litigation were those used by private and public elite universities that processed thousands of applications for a limited number of seats. In both cases, the trial courts upheld the constitutionality of the admissions programs, and the First Circuit affirmed the district court's ruling in the Harvard case. In the highly anticipated decision, *Students for Fair Admissions v. Harvard College* (2023), the court ruled that the use of race-conscious admissions by both universities was unconstitutional in a decision that exceeded 200 pages.

Chief Justice Roberts wrote the 6–3 majority opinion, which mirrored his *Parents Involved* opinion in certain respects. At the outset, Roberts presented a minimalist historical account of the Fourteenth Amendment until *Brown* was decided. He asserted that the core purpose of the equal protection clause was to do away with all governmentally imposed discrimination based on race. Roberts's application of a race neutral approach to the Fourteenth Amendment meant that there was no legal distinction between invidious and benign racial classifications, and that "eliminating racial discrimination means eliminating all of it." He asserted that all uses of race must satisfy the strict scrutiny standard with the exception of remediating identified instances of past discrimination that violated the Constitution or a statute, and avoiding imminent and serious risks to human safety in prisons.

Without explicitly overruling *Bakke*, *Grutter*, and *Fisher*, Roberts applied a more restrictive strict scrutiny standard that would make it extremely difficult for universities to create race-conscious admissions programs. The universities argued that they had a compelling interest in the educational benefits of diversity, such as training future leaders in the public and private sectors, preparing graduates to adapt to an increasingly pluralistic society, producing new knowledge stemming from diverse outlooks, promoting the robust exchange of ideas, promoting cross-racial understanding, and breaking down racial stereotypes. Roberts described the universities' "compelling reason to racially discriminate" as a "grab bag of interests" to justify their programs. He found that the goals were "commendable," but they were not "sufficiently coherent for purposes of strict scrutiny." Roberts believed that the goals were too vague to be reviewed by courts.

Chief Justice Roberts found that the means used by the universities to achieve the educational benefits of diversity failed the second part of the strict scrutiny test. The University of North Carolina argued that it worked to avoid the underrepresentation of minority groups, while Harvard guarded against the inadvertent drop-offs in representation of certain minority groups. Both universities classified students into six broad categories: Asian, Native Hawaiian or Pacific Islander, Hispanic, White, African American, and Native American. Roberts criticized the racial categories used by the universities because they were overbroad—they grouped together all Asian students without determining whether South Asian or East Asian students were adequately represented, and racial categories such as Hispanic were arbitrary or undefined. Roberts established that "courts may not license separating students on the basis of race without an exceedingly persuasive justification that is measurable and concrete enough to permit judicial review." Roberts also found that the admissions programs failed to comply with the twin commands of the equal protection clause that race may never be used as a negative and that it may not operate as a stereotype. He explained that when a university admits students on the basis of race, it engages in the offensive and demeaning assumption that students of a particular race, because of their race, think alike in the sense of being different from nonminority students.

Roberts identified two additional problems with the universities' admissions policies: the programs lacked a logical endpoint, and they constituted racial balancing. Roberts was not persuaded by the universities' argument that the use of race in admissions will end when there was meaningful representation and diversity. After examining their admissions percentages by race, Roberts characterized them as outright racial balancing. He did not believe that the universities would act in good faith to "comply with the Equal Protection Clause any time soon." In a footnote, Roberts indicated that the use of race in military academy admissions may be an exception "in light of the potentially distinct interests" they may present. He also pointed out that the decision did not prevent applicants from discussing race in their personal essays and universities may consider them in the limited context of individualized assessments of the applicants' personal qualities but not to thwart compliance with the decision.

Justices Gorsuch, Kavanaugh, and Thomas wrote separate concurring opinions. Gorsuch asserted that the race-conscious admissions programs violated Title VI of the Civil Rights Act of 1964. He took the extreme position that the racial categories used by universities came from bureaucrats who devised the scheme of racial classifications to facilitate data collection. Citing an amicus curiae brief, Gorsuch criticized the current system of self-reporting racial identity because it leads to fraud, exaggeration, confusion about how to self-identify, and the inconsistent treatment of multiracial applicants. Although Justice Kavanaugh acknowledged that "racial discrimination still occurs and the effects of past racial discrimination still persist," he asserted that "federal and state civil rights laws serve to deter and provide remedies for current acts of racial discrimination." Justice Thomas's lengthy concurrence recounted his well-known contempt for race-conscious policies, and he argued that they were the same as racial segregation. Thomas's originalist defense of color-blind constitutionalism was based on a fundamentally flawed and ahistorical interpretation of the Fourteenth Amendment and Reconstruction era civil rights statutes. He supported his arguments by twisting the meaning of precedents, taking statements out of context, making preposterous claims, citing flawed studies, and making incoherent legal positions. In a footnote, Thomas made the false claim that Thurgood Marshall and other LDF counsel who participated in the *Brown* litigation were adherents of his version of color-blind constitutionalism. Marshall, who was on the court when *Bakke* was decided and participated in several affirmative action cases, was a harsh critic of color-blind constitutionalism.

Justice Sonia Sotomayor wrote a penetrating critique of Chief Justice Roberts's restrictive views of the Fourteenth Amendment in a lengthy dissenting opinion joined by Justices Kagan and Jackson. Sotomayor's dissent ranks alongside Justice John Marshall Harlan's dissenting opinion in *Plessy* and Justice Thurgood Marshall's opinion in *Bakke* in their support of a broad interpretation of the equal protection clause. Sotomayor rejected Roberts's imposition of a color-blind interpretation on the Fourteenth Amendment to invalidate the use of race-conscious means "in a society that is not, and has never been, colorblind." Turning to Roberts's specific criticisms of the universities' admissions policies, Sotomayor explained that the requirement that the universities' interests must be measurable and require a precise definition was not only unworkable but it was created to ensure that all race-conscious plans fail. She pointed out that the exemption of military academies from its ruling "further proves that the Fourteenth Amendment does not categorically prohibit the use of race in college admissions." Sotomayor disputed Roberts's claim that the decision did not prohibit universities from considering race in student application essays as "nothing but an attempt to put lipstick on a pig." She criticized Roberts's assertion that recognition of racial identity amounts to a stereotype by countering that it was the absence of racial diversity that actually contributed to stereotyping.

Sotomayor rejected Roberts's contention that the racial categories used by the universities were imprecise, opaque, and arbitrary. She noted that the majority failed to identify a single instance where the universities' data collection methods prevented any student from reporting their race with the level of detail they preferred, and students had the option to choose whether to identify as one, multiple, or none of the racial categories on the application. She dismissed Roberts's assertion that the universities were engaging in racial balancing on the ground that they had to pay some attention to the numbers; otherwise, they would "blindly operate their limited race-conscious programs without regard for any quantitative information" and therefore lack the ability to assess the success of their programs and meet their diversity goals. Sotomayor concluded that the decision will slow the significant progress already achieved in the enrollment of underrepresented minorities on college campuses, it will decrease the pipeline of racially diverse college graduates to crucial professions, and it will further entrench racial inequality by lessening opportunities to benefit from powerful networks and the opportunity for socioeconomic mobility.

The landmark *Fair Admissions* decision was a significant turning point in the doctrinal development of the court's equal protection jurisprudence. An unconstrained, hard right supermajority found that any racial sorting of people was unconstitutional unless it was done to remediate identified instances of past discrimination. The decision was a significant victory for opponents of race-conscious policies because it provided a constitutional basis to attack diversity, equity, and inclusion policies outside of the higher education context.

Table 8.1. Roberts Court Education Cases, 2005–2025

Case	Vote	Outcome
Parents Involved in Community Schools v. Seattle School District No. 1 (2007)	5–4	Held that school districts' use of race in making school assignments violated the equal protection clause (C)
Fisher v. University of Texas (2013) (*Fisher I*)	7–1	Held that the lower court should have applied strict scrutiny to determine the constitutionality of the university's race-conscious admissions program (C)
Schuette v. Coalition to Defend Affirmative Action (2014)	6–2	Held that the political process rule did not apply to a state constitutional amendment that banned the use of racial preferences in public university admissions (C)
Fisher v. University of Texas (2016) (*Fisher II*)	4–3	Held that the university's use of race in the admissions process was constitutional under strict scrutiny (L)
Students for Fair Admissions v. Harvard College (2023)	6–3	Held that the universities' race-conscious admissions program was unconstitutional under the equal protection clause (C)

Source: Created by the author.

Note: C for conservative outcomes, and L for liberal outcomes.

Voting Rights

In May 2006, a bill was introduced in Congress to extend the temporary provisions of the Voting Rights Act for twenty-five years. The bill kept the law's current coverage formula, and it overturned two Rehnquist Court cases, *Reno v. Bossier Parish School Board* (2000) and *Georgia v. Ashcroft* (2003), which were viewed as attempts to weaken § 5's preclearance provision. The House Judiciary Committee hearings revealed that despite the significant progress made in eliminating first generation barriers to voting, second generation barriers persisted and prevented voters of color from fully participating in the electoral process. Opponents of the reauthorization bill mobilized to end their protections, but they were countered by a broad coalition of civil rights groups, grassroots organizations, and voting rights advocates who sought to strengthen them. The Voting Rights Act Reauthorization and Amendments Act of 2006 was passed with overwhelming bipartisan support in both houses and President George Bush signed the bill into law on July 27, 2006.

Vote Suppression

In *Crawford v. Marion County Election Board* (2008), the Roberts Court made it more difficult to challenge facially neutral voter identification laws that had a disproportionate effect on the ability of minority and poor citizens to participate in elections. The Republican controlled Indiana legislature enacted a strict photo ID law that required voters to produce a state or federal government-issued photo ID to vote in person in primary and general elections. Indigent voters or voters who had religious objections to being photographed could cast a provisional ballot that would be counted only if they executed a sworn affidavit before the circuit clerk within ten days following the election. The state claimed that the law was necessary to deter and detect voter fraud, but the NAACP and other groups challenged the law on the ground that it constituted an unconstitutional undue burden on the right to vote. Justice John Paul Stevens acknowledged that the record contained no evidence of voter fraud actually occurring in Indiana at any time in history, but the risk of voter fraud was real. Stevens dismissed the burdens placed on voters to obtain a photo ID as "that sort arising from life's vagaries," and they were not so serious or frequent as to question the constitutionality of the law. In his dissent, Justice Souter argued that the law imposed economic burdens on tens of thousands of Indiana's citizens who were mostly poor, old, and disabled voters who did not drive. He explained that the law left untouched other problems associated with elections: absentee ballot fraud, vote buying, ballot stuffing, and other forms of corruption. The *Crawford* decision allowed Republican controlled state legislatures to enact strict photo ID laws based on the myth of widespread voter fraud in elections held in communities of color.

Section Five Preclearance

Ten days after the Voting Rights Act reauthorization bill became law, Edward Blum, the architect behind the *Fisher* and *Fair Admissions* lawsuits and head of the conservative activist organization Project on Fair Representation, recruited a small Texas water district with an electoral board to challenge the constitutionality of the law's preclearance provision (Biskupic 2012a, 2012b). The Northwest Austin Municipal Utility District asked the federal district court to declare § 5 unconstitutional if it found the utility district ineligible for bailout under § 4(a) of the law. In *Northwest Austin Municipal Utility District No. One v. Holder* (2009), the court ruled that all political subdivisions, including a water district, were eligible to file a bailout lawsuit. Chief Justice Roberts avoided the constitutional challenge to § 5, but he issued a warning about the Voting Rights Act's coverage formula:

> Things have changed in the South. Voter turnout and registration rates now approach parity. Blatantly discriminatory evasions of federal decrees are rare. And minority candidates hold office at unprecedented levels. These improvements are no doubt due in significant part to the Voting Rights Act itself, and stand as a monument to its success. Past success alone, however, is not adequate justification to retain the preclearance requirements. It may be that these improvements are insufficient and that conditions continue to warrant preclearance under the Act. But the Act imposes current burdens and must be justified by current needs. . . . The statute's coverage formula is based on data that is now more than 35 years old, and there is considerable evidence that it fails to account for current political conditions.

After Blum lost the *Northwest Austin* case, he convinced the Calera, Alabama, city attorney to challenge the constitutionality of the preclearance and coverage formula provisions—the heart of the Voting Rights Act. In *Shelby*

County v. Holder (2013), the Roberts Court struck down the law's coverage formula, which automatically made the preclearance provision inoperable. Chief Justice Roberts found that the Voting Rights Act sharply departed from the principles of federalism and equal state sovereignty based on the operation of the preclearance process, which applied only to nine states. He cited the 2006 congressional reauthorization findings to support his assertion that "the Act has proved immensely successful at redressing racial discrimination and integrating the voting process." Roberts berated Congress for not easing the preclearance restrictions or narrowing the scope of the coverage formula. He found that the coverage formula was based on "decades-old data and eradicated practices" and that the Fifteenth Amendment was "not designed to punish for the past; its purpose is to ensure a better future." He explained that Congress's failure to act left the court "no choice but to declare § 4(b) unconstitutional. The formula in that section can no longer be used as a basis for subjecting jurisdictions to preclearance." The decision did not affect § 2's permanent nationwide ban on racial discrimination in voting, and Roberts left it up to Congress to draft another coverage formula based on current conditions.

Writing for the dissenters, Justice Ruth Bader Ginsburg framed the question as one of congressional power to enforce the Fifteenth Amendment. After presenting an extensive overview of the history of racial discrimination in voting, Ginsburg asserted that *South Carolina v. Katzenbach* (1966), which upheld the Voting Rights Act's coverage formula and preclearance provisions, established that "Congress may use any rational means to effectuate the constitutional prohibition of racial discrimination in voting." Ginsburg explained that the 2006 congressional reauthorization satisfied the rational means test and that the burden on the statute's challenger should be higher when the court has previously affirmed the reauthorization of a remedy based on exhaustive evidence gathering and a bipartisan deliberative process.

Republican-controlled state legislatures responded to the *Shelby County* decision in ways that indicated that conditions in the South had not changed that much after all. Previously covered states enacted restrictive laws that targeted every aspect of voting: strict voter ID laws, making voter registration more difficult, curtailing early voting, closing polling places, limiting voter assistance, limiting vote by mail, and criminalizing the voting process (Singh and Carter 2023; McChristian and Kane 2023). Previously covered jurisdictions could draw new redistricting maps without preapproval (Williams 2022). The John Lewis Voting Rights Advancement Act was reintroduced in 2023 to restore the preclearance requirement and update the coverage formula, but hyperpartisanship and polarization in Congress have prevented its passage.

Table 8.2. Roberts Court Vote Suppression and Preclearance Cases,
2005–2025

Case	Vote	Outcome
Riley v. Kennedy (2008)	7–2	Held that Alabama's reinstatement of its prior practice of gubernatorial appointment to the Mobile County Commission did not constitute a change that required preclearance (C)
Crawford v. Marion County Election Board (2008)	6–3	Held that an Indiana law that required voters to show a government-issued photo ID prior to casting a ballot did not burden the right to vote under the Fourteenth Amendment (C)
Northwest Austin Municipal Utility District No. One v. Holder (2009)	8–1	Held that § 4's bailout provision applied to all political subdivisions, including utility districts, seeking bailout (L)
Shelby County v. Holder (2013)	5–4	Held that the Voting Rights Act's coverage formula was unconstitutional, which made the preclearance provision inoperable (C)
Berger v. North Carolina State Conference of the NAACP (2022)	8–1	Held that two Republican North Carolina legislators could intervene in a lawsuit to defend the constitutionality of the state's voter ID law (C)

Source: Created by the author.

Note: C for conservative outcomes, and L for liberal outcomes.

RACE-CONSCIOUS REDISTRICTING

After the *Shelby County* decision, minority voters turned to § 2 of the Voting Rights Act to challenge discriminatory voting schemes. The Roberts Court's response to § 2 lawsuits was mixed. In *Abbott v. Perez* (2018), Justice Samuel Alito reversed the district court's findings that Texas intentionally discriminated against black and Latino voters when the state adopted the 2013 congressional and state house maps. He asserted that the district court disregarded the presumption of legislative good faith and improperly placed the burden of proof on the state to show a lack of discrimination. *Brnovich v. Democratic National Committee* (2021) considered a challenge to two restrictive voting policies enacted by the Republican Arizona legislature: an out-of-precinct policy that required the discarding of the entire ballot if the voter cast the ballot outside of a voter's assigned polling place on election day and a policy that banned the practice of collecting and delivering mail-in ballots for voters. The Democratic Party argued that both policies operated unequally to the disadvantage of Latinos, blacks, and Native Americans, because their ballots were thrown out at a statistically higher rate than whites and rural Native American communities lacked access to mail service. Alito upheld the legality of both policies under § 2 on the ground that they were facially neutral time, place, or manner voting rules. He explained that the *Thornburg v. Gingles* (1986) factors did not apply to the case, and the policies were unremarkable burdens that merely inconvenienced some voters.

There was considerable speculation that the court would use an Alabama redistricting case to eviscerate § 2's vote dilution jurisprudence. Alabama was required to redraw its seven congressional districts after the 2020 census showed a 5 percent population growth in the state that was unevenly distributed. Black plaintiffs sued the state after the legislature drew a map that included one majority black district in a state where blacks comprised over twenty-seven percent of the population. They argued that the map was an intentional discriminatory scheme to pack and crack black voters into four congressional districts to prevent the creation of a second majority black district. A three-judge district court comprised of two Trump appointees found that a second majority black district could have been drawn that would satisfy the *Gingles* framework for proving vote dilution.

In *Allen v. Milligan* (2023), Chief Justice Roberts and Brett Kavanaugh voted with the three liberal justices, Kagan, Sotomayor, and Jackson, to reject an interpretation of § 2 that would revise and reformulate the four decades old *Gingles* framework. Roberts found that the plaintiffs presented examples of redistricting maps that contained two majority-black districts that were roughly compact, contained equal populations, were contiguous, respected existing political subdivisions, and they joined a community of interest called the Black Belt that contained a high proportion of black voters. With regard to the second and third *Gingles* preconditions, Roberts found that there was no serious dispute that black Alabama voters were politically cohesive and the white majority voted as a bloc to usually defeat black voters' preferred candidates. Roberts flatly rejected "Alabama's attempt to remake our § 2 jurisprudence anew" by proposing a novel approach to vote dilution cases—a race-neutral benchmark theory based on the use of computer technology that would allow mapmakers to generate millions of possible districting maps according to traditional districting criteria but race would not be considered. His conclusion ran counter to Justice Clarence Thomas's support for a meaningful race-neutral benchmark to resolve vote dilution claims under § 2 and Justice Alito's desire to require the district court to determine whether race played a predominant role in the production of the plaintiffs' illustrative maps.

The NAACP challenged a map drawn by the South Carolina state legislature that moved almost two-thirds of the black voters in District 1 into District 6, which was represented by James Clyburn, the only Democrat and black representative in the South Carolina congressional delegation. After an extensive hearing process, the three-judge district court comprised of Democratic appointed judges found that the legislature engaged in race-based districting in violation of the equal protection clause. In *Alexander v. South Carolina State Conference of the NAACP* (2024), the court ruled that the district court's finding that race predominated in the design of District 1 was clearly erroneous. Justice Alito rejected the district court's presumption that the legislature had acted in bad faith, he criticized the expert reports as being deeply flawed because they ignored traditional districting criteria, and he added that the plaintiffs failed to meet the high bar for a racial gerrymander claim because they did not produce an alternative map showing that "a rational legislature sincerely driven by its professed partisan goals would have drawn a different map with greater racial balance." Alito explained that a vote dilution claim was analytically distinct from a racial gerrymandering claim and the plaintiffs were required to show that the state's districting plan had the purpose and effect of diluting the minority vote. The court remanded the case in light of the district court's errors.

In her scathing critique of Alito's opinion, Justice Elena Kagan pointed out that the district court resolved the factual dispute between the parties—whether race was used to expel residents out of District I—correctly after overseeing broad discovery, holding a nine-day trial that featured two dozen witnesses and hundreds of exhibits, evaluating evidence about the state's geography and politics, hearing firsthand testimony about the redistricting process, and considering the views of statistical experts. She reminded Alito that electoral districting factfinding was reversible only for clear error, and the majority should have given the district court's findings significant deference. In his concurrence, Justice Thomas responded to Alito's opinion by stating that clear error review was not an invitation for the court to sift through volumes of facts and argue its interpretations of the facts. He believed that Alito's searching review of the expert reports exceeded the proper scope of clear error review.

At the end of the 2024–2025 term, the court announced without explanation that it would rehear a case to decide whether the creation of a second majority-black congressional district in Louisiana was constitutional under the Fourteenth and Fifteenth Amendments. The Roberts Court's restrictive voting rights decisions permitted Republican-controlled state legislatures to engage in raw political power grabs to dilute the votes of communities of color in ways that resembled the power grabs by Southern white Democrats during and after Reconstruction. Voter suppression schemes and manipulation of the redistricting process constitute an assault on the democratic value of political equality.

Table 8.3. Roberts Court Race-Conscious Redistricting Cases, 2005–2025

Case	Vote	Outcome
LULAC v. Perry (2006)	5–4	Held that the creation of a Texas congressional district diluted the voting power of Latinos in violation of § 2 (L)
Bartlett v. Strickland (2009)	5–4	Held that § 2 does not require crossover districts where a racial minority makes up less than 50% of the district's voting age population (C)
Bethune-Hill v. Virginia Board of Elections (2017)	8–0	Held that the lower court applied the wrong legal test when it upheld twelve Virginia legislative districts against an unconstitutional racial gerrymandering challenge (L)
Cooper v. Harris (2017)	5–3	Held that North Carolina's two congressional gerrymandered districts were drawn primarily by race and not party in violation of the equal protection clause and the Voting Rights Act (L)
Abbott v. Perez (2018)	5–4	Held that Texas's redistricting plans for congressional and statehouse seats did not intentionally discriminate against black and Latino voters, and three districts did not dilute the votes of Latinos (C)
Brnovich v. Democratic National Committee (2021)	6–3	Held that Arizona's out-of-precinct and ballot harvesting policies did not violate § 2 (C)
Allen v. Milligan (2023)	5–4	Held that Alabama's congressional map violated § 2 because it diluted the black vote by cracking and packing black voters in one district to limit their voting power (L)
Alexander v. South Carolina State Conference of the NAACP (2024)	6–3	Held that plaintiffs must meet a high bar in bringing racial gerrymandering cases, and courts must disentangle race and politics in constitutional challenges (C)

Source: Created by the author.

Note: C for conservative outcomes, and L for liberal outcomes.

Economic Equality

During its first term, the Roberts Court advanced Title VII's antidiscrimination principle to cover protected employees who experienced retaliation at the workplace for filing discrimination charges in *Burlington Northern & Santa Fe Railway Company v. White* (2006). Two years later, the court ruled that § 1981 encompassed retaliation claims in *CBOCS West v. Humphries* (2008). *Burlington Northern* and *CBOCS West* were consequential employment discrimination decisions, because the guarantee of economic equality would be significantly weakened without protections from employer retaliation and unlawful racial discrimination in the workplace would go unreported and unremedied.

In *Ricci v. DeStefano* (2009), the court took a step backward when it adopted a restrictive interpretation of Title VII's disparate impact standard while broadening the disparate treatment standard in a way that benefitted white employees. The New Haven, Connecticut, fire department had few blacks and Latinos in the command ranks of lieutenant and captain. Under a contract between the city and the firefighters' union, vacancies for command positions were filled by firefighter candidates who performed well on a job-related examination administered by the civil service board. In 2003, the board refused to certify the results of a promotional exam because they produced a significant disparate impact on black and Latino candidates. Frank Ricci and other white firefighters sued city officials on the ground that discarding the test results intentionally discriminated against them on account of their race in violation of Title VII's disparate treatment standard. City officials defended the decision to throw out the test results because they could have faced liability under Title VII for adopting a practice that had a disparate impact on minority firefighter candidates.

In *Ricci*, the court found that discarding the promotional exam results violated Title VII. Justice Kennedy required employers to have a strong basis in evidence that they would be subject to disparate impact liability before they resort to remedial action. He asserted that "examinations like those administered by the City create legitimate expectations on part of those who took the tests." Kennedy pointed out that some firefighters invested substantial time, money, and personal commitment in preparing for the exam, and they saw their efforts invalidated by the city "in sole reliance upon race-based statistics." Writing for the dissenters, Justice Ginsburg recounted the long history of racial discrimination lawsuits against the New Haven fire department, and she pointed out that minority firefighters were starkly underrepresented at the entry-level and supervisory positions. Ginsburg explained that the promotion exam results indicated stark disparities that were enough to state a prima facie case under Title VII's disparate impact provision.

Title VII's disparate impact and disparate treatment standards were intended to advance the same policy objective—to end racial discrimination in the workplace. Until *Ricci*, the court had never ruled that an employer who complied with the disparate impact provision may violate the disparate treatment provision without a strong basis in evidence. The majority reframed the *Ricci* case as a reverse discrimination case to preserve the rights of innocent white firefighters to receive their promotions.

Table 8.4. Roberts Court Employment Discrimination Cases, 2005–2025

Case	Vote	Outcome
Burlington Northern & Santa Fe Railway Company v. White (2006)	9–0	Held that Title VII's antiretaliation provision covers only those employer actions that would have been materially adverse to reasonable employees (L)
CBOCS West v. Humphries (2008)	7–2	Held that § 1981 includes retaliation claims (L)
Ricci v. DeStefano (2009)	5–4	Held that the city must have a strong basis in evidence to discard firefighter command exam results that it believes would subject it to disparate impact liability (C)
Vance v. Ball State University (2013)	5–4	Held that an employer's vicarious liability for racial harassment under Title VII extends to supervisors and not coworkers (C)
Comcast v. National Assn. of African American-Owned Media (2020)	9–0	Held that a plaintiff must show "but-for" causation under § 1981 (C)
Muldrow v. City of St. Louis (2024)	9–0	Held that a black female employee who challenged a transfer decision did not have to show the transfer caused her significant harm (L)

Source: Created by the author.

Note: C for conservative outcomes, and L for liberal outcomes.

Jury Discrimination

The Roberts Court's jury discrimination cases did not break new legal ground, but they did reveal the alarming extent to which the peremptory challenge system was marred by prosecutors' racially discriminatory actions. In *Foster v. Chatman* (2016), eighteen-year-old Timothy Foster was indicted for the murder of an elderly white woman in Rome, Georgia, in 1986. After the prosecutor exercised nine of his ten strikes to remove prospective black jurors, Foster's attorney immediately lodged a *Batson* challenge, which was rejected by the trial court. Foster was found guilty and sentenced to death by an all-white jury. For almost twenty years, Foster's attorneys argued that his trial was unfair because prosecutors used their peremptory strikes to exclude blacks from the jury. The attorneys eventually gained access to the 1987 trial file under the Georgia Open Records Act. The contents of the prosecutor's file revealed a racial motive based on clear markings next to the names of qualified black jurors who were removed from the jury pool. In *Foster*, the court rejected the state's claim "that it exercised its strikes in

Table 8.5. Roberts Court Jury Discrimination Cases, 2005–2025

Case	Vote	Outcome
Synder v. Louisiana (2008)	7–2	Held that it was clear error for a trial judge to reject a *Batson* challenge to the strike of a black juror based on his demeanor (L)
Davis v. Ayala (2015)	5–4	Held that a Latino death row prisoner could not prove that the trial court committed reversible error by excluding the defense from part of the *Baston* hearing (C)
Foster v. Chatman (2016)	7–1	Held that the prosecutor's peremptory strikes to exclude blacks from the jury constituted purposeful discrimination based on evidence uncovered in the state's trial file (L)
Flowers v. Mississippi (2019)	7–2	Held that the trial judge erred in concluding that the state's strike of a black prospective juror was not motivated by discriminatory intent during the sixth murder trial of a black defendant (L)

Source: Created by the author.

Note: C for conservative outcomes, and L for liberal outcomes.

a 'color-blind' manner." Chief Justice Roberts found that the sheer number of references to race and the prosecution's focus on race in the file "plainly demonstrates a concerted effort to keep black prospective jurors off the jury." A similar pattern of prosecutorial misconduct was found in *Flowers v. Mississippi* (2019). Curtis Flowers, a 26-year-old black man, was tried six times and received four convictions over a span of twenty-three years for the 1996 execution style murders of the owner and three employees of a furniture store. The Roberts Court found that at the sixth trial, the court committed clear error when it found that the striking of a black potential juror was not motivated by discriminatory intent. Both cases demonstrated how prosecutorial misconduct was allowed to flourish for decades without any accountability.

Fair Housing

When the Roberts Court accepted *Texas Department of Housing and Community Affairs v. Inclusive Communities Project* (2015) for review, fair housing advocates feared that the court would extend the disparate impact reasoning of *Ricci v. DeStefano* to fair housing cases. The Inclusive Communities Project brought a disparate impact lawsuit against the Texas housing department on the ground that its policies perpetuated racially segregated housing patterns in the Dallas metropolitan area by allocating too many tax credits to housing in predominantly black inner-city areas and too few in predominantly white suburban areas in violation the Fair Housing Act. The district court ruled that the fair housing organization established a prima facie case of disparate impact based on statistical evidence, and the housing department failed to meet its burden of proof that there were no less discriminatory alternatives. Writing for the 5–4 majority, Justice Kennedy upheld the disparate impact claim on narrow grounds. Kennedy found that the Fair Housing Act targeted unlawful discriminatory practices such as zoning laws that "unfairly exclude minorities from certain neighborhoods without any sufficient justification," and such practices "reside at the heartland of disparate-impact liability." Kennedy explained that the use of race-neutral tools to foster diversity and combat racial isolation were permitted, but he cautioned that a disparate impact claim must fail if race is used in a way that leads to numerical quotas. Justice Alito took the hardline position that "the FHA does not authorize disparate-impact claims" despite a consensus among all nine circuits that the Fair Housing Act encompassed disparate impact claims. The *Inclusive Communities* decision was an important victory for fair housing advocates, but the decision placed limitations on the use of the disparate impact standard under the Fair Housing Act.

Conclusion

The Rehnquist and Roberts Courts were strongly committed to advancing the anti-civil rights agenda of the New Right alliance and movement conservatism. The Roberts Court was more successful in achieving its policy objectives over time for several reasons: the hyperpoliticized and hyperpolarized nomination and appointment process that prevented President Obama from placing Merrick Garland on the court, the expedited Amy Barrett confirmation hearing prior to the November 2020 election to guarantee Trump a third appointment, and, most importantly, the failure of Congress to check the excesses of the Roberts Court's exercise of power. Greenhouse (2022, 233) found that "2020–21 was the term the fourth wall disappeared" on the court. Barrett's appointment resulted in a court that lacked an ideological center or a swing justice. The six Republican appointees on the Roberts Court were free to vote their raw preferences into law without fear of external constraints. During its twenty-year operation, the Roberts Court decided significantly fewer race cases than the Rehnquist Court (55). The outcomes of the twenty-nine cases covered in this chapter reveal that 55 percent were decided in a conservative direction and 45 percent were decided in a liberal direction in favor of people of color or pro–civil rights plaintiffs. The defining characteristic of the court's policymaking approach to race cases was the application of the principle of race neutrality grounded in a misguided and twisted historical understanding of the Fourteenth and Fifteenth Amendments and the *Brown* decision. The court's decisions had the effect of rebuilding the legal foundations of the modern white supremacist racial order that transformative egalitarian civil rights legislation and Warren Court precedents sought to deconstruct.

Recent Gallup and Pew Research Center public opinion surveys show that the Roberts Court experienced historic lows with regard to public trust, job approval, and favorability ratings (Jones 2024; Copeland 2025). The polling organizations found that public perceptions of the court were influenced by political party affiliation and ideology. The Pew survey results found that 71 percent of Republicans viewed the court favorably while only 26 percent of Democrats and Democrat-leaning Independents viewed the court in a favorable light (Copeland 2025). A vast majority of Democrats, 82 percent, described the court as too conservative while only 4 percent of the Republicans believed that the court was too conservative (Jones 2024; Brenan 2025). The partisan sorting was not surprising given Devins and Baum's (2016, 361) finding that the "growing ideological polarization of the parties at the elite level has given presidents stronger incentives to choose nominees whose ideological orientations match those of the president's own party." Conventional wisdom posits that the Supreme Court must have robust levels of institutional legitimacy to facilitate compliance with its decisions.

Allegations of questionable institutional practices and unethical behavior have contributed to the loss of confidence in the Roberts Court. Vladeck (2023) exposed how the court's use of the shadow docket helped drive its right-wing agenda by deciding procedural matters involving emergency appeals to halt lower courts' orders without briefings, oral arguments, and little or no explanations. *ProPublica* magazine reporters Kaplan, Elliott, and Mierjeski (2023) revealed explosive revelations that Justice Clarence Thomas and his wife, Virginia Thomas, were the recipients of numerous luxury trips from conservative Texas billionaire Harlan Crow for more than two decades. A follow-up report revealed that other conservative billionaire benefactors treated Thomas to an ultrawealthy lifestyle (Murphy and Mierjeski 2023). Thomas failed to disclose the luxury travel, gifts, and other financial arrangements as required by federal ethics law that applied to members of Congress, federal officials, and federal judges. The negative publicity about allegations of corrupt behavior put Chief Justice Roberts on the political hotseat because the court had operated without a binding code of ethics. In November 2023, the court responded to political pressure by announcing a code of conduct for the justices. The new code had a serious flaw—it gave the appearance of accountability but it lacked any enforcement mechanism.

Conclusion

The main objective of this book has been to present a systematic and comprehensive account of the origins and development of Supreme Court policymaking in race cases. The recurrent question about the nature and extent to which the court has exercised its power to protect the rights of racial minorities has been a subject of extensive scholarly examination and debate. My book departs from prior works that approached the topic from the limited lens of leading race precedents analyses, studies restricted to particular historical periods, and normative debates about the constitutional role of the court in protecting the rights of minorities in a democracy. To the extent possible, I let the justices speak for themselves to explain their opinions. My research goal was to compensate for gaps in the literature to provide greater empirical scrutiny and clarity to an appraisal of the court's exercise of power in race cases over time.

I approached the problem from two competing organizing frameworks—the Hamiltonian model and the racial institutional orders framework. The Hamiltonian model maintains that the granting of life tenure to federal judges insulates them from majoritarian political pressures to protect the rights of minorities from the effects of oppression by unjust laws. An influential variant of this model asserts that the court's constitutional role is to protect the rights of racial minorities from tyrannical lawmaking majorities. King and Smith (2005) presented a racial institutional orders framework to analyze the issue of race in American political development. They argued that American politics has historically been constituted by two sets of evolving but linked racial institutional orders: a set of white supremacist racial orders and a competing set of transformative egalitarian racial orders that have shaped policy debates about race over time.

Racial institutional orders are comprised of political actors and governing institutions that take opposing positions on the predominant racial issues of their era. To position the court within the racial institutional orders framework, I resorted to regime politics theory to explain how partisan coalitions direct their power to strategically populate courts to advance their racial policy agenda. The court is inevitably part of the ruling regime, and its decisions are expected to advance the regime's policy agenda. This study assumed that the justices' policy preferences influence their decision-making behavior, and, as strategic actors, the justices must take the preferences of other actors into account to maximize their policy goals. To present a substantive treatment of the court's policies and how they affected the development of the law, I applied the basic tenets of jurisprudential regimes theory to identify and explain how landmark precedents and doctrines structure the way justices arrive at their decisions.

To assess court policymaking as a dynamic process, I placed the fourteen chief justice tenures into six historical periods: the Marshall and Taney Courts (slavery era), the Chase and Waite Courts (Reconstruction era), the Fuller, White, and Taft Courts (progressive era), the Hughes, Stone, and Vinson Courts (New Deal era), the Warren and Burger Courts (civil rights movement era), and the Rehnquist and Roberts Courts (New Right conservatism era). My assessment of court policymaking was centered on the policy dichotomies that represented the opposing positions adopted by the rival racial orders: slavery versus emancipation, formal equality versus civil rights, caste and exclusion versus rights of American citizenship, racial discrimination versus equal rights under law, and color-blindness versus race consciousness. I selected 441 cases from the Supreme Court Database to determine whether the decisions were decided in a liberal direction in favor of people of color or pro–civil rights claimants or in a conservative direction.

The main finding that emerged from this 224-year policymaking study was that the Supreme Court has consistently exercised its power as a foe, not a friend, to the rights of people of color. The court advanced the policy goals of the white supremacist racial order and its modern variants in a majority of the cases except for a fifty-six-year period (1930–1986) when the transformative egalitarian alliance was strengthening or becoming predominant at the national level. I found little empirical evidence to support the Hamiltonian view of court policymaking in race cases, with the exception of the court's exercise of power during the New Deal and civil rights movement eras. As a result, the Hamiltonian model was rejected as an analytically useful framework to appraise court policymaking in race cases. Dahl (1957, 291) argued that it would be unrealistic to articulate a theory of court policymaking "at odds with the rest of the political elite" given how justices are recruited to office. Dahl (294) explained that the "main task of the Court is to confer legitimacy on the fundamental policies of the successful coalition." With regard to race and rights, the Hamiltonian model stands on firmer normative grounds. Without explicitly linking his argument to the Hamiltonian model, Chemerinsky (2014, 10) asserted that "the two preeminent purposes of the Court are to protect the rights of minorities who cannot rely on the political process and to uphold the Constitution in the face of any repressive desires of political majorities." Despite his claim, Chemerinsky's examination of the leading race decisions from the era of racial slavery to 2013 indicated that the Supreme Court had repeatedly failed to carry out its important responsibilities, and my findings revealed that the court continued to advance a negative racial agenda after 2013.

This study revealed that the extent to which the court will rule favorably on behalf of the rights of people of color is dependent on the strength of the ruling regime's commitment to the democratic values of freedom, equality, and political representation. The court's protection of the rights of people of color reached its highest levels when transformative egalitarian alliances were gaining strength or were in power at the national level. The jurisprudential shift away from the white supremacist racial order that had been in place since the late 1880s can be traced to the return of Charles Evans Hughes to the court in 1930. Prior to FDR's first appointment to the court in 1937, the Hughes Court had amassed a liberal record in correcting racial injustices in the criminal justice system, jury discrimination cases reappeared on the court's docket, and it signaled that a more demanding level of judicial scrutiny would be applied to racial classifications under the equal protection clause. The Hughes, Stone, and Vinson Courts' policy responses to the demands for equal rights under law produced transformational change—the court decided 81 percent of the race cases in a liberal direction in favor of people of color. From 1930 until 1953, the court's decisions struck down the use of the white primary to maintain black disenfranchisement, and decisions in the areas of education, transportation, and housing undermined the system of apartheid. The court also supported the negative racial policy agenda of the executive and legislative branches to exclude and incarcerate over 120,000 members of the west coast Japanese community based on unsubstantiated claims of threats to national security.

Dahl (1957, 293) argued that the Supreme Court is an essential part of the ruling regime, and it "possesses some bases of power of its own, the most important of which is the unique legitimacy attributed to its interpretations of the Constitution." During the civil rights movement era, the

Warren Court exercised its power to "confer legitimacy on the fundamental policies of the successful coalition" (294). Earl Warren's lack of prior judicial experience mattered less than the political and leadership skills he brought to the court when he became chief justice in 1953. The Warren Court was a fully committed partner of the transformative egalitarian racial order that had gained predominance during the civil rights movement era. From 1953 until 1969, the Warren Court decided 92 percent of the race cases in a liberal policy direction. The decisions produced jurisprudential regime change, and they made the American political system more democratic by dismantling the institutional structures that supported the regime of white supremacy.

The most impactful human rights decisions of the twentieth century, *Brown v. Board of Education* (1954) and *Bolling v. Sharpe* (1954), brought about the constitutional demise of apartheid in America. The court partnered with Congress and the executive to dismantle a powerful instrument of white supremacist oppression—black disenfranchisement in the South. For the first time, the court recognized the relationship between the fundamental rights of the First Amendment and the equality goals of the Fourteenth Amendment. The Warren Court supported the racial justice goals of the civil rights movement by reversing the convictions of civil rights protestors, it expanded the meaning of the First Amendment to include the right of association to protect members of the NAACP and the organization's litigating activities from Southern legislatures that attempted to put the organization out of business, and it protected civil rights leaders and the press from the weaponization of state libel law when they expressed views critical of the actions of Southern officials and public issues about race. The court made federal prosecution of white supremacist officials and private actors who committed brutal acts of terrorism against blacks easier by applying liberal interpretations to Reconstruction era civil rights enforcement laws. The court also applied an expansive interpretation to § 1982 to reach all private and public racial discrimination in the sale or rental of housing, and it rejected the use of referenda that made it easier for political majorities to restrict or repeal fair housing laws.

Dahl (1957, 293) asserted that the court "is inevitably a part of the dominant alliance, except for short-lived transitional periods when the old alliance is disintegrating and the new one is struggling to take control of political institutions." The tenure of the Burger Court (1969–1986) coincided with the rise of conservative opposition to the policies of the transformative egalitarian alliance. The Nixon and Reagan administrations resisted the liberal jurisprudence of the Warren Court by exercising their executive powers of appointment to shift the policy direction of the court to the right. As the New Right's anti–civil rights agenda gained prominence in public and legal discourse, the justices became more ideologically divided in their decision-making. The ideological divisions were reflected in the court's weaker response to the policy demands for equal rights under law compared to the New Deal and Warren Courts—the Burger Court decided 68 percent of the race cases in a liberal direction in favor of people of color or pro–civil rights claimants. During its early operation, the Burger Court advanced the policy goals of the transformative egalitarian alliance, but by the mid-1970s, the court's decisions became increasingly conservative. Decisions such as *Milliken v. Bradley* (1974), *Washington v. Davis* (1976), *Mobile v. Bolden* (1980), and *Wygant v. Jackson Board of Education* (1986) made it more difficult for people of color to challenge discriminatory laws and practices under the Constitution.

This study found that the Supreme Court was hostile to the rights of people of color when white supremacist regimes and their modern variants were in power. During the era of racial enslavement, the Marshall and Taney Courts (1801–1864) ruled in favor of the pro-slavery policies of the slaveholding republic in 64 percent of the cases. Neither court decided a single case that threatened the institution of racial slavery. In the *Antelope* (1825) case, the Marshall Court sanctioned the economic enterprise of the international slave trade. The Taney Court's landmark cases, *Prigg v. Pennsylvania* (1842) and *Dred Scott v. Sandford* (1857), guaranteed that national power would be used to protect the South's property right in slaves and that blacks, whether free or enslaved, would never become citizens of the United States. After the Civil War, the first transformative egalitarian racial order became predominant, and the Radical Republican alliance added the Thirteenth, Fourteenth, and Fifteenth Amendments to the Constitution. For the first time, democratic principles of freedom, the privileges and immunities of citizenship, the equal protection of the laws, and the right to vote unencumbered by race were written into the Constitution. The amendments empowered Congress to enact legislation to protect and enforce civil rights from state infringement.

During Reconstruction, the court exercised its power independently of the policy goals of the transformative egalitarian racial order, which was predominant until 1877. In the first race cases after the second founding, the Chase and Waite Courts (1864–1888) ruled against the egalitarian goals of the Radical Republican alliance in 65 percent of the cases. The justices made policy choices that favored prewar interpretations of federalism advanced by southern Democrats while ignoring the intentions of the Radical Republican alliance. In the *Slaughter-House Cases* (1873), *United States v. Cruikshank* (1876), *United States v. Reese* (1876), and the *Civil Rights Cases* (1883), the justices applied restrictive interpretations to the newly added amendments and struck down their enforcement statutes. The decisions favored the South's policy interests, and they provided the constitutional foundation for the second phase of the ruling regime of white supremacy.

The three courts that operated during the progressive era—the Fuller Court (1888–1910), the White Court (1910–1921), and the Taft Court (1921–1930)—ruled against the rights of people of color in 72 percent of the cases. The Fuller Court's ultraconservative policymaking stands out for several reasons. Over half of all progressive era race cases were decided by the Fuller Court, and almost all of them were decided in a conservative direction. The Fuller Court finalized the Waite Court's anti–civil rights agenda by fashioning judicial doctrines that sanctioned apartheid in *Plessy v. Ferguson* (1896), race-based exclusion in *Chae Chan Ping v. United States* (1889), and the plenary power to exclude and expel immigrants based on race in *Fong Yue Ting v. United States* (1893). The Fuller Court abdicated its judicial authority to decide cases challenging massive black disenfranchisement in *Williams v. Mississippi* (1896) and *Giles v. Harris* (1903). The White and Taft Courts' race decisions advanced the policy goals of the white supremacist racial order, but both courts made limited concessions to the transformative egalitarian alliance in the areas of voting rights, peonage, housing segregation, and the fair administration of criminal proceedings.

The Rehnquist and Roberts Courts were not treated as analytically distinct courts to assess their policymaking role. The Rehnquist Court (1986–2005) laid the doctrinal foundation for the Roberts Court (2005–2025) to finalize what it began—to advance the racial policy agenda of the New Right alliance. Both courts applied ahistorical and revisionist interpretations to the Fourteenth and Fifteenth Amendments and the *Brown* precedent to restrict the constitutional and statutory rights of people of color. The Rehnquist Court decided 51 percent of its race cases in a conservative direction, and policymaking by the Roberts Court was slightly more conservative—55 percent of its cases were decided against people of color or pro–civil rights claimants. In *Shaw v. Reno* (1993), the Rehnquist Court ruled that white plaintiffs had standing to challenge race conscious redistricting plans under the equal protection clause, and in *Adarand Constructors v. Peña* (1995), the court required the use of the strict scrutiny test to all cases challenging the constitutionality of racial classifications under the Fifth and Fourteenth

Amendments, including race conscious policies. The Roberts Court restricted the use of race to voluntarily desegregate public schools in *Parents Involved in Community Schools v. Seattle School District No. 1* (2007), and the court made it more difficult for universities to pursue race conscious admissions under a more restrictive strict scrutiny test in *Students for Fair Admissions v. Harvard College* (2023). In *Shelby County v. Holder* (2013), the court declared the coverage formula in the Voting Rights Act of 1965 unconstitutional, which automatically made the preclearance provision inoperable. The Rehnquist and Roberts Court decisions had the effect of rebuilding the legal foundation of the white supremacist racial order that transformative egalitarian civil rights legislation and Warren Court precedents had sought to deconstruct.

Two factors prevented the Rehnquist Court from successfully carrying out its agenda to advance the policy goals of the New Rights alliance. First, Congress was receptive to the demands of civil rights groups to override adverse statutory rulings of the court. Second, some justices on the Rehnquist Court behaved independently of the preferences espoused by the ruling partisan regimes that appointed them. Epstein et al. (1998) found that policy preferences were not always stable for some justices, and they may change in linear or nonlinear ways over time. Harry Blackmun, John Paul Stevens, David Souter, and Anthony Kennedy did swing or drift to the left in race cases, which defied the expectations of the Republican regimes that appointed them (Epstein et al. 2007). The justices who coalesced with the liberals were able to slow down the Rehnquist and Roberts Courts' negative racial agenda to a certain extent, but they ultimately could not prevent it from becoming law due to the appointment of more conservative successors by Republican regimes. Because Republican appointees are consistently more conservative and Democratic appointees are consistently more liberal, ideological drift on the court may become a phenomenon of the past.

Given the Supreme Court's abysmal record at protecting the rights of people of color, the question becomes what can be done to alter the court's trajectory of ultraconservative policymaking in the issue area of race. Dahl (1957, 293) observed that national politics in the United States "is dominated by relatively cohesive alliances that endure for long periods of time," and "each is marked by a break with past policies, a period of intense struggle, followed by consolidation, and finally decay and disintegration of the alliance." This pattern suggests that only a transformational electoral shift to a new egalitarian regime, such as what occurred during the New Deal era, will result in court decisions that reflect the egalitarian policy goals of the new regime. Democrats in Congress have proposed temporary policy solutions to counter the Roberts Court's ultraconservative policymaking, such as proposing legislation to expand the number of seats on the court from nine to thirteen to restore its ideological balance. Another proposal calls for legislation to impose lengthy term limits on the justices to regularize the appointment process.

Perhaps the most important and long-lasting solution to an ultra-conservative court is to amend the Constitution to make the court more accountable in our constitutional democracy. Ironically, it is the presence of anti-democratic features in the Constitution that makes this solution extraordinary difficult to implement (Dahl 2003). In the 2000 and 2016 presidential elections, Republican candidates George W. Bush and Donald Trump won the electoral college vote but not the popular vote, which gave the minority Republican Party an advantage in populating federal courts. Bush made two appointments to the court, John Roberts and Samuel Alito, and Trump made three appointments during his first term, Neil Gorsuch, Brett Kavanaugh, and Amy Barrett. Equal representation of the states in the Senate and the use of Senate rules and norms to manipulate the outcomes of the confirmation process have worked to the advantage of the Republican Party. The outcome of the 2016 presidential election guaranteed that the hard right supermajority on the Roberts Court will likely hold power for decades regardless of which political party wins the White House in 2028.

Article III implicitly grants life tenure to federal judges. The system of life tenure for federal judges, including Supreme Court justices, is indefensible during the modern era. While he was solicitor general, Robert Jackson (1941, 187) made the following observation about President Roosevelt's battles with the Hughes Court:

> Life tenure was a device by which the conservatives could thwart a liberal administration if they could outlive it. The alternations of our national moods are such that a cycle of liberal government seldom exceeds eight years, and by living through them the Court could go on without decisive liberal infusions. So well has this strategy worked that never in its entire history can the Supreme Court be said to have for a single hour been representative of anything except the relatively conservative forces of its day.

The United States stands out as an outlier among democratic political systems with regard to constitutional high courts populated with unelected judges who have life tenure. Life tenure for state supreme court justices is nonexistent in the United States except for Rhode Island and Massachusetts, and New Hampshire provides for life tenure after initial appointment until the judges reach the age of seventy (Milov-Cordoba 2024). The federal judiciary already consists of judges who lack life tenure. For example, US Court of Federal Claims judges are appointed by the president with Senate approval, and they serve fifteen-year terms that can be renewed.

On October 13, 1932, Chief Justice Charles Evans Hughes delivered a speech in Washington, DC, to celebrate the laying the cornerstone of the new Supreme Court building. Hughes led the court during a decade of transition from the old conservative political order to a new liberal political order. After making the case why the court needed a building of its own, Hughes (1932, 729) explained that the court symbolized "the national ideal of justice in its highest sphere of activity, in maintaining the balance between the Nation and States and in enforcing the primary demands of individual liberty as safeguarded by the overriding guarantee of a written constitution." Hughes asserted that during a time of keen distress, widespread misgiving, and world unrest, "the distribution and limitations of powers under a written constitution cannot be maintained without an arbiter, as far removed as is practically possible from the disputes of parties and the manipulations of groups dominated by selfish interests" (729). Hughes's insights about the state of current affairs were made ninety-three years ago, but they are fitting for this moment in time. At present, the policy goals and actions by President Trump and the ruling regime of MAGA Republicanism strongly resemble those of autocratic political systems. Dahl (1988, 44–61) maintained that nondemocratic political systems do not allow their citizens to have rights, including the fundamental right of racial equality. Hughes's speech serves as a reminder to the Roberts Court that it must act as an arbiter to prevent the absolute centralization of authority under a written constitution, to check the abuses of power, and the flagrant disregard of the rule of law to ensure that the "government of the people, for the people, and by the people, notwithstanding all shortcomings, is not to perish" (729).

References

Alschuler, Albert W., and Andrew G. Deiss. 1994. "A Brief History of the Criminal Jury in the United States." *University of Chicago Law Review* 61 (3): 867–928.

Aoki, Keith. 1998. "No Right to Own? The Early Twentieth-Century 'Alien Land Laws' as a Precursor to Internment." *Boston College Law Review* 40:37–72.

Baker, Liva. 1991. *The Justice from Beacon Hill: The Life and Times of Oliver Wendell Holmes*. HarperCollins.

Ball, Howard. 1991. "Judicial Parsimony and Military Necessity Disinterred: A Reexamination of the Japanese Exclusion Cases, 1943–1944." In *Japanese Americans: From Relocation to Redress*, rev. ed., edited by Roger Daniels, Sandra C. Taylor, and Harry H. L. Kitano. University of Washington Press.

———. 2004. *Murder in Mississippi: United States v. Price and the Struggle for Civil Rights*. University Press of Kansas.

Barnes, Catherine A. 1983. *Journey from Jim Crow: The Desegregation of Southern Transit*. Columbia University Press.

Bartels, Brandon L., and Andrew J. O'Geen. 2015. "The Nature of Legal Change on the U.S. Supreme Court: Jurisprudential Regimes and its Alternatives." *American Journal of Political Science* 59 (4): 880–95.

Baum, Lawrence, and Lori Hausegger. 2004. "The Supreme Court and Congress: Reconsidering the Relationships." In *Making Policy, Making Law: An Interbranch Perspective*, edited by Mark C. Miller and Jeb Barnes. Georgetown University Press.

Belz, Herman. 1976. *A New Birth of Freedom: The Republican Party and Freedmen's Rights, 1861–1866*. Greenwood.

Bethune, Brett. 2022. "Influence without Impeachment: How the Impeach Earl Warren Movement Began, Faltered, but Avoided Irrelevance." *Journal of Supreme Court History* 47 (2): 142–61.

Biskupic, Joan. 2012a. "Insight: From Alabama, an Epic Challenge to Voting Rights." Reuters, June 4. https://www.reuters.com/article/idUSBRE85304N/.

———. 2012b. "Special Report: Behind U.S. Race Cases, a Little-Known Recruiter." Reuters, December 4. https://www.reuters.com/article/us-usa-court-case-maker/special-report-behind-u-s-race-cases-a-little-known-recruiter-idUSBRE-8B30V220121204.

Blackmon, Douglas A. 2008. *Slavery by Another Name: The Re-enslavement of Black Americans from the Civil War to World War II*. Anchor.

Bowen, William G., and Derek Bok. 1998. *The Shape of the River: Long-Term Consequences of Considering Race in College and University Admissions*. Princeton University Press.

Boyd, Christina L., Lori A. Ringhand, and Paul M. Collins, Jr. 2018. "The Role of Nominee Gender and Race at U.S. Supreme Court Confirmation Hearings." *Law and Society Review* 52 (4): 871–901.

Brenan, Megan. 2025. "Democrats' Confidence in U.S. Institutions Sinks to New Low." Gallup News, July 17. https://news.gallup.com/poll/692633/democrats-confidence-institutions-sinks-new-low.aspx.

Brennan, William J., Jr. 1986. "The Constitution of the United States: Contemporary Ratification." *South Texas Law Review* 27 (3): 433–46.

Browne-Marshall, Gloria J. 2013. *Race, Law, and American Society: 1607 to Present*. 2nd ed. Routledge.

Burton, Orville Vernon, and Armand Derfner. 2021. *Justice Deferred: Race and the Supreme Court*. Belknap Press of Harvard University Press.

Canon, Bradley C., and Charles A. Johnson. 1998. *Judicial Policies: Implementation and Impact*. 2nd ed. CQ Press.

Carbado, Devon W. 2009. "Yellow by Law." *California Law Review* 97 (3): 633–92.

Carr, Robert K. 1947. *Federal Protection of Civil Rights: Quest for a Sword*. Cornell University Press.

Carson, Clayborne. 1981. *In Struggle: SNCC and the Black Awakening of the 1960s*. Harvard University Press.

Carter, Dan T. 1969. *Scottsboro: A Tragedy of the American South*. Louisiana State University Press.

Chafe, William H. 1980. *Civilities and Civil Rights: Greensboro, North Carolina, and the Black Struggle for Freedom*. Oxford University Press.

Chemerinsky, Erwin. 2014. *The Case Against the Supreme Court*. Penguin Books.

Chin, Gabriel. 2008. "Unexplainable on Grounds of Race: Doubts about *Yick Wo*." *University of Illinois Law Review* 2008:1360–92.

Clayton, Cornell, and David A. May. 1999. "A Political Regimes Approach to the Analysis of Legal Decisions." *Polity* 32 (2): 233–52.

Commission on Wartime Relocation and Internment of Civilians. 1982. *Personal Justice Denied: Report of the Commission on Wartime Relocation and Internment of Civilians*. US Government Printing Office.

Condon, Sean. 2001. " 'The Peculiar Circumstances of Their Unhappy Birth and Colour': Bennett Darnall's Children in the Early National Chesapeake." *Maryland Historical Magazine* 96 (3): 348–56.

Copeland, Joseph. 2025. "Favorable Views of Supreme Court Remain near Historic Low." Pew Research Center, September 3. https://www.pewresearch.org/short-reads/2025/09/03/favorable-views-of-supreme-court-remain-near-historic-low/.

Cover, Robert M. 1982. "The Origins of Judicial Activism in the Protection of Minorities." *Yale Law Journal* 91 (7): 1287–1316.

Cray, Ed. 1997. *Chief Justice: A Biography of Earl Warren.* Simon & Schuster.

Cross, Theodore. 1999. "African-American Opportunities in Higher Education: What Are the Racial Goals of the Center for Individual Rights?" *Journal of Blacks in Higher Education* 1999 (23): 94–99.

Curriden, Mark, and Leroy Phillips, Jr. 1999. *Contempt of Court: The Turn-of-the-Century Lynching That Launched 100 Years of Federalism.* Faber and Faber.

Dahl, Robert A. 1957. "Decision-Making in a Democracy: The Supreme Court as a National Policy-Maker." *Journal of Public Law* 6:279–95.

———. 1998. *On Democracy.* Yale University Press.

———. 2003. *How Democratic Is the American Constitution?* Yale University Press.

Daniel, Pete. 1972. *The Shadow of Slavery: Peonage in the South, 1901–1969.* University of Illinois Press.

Davidson, Chandler. 1992. "The Voting Rights Act: A Brief History." In *Controversies in Minority Voting: The Voting Rights Act in Perspective*, edited by Bernard Grofman and Chandler Davidson. Brookings Institution.

Davidson, Chandler, and Bernard Grofman, eds. 1994. *Quiet Revolution in the South: The Impact of the Voting Rights Act, 1965–1990.* Princeton University Press.

Davis, David Brion. 2006. *Inhuman Bondage: The Rise and Fall of Slavery in the New World.* Oxford University Press.

Derfner, Armand. 1973. "Racial Discrimination and the Right to Vote." *Vanderbilt Law Review* 26 (3): 523–84.

Devins, Neal. 2003. "Explaining *Grutter v. Bollinger.*" *University of Pennsylvania Law Review* 152 (1): 347–83.

Devins, Neal, and Lawrence Baum. 2016. "Split Definitive: How Party Polarization Turned the Supreme Court into a Partisan Court." *Supreme Court Review* 2016:301–65.

Douglas, Davison M. 2005. *Jim Crow Moves North: The Battle over Northern School Desegregation, 1865–1954.* Cambridge University Press.

Douglass, Frederick. (1883) 1966. "The Civil Rights Case." In *Negro Social and Political Thought*, 1850–1920. Edited by Howard Brotz. Basic Books.

Dreyfuss, Joel, and Charles Lawrence III. 1979. *The Bakke Case: The Politics of Inequality.* Harcourt Brace Jovanovich.

Du Bois, W. E. B. 1910. "Reconstruction and Its Benefits." *American Historical Review* 15 (4): 781–99.

———. (1935) 2007. *Black Reconstruction in America.* Edited by Henry Louis Gates, Jr. The Oxford W. E. B. Du Bois, vol. 7. Oxford University Press.

———. 1948. "Race Relations in the United States, 1917–1947." *Phylon* 9 (3): 234–47.

Dudziak, Mary L. 2000. *Cold War and Civil Rights: Race and the Image of American Democracy.* Princeton University Press.

Elliott, Mark. 2001. "Race, Color Blindness, and the Democratic Public: Albion W. Tourgée's Radical Principles in *Plessy v. Ferguson*." *Journal of Southern History* 67 (2): 287–330.

———. 2006. *Color Blind Justice: Albion Tourgée and the Quest for Racial Equality from the Civil War to Plessy v. Ferguson.* Oxford University Press.

Endersby, James W., and William T. Horner. 2016. *Lloyd Gaines and the Fight to End Segregation.* University of Missouri Press.

Epstein, Lee, Valerie Hoekstra, Jeffrey A. Segal, and Harold J. Spaeth. 1998. "Do Political Preferences Change? A Longitudinal Study of U.S. Supreme Court Justices." *Journal of Politics* 60 (3): 801–18.

Epstein, Lee, and Jack Knight. 1998. *The Choices Justices Make.* CQ Press.

Epstein, Lee, Jack Knight, and Andrew D. Martin. 2001. "The Supreme Court as a *Strategic* National Policymaker." *Emory Law Journal* 50 (2): 583–611.

Epstein, Lee, Andrew D. Martin, Kevin M. Quinn, and Jeffrey A. Segal. 2007. "Ideological Drift among Supreme Court Justices: Who, When, and How Important?" *Northwestern University Law Review Colloquy* 101 (4): 1483–1542.

Everett, Robinson O. 2001. "Redistricting in North Carolina—a Personal Perspective." *North Carolina Law Review* 79 (5): 1301–32.

Fairman, Charles. 1939. *Mr. Justice Miller and the Supreme Court, 1862–1890.* Harvard University Press.

———. 1987. *Reconstruction and Reunion, 1864–1888.* Vol. 6 of *The Oliver Wendell Holmes Devise History of the Supreme Court of the United States.* Macmillan.

Fede, Andrew T. 2017. "Not the Most Insignificant Justice: Reconsidering Justice Gabriel Duvall's Slavery Law Opinions Favoring Liberty." *Journal of Supreme Court History* 42 (1): 7–27.

Fehrenbacher, Don E. 1981. *Slavery, Law, and Politics: The Dred Scott Case in Historical Perspective.* Abridged ed. Oxford University Press.

Finkelman, Paul. 1994. "Story Telling on the Supreme Court: *Prigg v. Pennsylvania* and Justice Joseph Story's Judicial Nationalism." *Supreme Court Review* 1994:247–94.

———. 1997. *Dred Scott v. Sandford: A Brief History with Documents.* Bedford Books.

———. 2001. *Slavery and the Founders: Race and Liberty in the Age of Jefferson.* 2nd ed. M. E. Sharpe.

———. 2018. *Supreme Injustice: Slavery in the Nation's Highest Court.* Harvard University Press.

Foner, Eric. 1988. *Reconstruction: American's Unfinished Revolution, 1863–1877.* Harper and Row.

———. 2005. *Forever Free: The Story of Emancipation and Reconstruction.* Vintage.

————. 2019. *The Second Founding: How the Civil War and Reconstruction Remade the Constitution*. Norton.

Foner, Philip S., ed. 1999. *Frederick Douglass: Selected Speeches and Writings*. Abridged and adapted by Yuval Taylor. Lawrence Hill Books.

Francis, Megan Ming. 2014. *Civil Rights and the Making of the Modern American State*. Cambridge University Press.

Frankenberg, Erica, and Gary Orfield, eds. 2012. *The Resegregation of Suburban Schools: A Hidden Crisis in American Education*. Harvard Education Press.

Franklin, John Hope. 1974. *From Slavery to Freedom: A History of Negro Americans*. 4th ed. Knopf.

Gillman, Howard. 2002. "How Political Parties Can Use the Courts to Advance Their Agendas: Federal Courts in the United States, 1875–1891." *American Political Science Review* 96 (3): 511–24.

————. 2006. "Regime Politics, Jurisprudential Regimes, and Unenumerated Rights." *Journal of Constitutional Law* 9:107–19.

Goldstein, Leslie F. 2017. *The U.S. Supreme Court and Racial Minorities: Two Centuries of Judicial Review on Trial*. Edward Elgar.

Gordon-Reed, Annette. 2011. *Andrew Johnson*. Holt.

Graetz, Michael J., and Linda Greenhouse. 2016. *The Burger Court and the Rise of the Judicial Right*. Simon & Schuster.

Graham, Howard Jay. 1938. "Four Letters of Mr. Justice Field." *Yale Law Journal* 47 (7): 1100–1108.

Greenhouse, Linda. 2022. *Justice on the Brink: A Requiem for the Supreme Court*. Random House.

Grossman, James R. 2022. "A Pardon for Homer Plessy: The Long Arc of 'Pernicious' Jurisprudence." *Perspectives on History*, January 25.

Halpin, Dennis P. 2019. *A Brotherhood of Liberty: Black Reconstruction and Its Legacies in Baltimore, 1865–1920*. University of Pennsylvania Press.

Haney-López, Ian F. 1996. *White by Law: The Legal Construction of Race*. New York University Press.

Higginbotham, A. Leon, Jr. 1978. *In the Matter of Color: Race and the American Legal Process, the Colonial Period*. Race and the American Legal Process, vol. 1. Oxford University Press.

————. 1992. "An *Open Letter to Justice Clarence Thomas from a Federal Judicial Colleague*." *University of Pennsylvania Law Review* 140 (3): 1005–28.

Higginbotham, A. Leon, Jr., and William C. Smith. 1992. "The Hughes Court and the Beginning of the End of the Separate but Equal Doctrine." *Minnesota Law Review* 76 (5): 1099–1132.

Hilbink, Thomas M. 2002. "Defining Cause Lawyering: *NAACP v. Button* and the Struggle over Professional Ideology." *Studies in Law, Politics, and Society* 26:77–108.

Hine, Darlene Clark. 1979. *Black Victory: The Rise and Fall of the White Primary in Texas*. KTO Press.

Hogue, James K. 2006. *Uncivil War: Five New Orleans Street Battles and the Rise and Fall of Radical Reconstruction*. Louisiana State University Press.

Holt, Thomas C. 2021. *The Movement: The African American Struggle for Civil Rights*. Oxford University Press.

Howard, John R. 1999. *The Shifting Wind: The Supreme Court and Civil Rights from Reconstruction to Brown*. State University of New York Press.

Hughes, Charles Evans. 1932. "Address of Chief Justice Hughes." *American Bar Association Journal* 15 (11): 728–29.

Irons, Peter. 1983. *Justice at War: The Story of the Japanese Internment Cases*. Oxford University Press.

Jackson, Robert H. 1941. *The Struggle for Judicial Supremacy: A Study of a Crisis in American Power Politics*. Vintage.

Johnson, Robert David. 2016. "Lyndon B. Johnson and the Fortas Nomination." *Journal of Supreme Court History* 41 (1): 103–22.

Jones, Jeffrey M. 2024. "Party Divisions in Views of Supreme Court Keep Ratings Low." Gallup News, October 3. https://news.gallup.com/poll/651527/party-divisions-views-supreme-court-keep-ratings-low.aspx.

Jones-Correa, Michael. 2000. "The Origins and Diffusion of Racial Restrictive Covenants." *Political Science Quarterly* 115 (4): 541–68.

Kaczorowski, Robert J. 2005. *The Politics of Judicial Interpretation*. Fordham University Press.

Kalven, Harry, Jr. 1965. *The Negro and the First Amendment*. Ohio State University Press.

Kaplan, Joshua, Justin Elliott, and Alex Mierjeski. 2023. "Clarence Thomas and the Billionaire." *ProPublica*, April 6. https://www.propublica.org/article/clarence-thomas-scotus-undisclosed-luxury-travel-gifts-crow.

Karlan, Pamela S., and Peyton McCrary. 1988. "Without Fear and without Research: Abigail Thernstrom on the Voting Rights Act." *Journal of Law and Politics* 4 (4): 751–78.

Karst, Kenneth L. 1975. "Equality as a Central Principle in the First Amendment." *University of Chicago Law Review* 43 (1): 20–68.

Keith, LeeAnna. 2008. *The Colfax Massacre: The Untold Story of Black Power, White Terror, and the Death of Reconstruction*. Holt.

Kellogg, Charles F. 1967. *A History of the National Association for the Advancement of Colored People, 1909–1920*. Johns Hopkins University Press.

King, Desmond S., and Rogers M. Smith. 2005. "Racial Orders in American Political Development." *American Political Science Review* 99 (1): 75–92.

Klarman, Michael J. 2004. *From Jim Crow to Civil Rights: The Supreme Court and the Struggle for Racial Equality*. Oxford University Press.

Kluger, Richard. 2004. *Simple Justice: The History of Brown v. Board of Education and Black America's Struggle for Equality.* Vintage.

Kousser, J. Morgan. 1974. *The Shaping of Southern Politics: Suffrage Restrictions and the Establishment of the One-Party South, 1880–1910.* Yale University Press.

———. 1980. "Separate but *not* Equal: The Supreme Court's First Decision on Racial Discrimination in Schools." *Journal of Southern History* 46 (1):17–44.

———. 1999. *Colorblind Injustice: Minority Voting Rights and the Undoing of the Second Reconstruction.* University of North Carolina Press.

Lado, Marianne L. 1995. "A Question of Justice: African-American Legal Perspectives on the 1883 *Civil Rights Cases.*" *Chicago-Kent Law Review* 70 (3): 1123–95.

Lamb, Charles C. 1981. "Housing Discrimination and Segregation in America: Problematical Dimensions and the Federal Legal Response." *Catholic Law Review* 30 (3): 363–430.

———. 2005. *Housing Segregation in Suburban America since 1960: Presidential and Judicial Policies.* Cambridge University Press.

Lane, Charles. 2008. *The Day Freedom Died: The Colfax Massacre, the Supreme Court, and the Betrayal of Reconstruction.* Holt.

Larsen, Allison, and Neal Devins. 2016. "The Amicus Machine." *Virginia Law Review* 102 (8): 1901–68.

Leuchtenburg, William E. 1973. "A Klansman Joins the Court: The Appointment of Hugo L. Black." *University of Chicago Law Review* 41 (1): 1–31.

Levinson, Sanford V. 2018. "Why *Strauder v. West Virginia* Is the Most Important Single Source of Insight on the Tensions Contained within the Equal Protection Clause of the Fourteenth Amendment." *Saint Louis University Law Journal* 62 (3): 603–22.

Litwack, Leon F. 1961. *North of Slavery: The Negro in the Free States: 1790–1860.* University of Chicago Press.

Lofgren, Charles. 1987. *The Plessy Case: A Legal-Historical Interpretation.* Oxford University Press.

Logan, Rayford W. 1965. *The Betrayal of the Negro: From Rutherford B. Hayes to Woodrow Wilson.* Collier.

Lusky, Louis. 1982. "Footnote Redux: A Carolene Products Reminiscence." *Columbia Law Review* 82 (6): 1093–99.

Magrath, C. Peter. 1963. *Morrison R. Waite: The Triumph of Character.* Macmillan.

Maltz, Earl M. 1994. "The Federal Government and the Problem of Chinese Rights in the Era of the Fourteenth Amendment." *Harvard Journal of Law and Public Policy* 17 (1): 223–52.

Matthews, Donald R., and James W. Prothro. 1966. *Negroes and the New Southern Politics.* Harcourt, Brace & World.

McChristian, Andrea, and Kayla Kane. 2023. "A Decade Long Erosion: The Impact of the *Shelby County* Decision on Political Participation and Representation of Black People and Other People of Color in the Deep South." Southern Poverty Law Center, June 21. https://www.splcenter.org/resources/reports/shelby-county-decision-report/.

McClain, Charles J., Jr. 1984. "The Chinese Struggle for Civil Rights in Nineteenth Century America: The First Phase, 1850–1870." *California Law Review* 72 (4): 529–68.

———. 1985. "The Chinese Struggle for Civil Rights in 19th-Century America: The Unusual Case of *Baldwin v. Franks*." *Law and History Review* 3 (2): 349–73.

McCloskey, Robert G. 1960. *The American Supreme Court*. University of Chicago Press.

McCrary, Peyton, Christopher Seaman, and Richard Valelly. 2006. "The End of Preclearance as We Knew It: How the Supreme Court Transformed Section 5 of the Voting Rights Act." *Michigan Journal of Race and Law* 11:275–323.

McMahon, Kevin J. 2003. *Reconsidering Roosevelt on Race: How the Presidency Paved the Road to Brown*. University of Chicago Press.

McNeil, Genna Rae. 1983. *Charles Hamilton Houston and the Struggle for Civil Rights*. University of Pennsylvania Press.

McWhirter, Cameron. 2011. *Red Summer: The Supreme Court of 1919 and the Awakening of Black America*. Holt.

Meese, Edwin, III. 1986. "The Supreme Court of the United States: Bulwark of a Limited Constitution." *South Texas Law Review* 27 (3): 455–66.

Meier, August. 1957. "Toward a Reinterpretation of Booker T. Washington." *Journal of Southern History* 23 (2): 220–27.

Meier, August, and Elliot Rudwick. 2002. *Along the Color Line: Explorations on the Black Experience*. University of Illinois Press.

Meltsner, Michael. 1973. *Cruel and Unusual: The Supreme Court and Capital Punishment*. Quid Pro Books.

Messer-Davidow, Ellen. 2021. *The Making of Reverse Discrimination: How DeFunis and Bakke Bleached Racism from Equal Protection*. University Press of Kansas.

Milov-Cordoba, Michael. 2024. "Life Tenure Is a Rarity on State Supreme Courts." Brennan Center for Justice, October 2. https://www.brennancenter.org/our-work/analysis-opinion/life-tenure-rarity-state-supreme-courts.

Morris, Aldon. 1984. *The Origins of the Civil Rights Movement: Black Communities Organizing for Change*. Free Press.

Murphy, Brett, and Alex Mierjeski. 2023. "Clarence Thomas' 38 Vacations: The Other Billionaires Who Have Treated the Supreme Court Justice to Luxury Travel." *ProPublica*, August 10. https://www.propublica.org/article/clarence-thomas-other-billionaires-sokol-huizenga-novelly-supreme-court.

Murphy, Walter F. 1959. "The South Counterattacks: The Anti-NAACP Laws." *Western Political Quarterly* 12 (2): 371–90.

National Commission on Law Observance and Enforcement. 1931. *Report on Lawlessness in Law Enforcement, No. 11*. US Government Printing Office.

Nieman, Donald G. 2020. *Promises to Keep: African Americans and the Constitutional Order, 1776 to the Present*. 2nd ed. Oxford University Press.

O'Brian, John Lord. 1950. "In Memory of Charles Evans Hughes." *Proceedings before the Supreme Court of the United States*, May 8.

Olivas, Michael A., ed. 2006. *"Colored Men" and "Hombres Aquí": Hernandez v. Texas and the Emergence of Mexican-American Lawyering*. Arte Publio.

Orfield, Gary, and Danielle Jarvie. 2020. *Black Segregation Matters: School Resegregation and Black Educational Opportunities*. UCLA Civil Rights Project, December 17. https://www.civilrightsproject.ucla.edu/research/k-12-education/integration-and-diversity/black-segregation-matters-school-resegregation-and-black-educational-opportunity.

Oshinsky, David M. 2010. *Capital Punishment on Trial: Furman v. Georgia and the Death Penalty in Modern America*. University Press of Kansas.

Owens, Ryan J., and Lee Epstein. 2005. "Amici Curiae during the Rehnquist Years." *Judicature* 89 (3): 127–33.

Owens, Ryan J., and David A. Simon. 2012. "Explaining the Supreme Court's Shrinking Docket." *William and Mary Law Review* 53 (4): 1219–85.

Pacelle, Richard L., Jr. 2009. "The Emergence and Evolution of Supreme Court Policy." In *Exploring Judicial Politics*, edited by Mark C. Miller. Oxford University Press.

Peltason, Jack W. 1961. *Fifty-Eight Lonely Men: Southern Federal Judges and School Desegregation*. Harcourt, Brace & World.

Perea, Juan F. 1997. "The Black/White Binary Paradigm of Race: The 'Normal Science' of American Racial Thought." *California Law Review* 85 (5): 1213–58.

Peretti, Terri Jennings. 2020. *Partisan Supremacy: How the G.O.P. Enlisted Courts to Rig America's Election Rules*. University Press of Kansas.

Pildes, Richard H. 2000. "Democracy, Anti-Democracy, and the Canon." *Constitutional Commentary* 17 (2): 295–319.

Pope, James Gray. 2014. "Snubbed Landmark: Why *United States v. Cruikshank* (1876) Belongs at the Heart of the American Constitutional Canon." *Harvard Civil Rights–Civil Liberties Law Review* 49 (2): 385–447.

Power, Garrett. 1983. "Apartheid Baltimore Style: The Residential Segregation Ordinances of 1910–1913." *Maryland Law Review* 42 (2): 289–329.

Richards, Mark J., and Herbert M. Kritzer. 2002. "Jurisprudential Regimes in Supreme Court Decision Making." *American Political Science Review* 96 (2): 305–20.

Rosenberg, Gerald N. 2008. *The Hollow Hope: Can Courts Bring about Social Change?* 2nd ed. University of Chicago Press.

Rothstein, Richard. 2017. *The Color of Law: A Forgotten History of How Our Government Segregated America*. Liveright.

Rubinowitz, Leonard S., and James E. Rosenbaum. 2000. *Crossing the Class and Color Lines: From Public Housing to White Suburbia*. University of Chicago Press.

Schafer, Judith. 1994. *Slavery, the Civil Law, and the Supreme Court of Louisiana.* Louisiana State University Press.

Scheingold, Stuart A., and Austin Sarat. 2004. *Something to Believe In: Politics, Professionalism, and Cause Lawyering.* Stanford University Press.

Schindler, Sarah. 2015. "Architectural Exclusion: Discrimination and Segregation through Physical Design of the Built Environment." *Yale Law Journal* 124 (6): 1934–2024.

Schmidt, Benno C., Jr. 1982a. "Principle and Prejudice: The Supreme Court and Race in the Progressive Era. Part 1, The Heyday of Jim Crow." *Columbia Law Review* 82 (3): 444–524.

———. 1982b. "Principle and Prejudice: The Supreme Court and Race in the Progressive Era. Part 2, The *Peonage Cases.*" *Columbia Law Review* 82 (3): 646–718.

———. 1982c. "Principle and Prejudice: The Supreme Court and Race in the Progressive Era. Part 3, Black Disfranchisement from the KKK to the Grandfather Clause." *Columbia Law Review* 82 (5): 835–905.

———. 1983. "Juries, Jurisdiction, and Race Discrimination: The Lost Promise of *Strauder v. West Virginia.*" *Texas Law Review* 61 (8): 1401–99.

Schmidt, Christopher W. 2018. "The Sit-In Cases: Explaining the Great Aberration of the Warren Court." *Journal of Supreme Court History* 43 (3): 294–320.

Schnapper, Eric. 1985. "Affirmative Action and the Legislative History of the Fourteenth Amendment." *Virginia Law Review* 71 (5): 753–98.

Schwartz, Bernard. 1983. *Super Chief: Earl Warren and His Supreme Court—a Judicial Biography.* New York University Press.

———. 1985. *The Unpublished Opinions of the Warren Court.* Oxford University Press.

———. 2013. "Rehnquist, *Runyon,* and *Jones*—the Chief Justice, Civil Rights, and Stare Decisis." *Tulsa Law Journal* 31:251–73.

Scott, Rebecca J. 2020. "Discerning a Dignity Offense: The Concept of Equal 'Public Rights' during Reconstruction." *Law and History Review* 38 (3): 519–53.

Segal, Jeffrey A., and Harold J. Spaeth. 2002. *The Supreme Court and the Attitudinal Model Revisited.* Cambridge University Press.

Selmi, Michael. 2011. "The Supreme Court's Surprising and Strategic Response to the Civil Rights Act of 1991." *Wake Forest Law Review* 46:281–306.

Senate Judiciary Committee. 1991. Nomination of Judge Clarence Thomas to Be Associate Justice of the Supreme Court of the United States, 102nd Cong., 1st session, part 4, October 11. US Government Printing Office.

———. 2018. Confirmation Hearing on the Nomination of Hon. Brett M. Kavanaugh to Be an Associate Justice of the Supreme Court of the United States, 115th Cong., 2nd session, part 1, September 4, 5, 6, 7, and 27. US Government Printing Office.

Singh, Jasleen, and Sara Carter. 2023. "States Have Added Nearly 100 Restrictive Laws since SCOTUS Gutted the Voting Rights Act 10 Years Ago." Brennan

Center, June 23. https://www.brennancenter.org/our-work/analysis-opinion/states-have-added-nearly-100-restrictive-laws-scotus-gutted-voting-rights.

Smith, Rogers M., and Desmond King. 2024. *America's New Racial Battle Lines: Protect versus Repair*. University of Chicago Press.

Spaeth, Harold J., Lee Epstein, Andrew D. Martin, Jeffrey A. Segal, Theodore J. Ruger, and Sara C. Benesh. 2024. Supreme Court Database. Modern Database Version 2024, Release 1, and Legacy Database Version 2021, Release 7. http://supremecourtdatabase.org.

Spann, Girardeau A. 1993. *Race against the Court: The Supreme Court and Minorities in Contemporary America*. New York University Press.

Steiker, Carol S., and Jordan M. Steiker. 2016. *Courting Death: The Supreme Court and Capital Punishment*. Belknap Press of Harvard University Press.

Stone, Geoffrey R., and David A. Strauss. 2020. *Democracy and Equality: The Enduring Constitutional Vision of the Warren Court*. Oxford University Press.

Strum, Philippa. 2010. *Mendez v. Westminster: School Desegregation and Mexican-American Rights*. University Press of Kansas.

Sumner, Charles. 1865. *Congressional Globe*. US Senate, 38th Congress, 2nd Session, February 23.

Terrell, Mary Church. 1907. "Peonage in the United States." Mary Church Terrell Papers, Library of Congress. https://www.loc.gov/item/mss425490392.

Thernstrom, Abigail. 1987. *Whose Votes Count? Affirmative Action and Minority Voting Rights*. Harvard University Press.

Thomas, William G., III. 2020. *A Question of Freedom: The Families Who Challenged Slavery from the Nation's Founding to the Civil War*. Yale University Press.

Tourgée, Albion W. 1895. "Supreme Court Case No. 210: *Plessy v. Ferguson*." Brief for Plaintiff in Error. ProQuest: Supreme Court Records and Briefs. https://blackfreedom.proquest.com/supreme-court-case-no-210-plessy-v-ferguson-brief-for-plaintiff-in-error/.

Trelease, Allen W. 1971. *White Terror: The Ku Klux Klan Conspiracy and Southern Reconstruction*. Harper and Row.

Twitty, Anne. 2016. *Before Dred Scott: Slavery and Legal Culture in the American Confluence, 1787–1857*. Cambridge University Press.

Urofsky, Melvin I. 2020. *The Affirmative Action Puzzle: A Living History from Reconstruction to Today*. Pantheon.

VanderVelde, Lea. 2014. *Redemption Songs: Suing for Freedom before Dred Scott*. Oxford University Press.

———. 2015. "The *Dred Scott* Case in Context." *Journal of Supreme Court History* 40 (3): 263–81.

Vladeck, Stephen. 2023. *The Shadow Docket: How the Supreme Court Uses Stealth Rulings to Amass Power and Undermine the Republic*. Basic Books.

Vose, Clement E. 1955. "The NAACP Strategy in the Covenant Cases." *Western Reserve Law Review* 6 (2): 101–45.

Wang, Xi. 1995. "The Making of Federal Enforcement Laws, 1870–1872." *Chicago-Kent Law Review* 70:1013–58.

———. 1997. *The Trial of Democracy: Black Suffrage and Northern Republicans, 1860–1910*. University of Georgia Press.

Warren, Earl. 1969. "Retirement of Mr. Chief Justice Warren." Supreme Court of the United States, *U.S. Reports* 395 (June 23): vii–xiii.

———. 1977. *The Memoirs of Earl Warren*. Doubleday.

Watson Jr. Richard L. 1963. "The Defeat of Judge Parker: A Study in Pressure Groups and Politics." *Mississippi Valley Historical Review* 50 (2): 213–34.

Welke, Barbara Y. 2001. *Recasting American Liberty: Gender, Race, Law, and the Railroad Revolution, 1865–1920*. Cambridge University Press.

Wiecek, William M. 1977. *The Sources of Antislavery Constitutionalism in America, 1760–1848*. Cornell University Press.

———. 1989. "The Black Codes." In *Civil Rights and Equality: Selections from the Encyclopedia of the American Constitution*, edited by Leonard L. Levy, Kenneth L. Karst, and Dennis J. Mahoney. Collier Macmillan.

Williams, Ben. 2022. "Redistricting: It's All Over but the Suing." National Conference of State Legislatures, September 15. https://www.ncsl.org/state-legislatures-news/details/redistricting-its-all-over-but-the-suing.

Williams, Juan. 1998. *Thurgood Marshall: American Revolutionary*. Random House.

Woodward, C. Vann. 1951. *Origins of the New South, 1877–1913*. Louisiana State University Press.

———. 1974. *The Strange Career of Jim Crow*. 3rd rev. ed. Oxford University Press.

———. 1987. "The Case of the Louisiana Traveler." In *Quarrels That Have Shaped the Constitution*, rev. ed., edited by John A. Garraty. Harper and Row.

Case Index

Index